DUSTY

REFLECTIONS OF AN
AMERICAN DREAM

DUSTY RHODES
WITH HOWARD BRODY
FOREWORD BY GEORGE STEINBRENNER

SportsPublishingLLC.com

ISBN-10: 1-59670-160-9
ISBN-13: 978-1-59670-160-1
ISBN: 1-58261-907-7 (hard cover)

Front and back cover photos of Dusty Rhodes, PH: Nathan Bolster. Courtesy Turner South. © TRENI. A Time Warner Company. All Rights Reserved.

Interior photos provided by Dusty Rhodes unless otherwise noted.

Publishers: Peter L. Bannon and Joseph J. Bannon Sr.
Senior managing editor: Susan M. Moyer
Acquisitions editors: Nick Obradovich and Noah Amstadter
Developmental editor: Laura Podeschi
Art director: K. Jeffrey Higgerson
Cover/photo insert design: Joseph Brumleve
Interior layout: Kathryn R. Holleman
Photo editor: Erin Linden-Levy

Sports Publishing L.L.C.
804 North Neil Street
Champaign, IL 61820
Phone: 1-877-424-2665
Fax: 217-363-2073
www.SportsPublishingLLC.com

Printed in the United States of America

CIP data available upon request.

For Hoyt Richard Murdoch.

We grew up in the business together. You were my idol. You were my friend. I am carrying on for us both.

You lived life like there was no tomorrow. You were a Texan first and foremost. I want to tell you a secret, Hoyt, I miss you so much, but the road misses you most!

You were the greatest pro wrestler of all time. Together in the flesh we kicked some ass, raised some hell ... a lot of hell ... and you left me.

Well, at my age after all these years, I am out there alone again. But everywhere I go, you are with me.

You're a bastard for leaving me with this bunch of tick-turds, but you ride with me always.

Hoyt, you should have been world champ!

Thanks partner!

CONTENTS

FOREWORD

I am a fan of professional wrestling and a "big time" fan of "The American Dream" Dusty Rhodes. I saw my first live wrestling match in the 1950s and have remained a follower of the sport ever since. I was a regular at the wrestling matches when they were held in Tampa at the Sun Dome. I use to take my grandchildren when they were quite small (I think Stephen was four, and Haley about seven). I think it was Stephen's early exposure to wrestling at the Tampa Sun Dome that had him take up the sport when he entered high school.

Wrestlers are tremendous athletes and Dusty Rhodes was a tremendous wrestler and a tremendous showman. Strange as it may seem, the two don't always go hand in hand. Dusty had speed, strength and agility that you don't often see in men of his size, 6-foot-3 and 289 pounds. He had grace and agility inside and outside of the ring.

Dusty is also one of the most giving individuals in the world. There isn't anything that he wouldn't do for a friend, a child or a community. He spent a lot of time "doing good"—more than you would think possible for a professional athlete and the demands that they have to meet. You need something—you call Dusty Rhodes, his heart is as big as his girth. Dusty is a star in the wrestling world but an even bigger star to those who personally know him in the real world.

Dusty is a character—there's no doubt about it. He's very charismatic and very smart. Dusty had a lot of unique moves—that's obvious and that's why he held so many titles—but all his moves, in and out of the ring—were Dustified—you can be sure of it. Read and get to know the real Dusty Rhodes.

—GEORGE STEINBRENNER

ACKNOWLEDGMENTS

The authors wish to thank the following individuals for their participation and contribution in making Dusty: Reflections of an American Dream a reality: "Magnum TA" Terry Allen; Bill Apter; "Stone Cold" Steve Austin; Bill Behrens; Tully Blanchard; Jack Brisco; David Allan Coe; Steve Corino; Jim Cornette; Kristin Ditto; Jerry "J.D." Douthit; Janie Engle; Terry Funk; Sheldon Goldberg; "Superstar" Billy Graham; Mike Graham; Senator Richard Green; Jimmy Hart; "Playboy" Gary Hart; Monsignor Laurence Higgins; Sir Oliver Humperdink; Jerry Jarrett; Wanda Jenkins; Connie Jones; Paul Jones; Nikita Koloff; Captain Lewis; Dean Miller; Black Jack Mulligan; Michael O'Brien; Rikki Nelson; "Diamond" Dallas Page; Reggie Parks; David Qualls; Harley Race; Nickla Roberts; Randy Roberts; Jim Ross; Cody Runnels; Dustin Runnels; Larry Runnels; Michelle Runnels; Teil Runnels; Grizzly Smith; George South; George Steinbrenner; Kevin Sullivan; Greg Troupe; "Boogie Woogie" Jimmy Valiant; and last, but not least, all the fans of "the American Dream" Dusty Rhodes.

CHAPTER 1

I've seen the best of times. I've seen the worst of times. But this ain't no two-city tale, this is my tale. This is my story. This is my life. This is the story of how Virgil Riley Runnels Jr. was born to a proud Texan and went from being the son of a plumber to the last bull of the woods and lived the American Dream as Dusty Rhodes.

You see, this story isn't really about wrestling, if you will, but in a way it is, because it's about someone who lived his life as a wrestler in the wrestling business. A business, an industry that gave me nearly everything I ever wanted. A business that at times has brought out the very best and the very worst of people.

It all comes down to this. When the roaring crowds are no longer in the arena and the echoes that were cheers fade silently into the night, all you have left are your loved ones and your memories to reflect upon your life. You thank God for what you have been blessed with and curse the Devil for the scorn and agony he caused. You ask yourself, "Would I do it all again?" and you answer without hesitation, "Fuck, yeah!"

It was a Saturday night and I was sitting in the dressing room of an *NWA Wildside* show in Cordele, Georgia, not too far from my home in Atlanta. The little throwback arena and promotion was run by then NWA president Bill Behrens. I put my boots on the same way I always have—the left one first and then the right one. As I looked around the room, I saw all of these young lions chasing their dreams. It was 36 years ago that I was one of them, chasing mine.

That particular dressing room was small and gloomy. But it was no different than the hundreds of dark basements or makeshift locker rooms I had sat in before.

1

Settling in across from me was a young man lacing up a new pair of wrestling boots he had bought off of a web site. Tonight was going to be his first match. All I could think of was how was he feeling? Everyone came up to him and wished him luck. He made sure not to get too close to me. I then wondered what he thought about me . . . too young to have seen me in my prime to offer an opinion—he'd probably only seen me on videotapes . . . but you could tell that the respect he had for me was overwhelming.

It seemed all too familiar to me and it took me back.

It was 1968 and the place was Harlingen, Texas. This was going to be my first match and my first match for Joe Blanchard. This was his promotion, his town, and his building for this Friday night.

Joe trained me somewhat about the business—I had actually stepped into a pro ring a year earlier—but this was the real deal. As far as I was concerned, this was my first real match.

It was a small, smelly, gloomy dressing room. As I looked around the room, the old timers sat around talking shit; but they were my heroes. Others were getting ready and paying attention to the time. I was putting on my boots for the very first time before a real match—the left one first and then the right one; I had bought them from K&H Wrestling Wear.

My opponent sat across the room. He was a young, good-looking athlete with what I thought to be a Herculean body. His name was Reggie Parks.

No one had come up to me to wish me luck.

Reggie was laughing and joking with the rest of the veterans. In those days the old timers hated the new kids. I remember thinking, "I must gain their respect!" I didn't know how I was going to make it through the night—but I was ready. "Dirty" Dusty Rhodes was ready to wrestle Reggie Parks. It was finally my turn to chase my American Dream.

My stomach was in a knot—the same feeling I get today—but there was no talk between us, just a one-fall, 20-minute match. We were scheduled second up and had about an hour to wait.

The arena was small, and the smoke made it look like something out of a science fiction movie. My legs were like rubber. The ref finally said, "You're up, kid!" Could I stand up? Could I walk? Could I even breathe? My mouth felt like the movie *Ben-Hur* had been made inside of it and it was the dry desert scene. Fuck, I couldn't even spit!

I can remember bits and pieces of it like it was yesterday. Walking to the ring, my mind was going a million miles a minute, but my damn legs hadn't caught up with my head. All I can remember saying was, "Man, I have to get through this!" Should I try to street fight him, or just do what I had learned? In my state of mind he could have beaten me in 30 seconds.

The crowd was 95 percent Mexican Americans. They were full of Lone Star beer, smoking, spitting, and yelling at me as if I were El Diablo—the fucking Devil himself! Again, I couldn't breathe, I couldn't spit . . . but wow man, I loved it! What a rush!

After locking up with Reggie, he backed me into the ropes and without a word of warning, he slapped me on my ear—it sounded like a shotgun went off in my head. I remember nothing of the rest of the match. All of a sudden the bell rang. ... I could barely walk as it did. "This match is a draw." Holy shit, a draw!

My legs came back, my mind was clear, but my ear hurt like hell. As I walked down the steps to the jeers of the crowd, I soaked them up as if I were down on Miami Beach soaking up the sun. I made my way back to the dressing room and to my chair. Then Reggie walked past me looking like he had just stepped out of a five-star restaurant, every hair in place. He simply said: "Thanks, kid! Business is business . . ."

Thirty-seven years later, it's 2006 and there I am back in the same place, but this time around I'm doing the ear-slapping and throwing the elbow that I have made so famous.

On this Saturday night on *Wildside* I made my way from the dressing room to the entrance way leading to the ring as Kid Rock belted out the song "Midnight Rider". I stepped into the arena again. The roar of the crowd was loud. Some say they had never heard it so loud in these parts! My quest, my dream once again captured the night. I was home. I was with my family.

Despite what others may say, once you step into the squared circle, you can never get out! Make no mistake, the pro wrestling business is like a mistress from some Texas whorehouse, loving and kind in a strange way, but because of money, not only brings you up but so damn mean as to talk you to the bottom of despair. Yet even with all that, you always come back. It's like a drug ... a rush. It's lonely sometimes, but always you return. You offer up your innocence, only to be paid back in scorn! Sometimes I think I'll die in the ring.

Just like Kris Kristofferson sang, "Some people say I'm a walking contradiction; partly true and partly fiction." Some people in the wrestling business love me. Others hate my fucking guts. But, whatever I am, I know

I'm a man who has lived a dream through millions of fans; fans who've supported me over and over again throughout the years and still going strong like the Energizer bunny.

Even though I signed with WWE in late 2205, I still find myself playing to the small town as a drunk would play to a half bottle of cheap wine; still entertaining the fans when I do independant shows. I am a storyteller, and the tale I tell is good versus bad, bringing hope to those who can see me in that American Dream, because they see that I'm one of them.

Some mornings my knees hurt so badly I don't think I can walk ... but I do. And so I give back to the ones who made me the champion of the people before it was fashionable ... "The Dream" for many ... I thank God for that.

Truth be told, I've made enough money to buy Miami and I pissed it all away. But man, what a piss it was!

I once saw a sign that read: "Don't just dream it, be it." Well, I am it! The business is my life, the ring my salvation, the locker room and roads my nourishment.

And so my real story begins; not only the story of Dusty Rhodes, the creation of "The Dream," my life on the road and the events that have been flowing through my mind these many years, but the story about the power behind the scenes and the everyday struggle to stay on top of your industry ... the story about complete domination by one company and how it came to pass.

Wrestling fans have a real fascination with the once-secret organization known as professional wrestling. My business is the purest form of visual storytelling; it's the good, the bad, and the ugly, if you will. What takes Hollywood weeks and months to film takes professional wrestlers and the companies behind them literally minutes to put together. A spontaneous explosion of emotion unleashed before your very eyes. With apologies to P.T. Barnum, it truly is "The Greatest Show on Earth."

Before all of the independent promoters of today, the wrestling business was designed and run on an American blueprint. That blueprint mimicked the Mafia.

Mafia, you say? How's that?

Professional wrestling was made up of more than 20 regional promotions run by families under a code, and that code was, "Take care of your own territory, keep your business within the family, and hold your ground." Sound like a movie? Marlon Brando and Al Pacino were nowhere to be found. Some of the old territories were taken by force, some by legitimate business deals and others by lies and violent acts. This was real, man!

The map was carved up like a Thanksgiving turkey. Florida was run by Eddie Graham, the Northeast corridor was controlled by Vincent McMahon Sr., and men like Don Owens, Stu Hart, and Jim Crockett, Sr. ran the Portland, Calgary, and Mid-Atlantic regions, respectively. But there were others, too. Frank Tunney in Toronto, Fritz von Erich in Texas, Bob Geigel in Kansas City, Sam Muchnick in St. Louis, Jerry Jarrett in Tennessee, Jim Barnett in Georgia and Australia, Paul Boesch in Houston, and Joe Blanchard in West Texas were just a few of pro wrestling's Godfathers.

Oh, and like the Mafia, there was another unwritten rule, but one that was spoken frequently, one rule that was never questioned by anybody. "Business is business."

As a promoter, being part of "the family" meant you did not stray into any other territory without paying some price. And if you were not part of "the family," you were considered an "outlaw"—fair game for any "legit" promoter to simply take you out. This was until one man, however, one family if you will, tried to and succeeded in putting to death the territorial system by totally dominating it. I'm sure you know who I'm talking about. More on him and on that later.

I was running Championship Wrestling for Eddie . . . he was my boss, my Godfather, and he was the smartest person I knew when it came to the wrestling business. I loved him very much. He was my mentor, and even though he is no longer with us, I still consider him to be so today. His son Mike, or "Banny Rooster" as I call him because of his "cock of the walk" attitude which I like, remains one of my five closest friends. Anyway, I had just created the first super show for Florida, called the "Last Tango in Tampa" with 35,000 people witnessing me and Harley Race wrestling an hour for the NWA World Heavyweight title.

We had a second super show set for Hollywood, Florida, at the Hollywood Sports Stadium outside of Miami called "Battle Stars" with Race and me again in the main event. The building held about 18,000. Banny rented two Rolls Royces for the show so the dignitaries would arrive in style. Aside from some local political figures, heading to the building were Jim Barnett, my wife, Michele, and I think Eddie, although he might have been in the other car with Vince McMahon Sr. and his wife.

Leading up to the show, I checked the ticket sales every day. They were moving well. This could be our biggest indoor show ever. Man, I was on a fucking roll. Anyway, as the final day came I spent the day in the building and our office boy Pat Tanaka—Duke Keomuka's son—checked our advance. The building manager and Pat told me our advance was $75,000. Wow! A new indoor record! The Godfathers were there, Graham, McMahon Sr.; this was truly living the American Dream. However, I was about to be taught a valuable "family business" lesson.

After the show I was on the way to the post party with Barnett and asked Pat what the house was. I will never forget Tanaka saying, "$52,000." What the fuck did he say?! Shit, at five o'clock we had $75,000 and now we had $52,000? How the fuck did we lose $23,000? Fuck, you could have burned down Atlanta with the amount of heat coming from my body. Needless to say I went nuts and I made a complete ass out of myself at the party.

The next morning I was still hot as we flew back to Tampa on Eddie's plane. I still couldn't get over the feeling that I'd been fucked. So much hard work went into that show. On landing, Eddie called me to the back of the plane as we got our bags. He looked like Brando from *Apocalypse Now*. He handed me a paper sack. It was full of money; lots of money. He said, "This is the way we do business, we take care of family."

I knew not to mention it again, but one time I said about a new talent, "Fuck, let's book this guy."

He said, "No, let's book him … then fuck him."

Business is business.

CHAPTER 2

Growing up in Austin, Texas, was a blast! I don't believe that anywhere in the world can compare to Texas, and when you talk about the Lone Star State, it's like a different country, a whole other universe, a whole other way of life. Austin was a special place to me, and everybody who knows me knows that if you're not in Texas, you are just passing through. There's nothing like being a Texan, and I'm proud to be one.

The east side of Austin can best be described as a small version of East Los Angeles, made up predominately of Mexican Americans and African Americans. There were old school houses that were painted green and yellow and all different colors.

My family and I lived at 1619 Willow Street, and that's where my dreams and hopes and my future were forged.

One of the first things I can recall about Willow Street is that there were cars propped up on cinderblocks. It's a wonder that the cars in the neighborhood had any fucking wheels at all. I remember in our yard was an old Ford that had three blocks and one wheel, so it was my belief that if you had all four wheels set up on cinderblocks, then you were really well off.

There were carts, blocks, wheels, and all sorts of shit everywhere. We had different dogs in and out of the yard and we had some great neighbors.

Down the block there was a man named Alfonso Ramos, who had a band with his brothers. Our summer nights would be filled with the music of his band practicing. All of the kids from the neighborhood would be out in the streets and we would just listen and have a great time. The sound filled the Texas night air, and the fireflies that flew around shone like spotlights on the Ramos house. Today Alfonso Ramos is known as "El Mero Leon de la Sierra" or "the distinguished silver-headed living legend" among Tejano music fans. I understand he was inducted into the Tejano Music Awards Hall of Fame in 1998 and the Tejano R.O.O.T.S. Hall of Fame in 2002.

Imagine that, two living legends having grown up on the same block.

Our household was made up of my dad, Virgil Runnels Sr., my mom, Katherine, my sister, Connie, my brother, Larry, and me. I was the oldest, Larry was the middle child, and Connie was the youngest.

My dad was a plumber, of course. However, he wasn't a union plumber or a plumber of great wealth at $12 or $14 an hour like they were making in California. He was a plumber of $3.50 an hour. I think the most he ever made was $4 an hour. He was a hard-working man and he worked from 6 a.m. to 5 p.m. five days a week and worked extra on the weekends. To me, he was a man's man, making sure his family was provided for.

Virgil Runnels was also a bit colorful. He had his own take on the English language that was like no other. That is the one thing that has rubbed off on me, because we would use the words *fuck* and *ass*, like someone would use the sentence, "The dog ran across the street." I mean, it was amazing.

Unfortunately, he could also be a very violent man. At 6 foot 3 and 280 pounds, he was a real bad ass. He was of Choctaw Indian heritage from Paul Valley, Oklahoma, and his skin had that constant red color. He also had no fear.

My mom was from Germantown and was of German descent. She was a real force behind me and my dream. She was always my biggest fan, even when I was wrestling at an early age. She worked different jobs and was a typical housewife, hanging the Levis on the line out back. She was a wonderful, wonderful person who was very dear to me. I was her boy, and she would do anything possible to keep me out of trouble, anything possible to see that I did well. I always thought I was her favorite, but I knew she loved all her kids the same. On numerous nights when she told me I was her favorite, I always wondered if Larry was hearing it, as I would hear them when they talked.

"Dusty always liked to be the center of attention. One of my mother's favorite pictures of him was from when he was in a high school play and was wearing a red fringe dress, a little 1920s headband, flapper shoes, and was dancing the Charleston."

—CONNIE JONES, SISTER

CHAPTER TWO

My brother, Larry, was the brains of the family and he grew up to be a successful teacher and football coach in Colorado. But despite his success, I always considered him to be an underachiever. I say this because I always thought he had the ability to move to a different level ... to a higher level. I wanted to see him coach college ball instead of junior high or high school. But this ain't a knock on him. I've said this before, if I had the opportunity to go to a small town and coach high school football for $20,000 a year, I'd sign the contract without even reading it. Anyway, today Larry is well respected, and his wife, Denay, has been with him since grade school. They went around the country during an era when you could safely hitchhike, ride bikes, and smoke pot. They were hippies, and that's cool. Larry always reminded me of the Donald Sutherland character in the movie *Kelly's Heroes*, and if you've seen the movie, you know the character was a wild man. All I'm saying is that was how my brother was and I love him dearly. They've got a wonderful son, Travis, who made All-State high school football and now plays for West Texas State University.

Larry and I were close as kids. We had a Chinaberry tree in the backyard and sometimes we used to have fights with homemade slingshots. Well, one year Larry hit me in the eye and blinded me. I couldn't see at all and the doctors bandaged both eyes. They thought I might never see again.

"The thing I remember the most about that was how Dusty relieved me of feeling guilty. He never blamed me. He was laid up in bed from it for some time, and I felt horrible."

—LARRY RUNNELS, BROTHER

I used to lie in bed and try to peek out from under the bandages. One day I was finally able to see ... but I didn't tell anyone because everybody used to wait on me hand and foot to do everything for me. They'd serve me in bed, read to me, you name it. I eventually 'fessed up, though.

My sister, Connie Jones, born Constance Nevada Runnels, was named after my Aunt Vada, who was a huge woman, easily over 300 pounds. Anyway, Connie was like my dad as she was the spitting image of him in a woman's outfit, if you can imagine that. Growing up she was so much like Virgil she should have been the junior instead of me. She's got this wonderful thing about her, in that she's got a huge heart where she would do anything for anybody, and although she's pretty mean too, underneath it all she's the sweetest of us all. Connie was strong enough and built enough to kick a man's ass, and I've actually seen her do it. She also had my dad's mouth, as every word she spoke was preceded by a cuss word—I guess I was more like my mom. My brother was caught somewhere in between. Anyway, as Connie got older, she became more refined and today is a very successful real estate broker in Panama City Beach, Florida.

"When I was a child, I thought being Dusty's sister was the worst thing that ever happened to me. Whatever was going on, the whole family would pile into the car and see Dusty playing football, Dusty playing baseball, Dusty playing basketball, it was always Dusty, Dusty, Dusty. So, I felt like I was a little stepchild pushed off into a back corner for so many years."

—CONNIE JONES, SISTER

As the years pass I realize just how much I really love my sister and brother. Connie took over as my biggest fan after my mom passed away … but maybe Connie was always one of my biggest fans.

For as long as I can remember, my nickname was Dusty. I remember my dad naming me that because of the streets where we lived. In Austin, if you crossed under the I-35 overpass—even before I-35 was built—you went into East Austin and you can very well picture in your mind how it was; I believe I was in my late teens when they finally paved the road. Anyway, I would walk with my dad nearly every day to the corner store where we would go to get an RC Cola, a Moon Pie, and a Dixie Cup ice-cream, the kind you used the little wooden spoon with.

We grew up Southern Baptist, but I'd hardly say we were religious. One time the preacher asked my dad to come to church, and I remember him saying, "Every morning at work, seeing the sun, hearing the birds sing, being able to smell the outdoors, that's my church. I sure don't need a building to go to when I have the outdoors!" Well, whatever that meant, it sounded good to me.

I remember very vividly growing up in that neighborhood. I remember the violence of the neighborhood, too, and I remember the good parts of the neighborhood where you could walk the streets at night until 10, 11, or midnight to visit your neighbor. And I still remember that music. One of the things that I grew up to love about the Mexican American people and their

Latino heritage was their music. If I could not be in this free and wonderful country—I wouldn't want to be anywhere else mind you—Mexico is where I would live. I love Mexico and I love the Mexican people. And I love the music because whenever I hear it, all I have to do is close my eyes and it draws me back to 1619 Willow Street on the east side of Austin.

Dad coached Little League and did the things that dads do, but he worked hard, and like I said before, he could be violent. Even when he was coaching Little League, he got thrown out for hitting an umpire. Now that I think back in the years after his death, I try to visualize the things he did and why he did them. Back then it wasn't like we're going to take your allowance away or cut off your cell phone. I mean when you got punished, you got the belt or you would walk out into the backyard and cut a switch off the tree and he would whup your ass … and I mean literally whup your ass. The only one who didn't get the switch was my sister, Connie. She always says he had an inner peace to him, something she claims I don't have. But I think Dad just kind of favored her a little bit.

From all I could make out being around him, Dad was the best plumber in the world. Like I said before, Virgil Sr. was paid by the hour and he worked sun up to sun down.

The heat and humidity in Texas during the summer were unreal. For a boy almost nine years old, I was about to learn just how hot Texas could really get. Dad put me to work.

The first real summer I can remember working with my dad was when I had just came off my bout with osteomyelitis, the same bone infection that plagued baseball's Mickey Mantle when he was young. I not only beat the odds of getting off those crutches that I used for two years, but I actually started working that summer. Little League baseball was finishing up, and I still didn't feel right to play. Not bad for a kid who wasn't ever expected to walk again.

Osteomyelitis is an acute or chronic infection in the bones. Often, the original site of infection is elsewhere in the body, and spreads to the bone by the blood. Bacteria or fungus may sometimes be responsible for osteomyelitis.

—NATIONAL INSTITUTE OF MENTAL
HEALTH MEDICAL ENCYCLOPEDIA

School was out for the summer, and I remember Dad getting me up around 5:30 in the morning; he was going to work and I was going with him. Since Dad usually brought the plumbing truck home with him, we took it to the shop where he worked at that time, Middleton Plumbing in Austin.

Across the street from the shop was a 7-11—nowadays there's a Quick Trip at that location—and I remember that on my first day of the job it was already 190,000 degrees and it wasn't even 6:30 yet. I had to go across the street when the store opened up to get a block of ice. I carried the ice back across the street and I put it in one of those old aluminum water coolers that was mounted up on the plumbing truck. I climbed up there and got an ice pick and chopped it all up and then ran fresh water in it right out of the tap ... and buddy, let me tell you ... at around 9:30 or 10 in the morning when the sun is beating down and you drank water out of that thing, man it was like the nectar of God ... it was unbelievable.

T.C. Lee was a black man who worked with my dad for years at Middleton Plumbing. He was ditch digger and became my friend. My job was simple; all day long I would help T.C. dig ditches. I helped dig ditches, get the pipes and other equipment off the truck, and basically was a gofer, running around and doing whatever I could. So I wasn't really a plumber. I did this as a teen, too, and even remember hitting the jackhammer with T.C. Our break came at lunch, and I couldn't wait because that's when we'd try to find the shade. He once told me, "Dusty, there's a dream out there ... you oughta get out of this ditch and live it."

I guess you could say it was my first time working on the road. We would go all over town, all over Austin to see the new houses and all these great places and that's where I'd watch my dad take care of business ... and I did what I could. I never learned a lot about plumbing, but I learned a lot about ditch digging, and I learned a lot about common labor. I could probably put in a bathroom if I had to, but I know that it was a rough, rough summer ... that first summer working.

It's not like I didn't have fun, too. I did play some baseball and I was always out of the house on the weekends playing with the kids from the neighborhood. But above anything else, I remember that the one thing that was really cool was that Friday night was a big night for my dad and the family.

He would get paid, and we'd go to Archie's Café for dinner, which was right down First Street from where we lived on the east side. Because I was really a little too heavy for Little League baseball, instead of going to the ball field, we would go to the city coliseum, where low and behold pro wrestling was held.

Once I was exposed to it, I was hooked from day one, and it was like a magnet that drew me to the characters like the people and the athletes in this industry.

I remember watching my dad at these things and I remember him screaming so loud. He was a tough son of a bitch, buddy, let me tell you, and he had that Indian heritage in him boy, so he could hoot and holler and he'd get madder than shit!

One of the regrettable things in my life is that my dad was not around to see my stardom, to see me wrestle, or to see what I achieved for the dream I had at an early age, influenced by where he would like to go.

So at the coliseum we would see the stars coming in and he would yell and scream and man he was crazy ... he always wanted to fight somebody there. But they were fun times and that was my exposure to pro wrestling, because that's all we did as a family. He worked hard and screamed hard. He always said that during the week he worked for a guy, and he did his work as he was told. While he was his own man and he lived by that code, Friday night was the night we'd go out to wrestling so he could yell and scream and take out all of that emotion he had bottled up inside of him.

Of course on Saturday night, it was much of the same. Whether it was going to San Antonio, which was 75 miles away, or Oak Hill down in Austin, we went to the jalopy races, the stock car races, or the dirt track. I remember those times, boy, and they were some great times. I remember that my dad and mom, whether the kids liked it or not, took us on outings. We didn't have money, but we went places like camping. And not camping like you might think of how it is today, I'm talking about a park with a built-in place to put your barbeque and shit.

Dad built a slab in the backyard when I started junior high school, and sometimes he would throw parties for all of my school friends. He always entertained them, whether he would dress up or do a funny dance —he loved to entertain—and I guess I got my entertaining from him. And he could do this even though he was a tremendously violent man, a tremendously angered man, a man who I've seen knock out motherfuckers colder than a wedge who interfered with him, and who when we did something wrong, would take his belt off or get a switch off a tree and whup our ass. It was just that simple. That's the way you were brought up, and that's the way it was. Period.

Every day there were ongoing non-stop arguments; yelling, screaming, and cursing between my mom and dad. I never saw him lay a hand on her, but I know it was verbally unbearable for her sometimes, especially considering we grew up in a small poor-ass looking house.

It's not that we were poverty stricken, it's just how it was; it was a pretty small dwelling, and Grandpa Sanders—my mom's dad—lived in the house with us for many years. Now Grandpa Sanders was cool. He was into politics, living and dying with Sam Rayburn and Lyndon Johnson, and he played dominoes down on Sixth Street almost every day. He also gave me a dollar for every home run I hit when I was in Little League.

Dad did a lot of extra plumbing to put an additional room on the house for my brother and me to have a real place to sleep. When the little room was complete, we finally had our own beds. Before that, we either slept on the couch or on rollaway beds.

I'm not saying I regret the way we lived, because that would be bullshit. Just like in the wrestling industry where the code is "business is business," well, "family is family." We all lived together, and as kids they were great times, especially when it was a clear Texas night and you could see all the colors in the sky… man, it was beautiful. We might have been poor, but we were rich in that each day brought hope for a new adventure, fame, fortune, and a love for life.

I've talked about the violence and all, and aside from us getting the belt, by now you must be wondering how violent could it have really been?

There was a family that lived down on the corner. They were a little bit older than us, and there was one kid my age and he had an older brother. Now when you talk about rednecks, this family was the deal, the kind you see in the movies. They were just trailer trash. But they were violent and we were violent. There was always something going on down around their place and something going on around our place. When I was real young, the two brothers caught me in an alley and put the boots to me. My dad came home and saw me with the old black eye, and asked me what happened. Well, I said so and so did this—I don't want to name names because it's not that important, and they probably own banks in Europe today or something—

and he just took the belt to me and gave me a whupping. I was crying, kicking, screaming, and coughing, and then he took a switch to me and kept it on me all the way down the block to that house. We passed houses that were pink, orange, blue … if you can imagine what old Mexico looked like back in that era, then you can picture my neighborhood.

So we went down to that house, and my dad went up and beat on the screen door. Their mom was there, and the kids were hiding inside because they were afraid of him. Meanwhile, a big group of kids from the neighborhood followed us there. So, I was standing on their front porch crying from the spanking my dad had just given me, and he was yelling through the screen door, "Well, get so and so out here, 'cause Dusty is going to kick his ass. And get the other boy out here 'cause I'm going to kick his ass and then I'm going to kick his daddy's ass, and my wife gets off work in a minute and she's going to be down here and she's going to kick your ass … let's get it on."

Good Lord, it was like a free for all.

The thing about my neighborhood was that it was rough living on the east side of Austin. You walked everywhere you went, and we kids had a bond. We were out on the streets at night but we weren't scared. Sure there were gangs and street fights and stuff like that, but it was survival and it was fun.

I think when I look back on those times the reason I started getting into athletics was really an outlet for me to get away and try to work myself into something that I loved.

"Dusty has always been his own man. He had to overcome a tremendous amount of adversity. He was a great role model and he's still a great role model, and I idolize him. I always looked up to him. I even played football at the same position he did."

—LARRY RUNNELS, BROTHER

One of the things I loved was wrestling. Pro wrestling had a tremendous influence on me, and because it did at an early age, I became the wrestling promoter of the neighborhood, something I did for about three years. There were a lot of kids who lived on that street. All the neighborhood kids would come out and Connie would charge them I think one penny apiece or whatever it was. This backyard wrestling wasn't jump-off-the-barn wrestling—the stunt maneuvers used by the majority of the young kids nowadays in the business. It was backyard professional wrestling. Professional wrestling is not stunts; it's storytelling in its purist form. I think stunts are great because I think it sometimes borderlines wrestling, but all it really, really is is stuntmen doing dangerous shit.

"When I was a little girl, my dad and grandfather got me a horse and the horse was really, really mean. We had this old shed out in the backyard and I'd do anything Dusty'd tell me to do so he got me on the roof of the shed and he and Larry would run the horse around and around in a circle and he'd be down on the ground hollering up to me, 'Jump! Jump! Just like on TV, jump!' He tried to kill me. Growing up with him was bad. There were times that I thought I was close to death."

—CONNIE JONES, SISTER

Anyway, we needed to build a ring and we only had two green water hoses, so I sent Connie next door to steal a couple of water hoses from our neighbor. She came back with this real long red one, and Larry came in the yard with some cedar posts he had gotten from somewhere. I had the shovel, the posthole digger if you will, and I began to bury the posts and build the ring. After we put the cedar posts in the ground, we nailed the water hoses around them to make our ropes. You couldn't hit them or anything, but now we had a ring. The grass was the canvas. I recruited the neighborhood kids to be on the card.

Like I said, it was always Friday nights when my dad would take us to the city coliseum to see pro wrestling. It was a thrill and it was always a tradition. So boy, this was great because I got to be the promoter, the booker, and the champion. I would also be the ring announcer.

It was 1957, and on this particular morning we were lucky because there were no rain clouds in sight; of course this was one of my first big "outdoor" shows.

We always had the kids play the different wrestlers like the Zebra Kid, who was a bad guy, or the Kozak brothers. On this one particular event, my brother, Larry, was Nick Kozak, who was a young wrestler in Texas at the time, and who I actually got to work with later on, along with his brother Jerry, when I started in the industry. The Kozaks ended up becoming friends of mine and they kind of helped me along.

Of course I was Lou Thesz, the champion. Whether he was champion or not at that time didn't matter. He was the big hero back then, and so I just beat the shit out of my brother because he was a little smaller than me. We then just paired up the other kids and let them go have a little time of it.

The ropes would always fall if you hit them, and the cedar posts were not dug in deep enough to stay straight. But none of it mattered as we had a tremendous amount of fun, and I cherish those times in the backyard with my family. The water hoses weren't worth shit after that, and as you probably guessed by now, I would get my ass whupped … literally get my ass whupped over it.

Of course back then as I got older I played in all sports, whether it was football, baseball, basketball, running, jumping, swimming. … I was an all-star baseball player and I really felt that I would play Major League Baseball. My dad, of course, believe that too, because in 1954 a big star for the New York Giants, Dusty Rhodes, became very famous for hitting home runs in the World Series. Since I've always been called Dusty because of the road outside our house and the fact I hit something like 16 home runs in 18 games one year, we thought that was my destiny. I was a real power hitter as far as that went.

> *"My dad was real superstitious and one time we were going over to Waco to see Dusty play football and a black cat ran across the road. Daddy almost wrecked the car and all the cars around him were trying to get off the road because he didn't want to cross the path. He actually drove around back to another highway and came around in another direction to get to Waco because he would not cross the road where that black cat had gone and he wasn't going to miss that game."*
>
> —CONNIE JONES, SISTER

I wasn't always Rhodes, but I was always Dusty. I was never called Virgil, not by my family, not by my friends. Even my teachers at school didn't call me Virgil. But I do remember very distinctly about the dusty roads thing and I know when I broke into the wrestling business, "Bulldog" Danny Pleaches—one of the lieutenants for the Dallas territory who took a liking to me—tagged that last name on when I told him the story of where we lived and my dad's favorite player. That's how I became "Dusty Rhodes." Thank God for "Bulldog" Danny Pleaches.

Anyway, those were times that I cannot forget. They were just amazing, and back then my dad was amazing. My God, when I realize what he was fighting for, what he was working for and he wasn't a drunk or an alcoholic … he was just a violent Indian, and that's what he was. And despite the whuppings, he loved his kids.

If he had only $14 and there was this red wagon you wanted and it cost $14, but that meant the whole week we would go with no food or anything, he would buy the wagon. Now that's not cliché or bullshit, because that actually happened, and I was the one who wanted the wagon.

He influenced me, but I wasn't as close to him as I should have been. I'm ashamed to say that I should have been closer to him growing up. Sure, I worked for him and deer hunted with him, but there's more to a father-son relationship than that. I wish I would have been closer to him as time went on, but I still remember him vividly when I think back about those times. I think I grew to love my dad more after he passed away than while he was alive. I know that whatever he did, he did because he loved his children very, very much. And that parent-child love goes both ways. I suppose that is why I am so grateful today that my son, Dustin, and I have been able to mend our differences and are closer today than ever before … but more on that later, too.

Virgil Runnels Sr. was only 56 years old when he passed away. Toward the end he was a very sick man, having smoked a box of Tampa Nugget cigars a day. He died of emphysema, but I think he was just worn out. The day he died, later that evening, his first grandson, Dustin, was born. That was an emotional time for me, and that's why I always said Dustin was a very special child; you learn a hell of a lot about yourself in a quick way.

As for Mom, she knew when her time was up. She told my sister, "Call Larry and Dusty. Get them here." How do people know it's the end?

Just three weeks earlier, I had walked in on her and her eyes had lit up. We played cards, laughed, and just talked. Driving home to Atlanta from Texas I thought I would see her again. I didn't.

On day two she was waiting on me. It went downhill quickly from there.

I was in a fucking dressing room with people I really didn't know when the call came from Connie that she was gone.

Say whatever you want about these two people, but I will always think of Bob Ryder and Bert Prentice as my mom's angels, because they were there emotionally for me when the call came. Bob offered to drive me from

CHAPTER TWO

Nashville to my home in Atlanta … and that wasn't some empty offer, it was genuine. Thank you, guys.

My mom knew … she knew and she wanted her sons by her side. We were too late. My mom was very special and even in the end she called the shots—she knew it was over. I love you, Mom.

Katherine Runnels, God bless her soul, passed away on June 7, 2203.

CHAPTER 3

I grew up, went to college, and became a pro wrestler! I wish my life was that simple to sum up.

Being able to talk about the past means we are here in the now! I really don't want to bore you, but some of the tales are really funny, sad, and at times unbelievable.

As I was kicking around West Texas State College in Canyon, Texas, in 1966 and '67, the school's favorite sons were Terry Funk and Dory Funk Jr., sons of the very famous Dory Funk.

They had the Amarillo Territory ... Amarillo, Lubbock, El Paso, Odessa, New Mexico, you get the picture.

Every Thursday night Amarillo ran at the fairgrounds and Frank Goodish—who would later become Bruiser Brody—Bobby Duncum, and others would go with me. Goodish bounced with me at the Bat Cave nightclub so we would have a little money. It cost about $1.50 to get in. Bobby would bale hay with me for some of the ranches in the area to get our money to go.

During that time I had a chance to see some great wrestlers, and young Terry was the Nick Barkley of pro wrestling. Nick Barkley was a character on the TV show *The Big Valley*, which was popular at the time. Terry would later become my rival and mortal enemy in the pro wrestling ring for more than 30 years.

We would wait to see who was coming in the next week. One time there was a sign hanging from the rafters with the date on it saying, "Coming: The Sheik." Man, that was promotion ... if you read the wrestling magazines, you knew that The Sheik was the baddest motherfucker this side of Saudi Arabia, much less Tulia, Texas. You also knew that he would kick the shit out of Terry, and the old man would meet him the following week! Man, I couldn't wait. ...

However, it would be another year or so before I crossed paths with the Funks.

Meanwhile, it was now 1967, and being fresh out of West Texas State University, I went to play football for the Hartford (Connecticut) Charter Oaks of the (now-defunct) Continental Football League. Twelve games into the season, however, with a record of 5-7, the team folded, and there I was, stuck in the fucking Northeast with a Mustang that had no heat or air conditioning and only $35 in my pocket.

I remember seeing a newspaper ad for pro wrestling at the Boston Arena Annex and decided to give it a shot. Hell, I knew I was big enough and tough enough, so I went down there, and wearing my boxing shoes from when I fought in the Golden Gloves, I made my pro wrestling debut against Bull Montana. The local champion was this cat Frank Scarpa. I wrestled three shots in the Massachusetts area and made a whopping $36! That's 12 dollars a fucking match! What the fuck is that? And those early matches were bullshit, because they were like my training. In my mind my first real match was the one I described earlier against Reggie Parks.

I will say this, though, even as shitty as it was back then, I was hooked. I was hooked on the business like a $20 whore on crack. But I was also broke as shit, and if not for my credit card—my Gulf Oil credit card, if you will—to get me by, I don't know what I would've done.

So, that's when I started my trip back home to Austin. "Get me the fuck out of Dodge!" And I almost made it home, too! But, really it wouldn't be as good a story of how I struggled to get where I am today if I had made it home without something happening along the way. So, I was just outside Dallas when I lost my credit card; that credit card was like my lifeblood. I figured I needed just about nine dollars' worth of gas to make it all the way home. Now, being the charismatic Texan I am, I flashed my million-dollar smile—I guess it was actually only worth nine dollars at the time—and I convinced the station attendant to let me pump gas in exchange for what I needed to get home. I told him I would pay him back someday and I meant it. He probably thought I was full of shit, but he gave me what I needed and I was on my way.

I can't explain it, but from the first day I stepped into a wrestling ring, I knew that one day I was going to be a big superstar. I knew that one day I would be the NWA World Heavyweight Champion like my hero, Lou Thesz. Call it ego or cockiness or whatever you want, but I just knew that I was destined to make more than eight dollars a match.

Like I said earlier, I made enough money to buy Miami but pissed it all away. Well, you can't buy Miami at eight dollars a match, you know? But you don't start at the top, either. You pay your dues and work your way up through the system, whatever system there is; something guys in the business today don't really understand, don't have a clue.

Anyway, the day I became the NWA World Heavyweight Champion, when I put that belt on, it was like, oh man ... it was real. It was real to me! It was real to me, because all the other guys knew they could not get that belt, politically or whatever the reason ... and when I put it around my waist, man, it was like you can't even imagine how it felt. It was a rush ... and I thought back to the first day I saw Lou Thesz, because growing up he was unbelievable as a champion.

So I was just a kid hanging over the side railing with an autograph book and I watched Lou walk in the back door of the city auditorium. Now, as a kid, the auditorium looked huge—and you see those buildings now, and they all look like little pieces of shit—but as a kid you see the auditorium as the Astrodome—and when he came in the door and he had this really fine suitcase ... not like the gym bags they use today ... how you compared yourself in the business back then was if you had a Haliburton briefcase, then you made it with the big guys. You can imagine back then how you got to work your way up the card and all ... that's the way the people in the business looked at it.

Anyway, you came in to the auditorium and it was always like 150 degrees and there was a hallway where I could lean over the railing and I could see the dressing room—at the time I didn't know that the babyfaces came out on one side and the bad guys came out on the other and in the middle they were all together and I didn't care—because there was Thesz, really stringy-looking to me but really cut, really ripped. He was the world champion and he looked like a champion.

I can remember that he was kind of muscled up, and while the matches were going on, I could hear the dressing room door open and I would be looking down that hall trying to peek into there like a kid at a baseball game trying to look in the dugout ... and he would be in the hallway back there

... he looked immaculate, he looked like he was the champion, every hair in place.

And every time I saw him, when it was show time, it was the same.

Years later, one night in Chicago, Murdoch and I were on a card with Lou and he was pissed at me, and Dick Murdoch was ragging his ass so bad, and even though he used to laugh at us, he would get pissed at us. Anyway, he had one of those rubber things where you hold it down with your foot and you work out your arms, doing curls. So he was pulling up, working out his arms and the thing slipped off his foot and came up and hit him right in the nose. I nearly died when it hit him. It was so funny!

But even though that happened to Lou, watching him when I was a kid and watching the crowd react when he was introduced, he carried himself like a champion, I remembered back to the old Austin city auditorium like it was yesterday, there he was, he had the blue robe on, and he had the old belt on, the original Ed "Strangler" Lewis belt, and he came out last because he was the champion.

That taught me something. I always made sure that I was over enough that I never came out before the other guy. You can go back and document everything that I've done ... never would I go into the ring before my opponent, because I always said that was how to stay over.

Thesz came out and they introduced the man and there was nothing hurried about him. He didn't get in the ring in a hurry. He would get in the ring, the referee would check the bottom of his shoes for tacks or whatever they had back then ... he'd check him all over ... and then Lou took the belt off and the referee held it up. Wow, man, this guy was unbelievable. Not knowing he couldn't work a lick—well, he could work, but it was not like what we call working today ... he was very old school, very old school ... that was old times, though—he was great!

Seeing Thesz and the way he carried and presented himself was why in the later years I said that Jack Brisco never knew how he guided my career. I looked up to Jack. I never told him this, but I'm telling him now as I write. I'm saying he was the one guy I respected more than anybody else. Not as a shooter, but from watching him. I learned so much from just watching him ... and he would be what you call just pretty bland by today's standards. You would ask, "How flamboyant is this Jack Brisco?"

Jack was the new era to me.

I was selling out these buildings with Jack and I couldn't get out of the car, the paparazzi would follow me everywhere I'd go. He helped make Dusty Rhodes the American Dream, and I'll get into that in a little bit. In the meantime, whether it was 30 minutes, 20 minutes, or whatever he would have, he would have a cigarette in his hand, have immaculate shoes just like Lou Thesz wore, and he would put on the Avis Rent-a-Car jacket—the little red and white one he usually wore—or if he didn't wear the jacket that night, he would just do two deep knee bends, take a puff of the cigarette, and be ready to go.

I would say, "Wow, man, shit…" He never knew I watched him so closely on how to present himself, but to me Jack was like Lou, and when I wrestled Lou, it was strange, because I was in there with him; in the ring with my idol.

I think it's important to know that when I stepped into the ring with Lou for the first time, it wasn't the American Dream stepping into the ring with him, but rather it was a very young, still sowing his oats, "Dirty" Dusty Rhodes … and I think it's important to understand the setup that allowed me to be in the ring with Thesz in the first place, because it came off a very hot angle.

I had literally just started, having the match with Reggie Parks, and Gary Hart was the hottest manager in Texas. He managed the Spoiler, who was Don Jardine, the Super Spoiler, and others. Gary was from Chicago and loved his wine. I called him "the wino from Chicago," and we had a great run later on as one of the greatest feuds of all time with me against Gary Hart's Army.

So I walked into the old Dallas Sportatorium for the first time and that place was hot—it was a hot territory doing great business—and there was Gary, like in *The Godfather* giving counsel to the Kentuckian, Grizzly Smith. Grizzly, or "Pops "as we called him, was over. He had been there five weeks and had beaten everybody within 40 seconds.

They did a little TV like they do nowadays, like at *Wildside* and other places, and there was a monitor on Fritz von Erich's desk.

Anyway, Fritz had never met me before, and I had just come out of Hartford with the Continental Football League. I was ripped pretty good and I looked good at about 245 pounds and I was going up against Grizzly Smith to help build up this angle with him against the Spoiler— a big fucking angle—so he beat everybody's ass, and there I was and they didn't know me from shit.

"Bulldog" Danny Plechas was the referee. So they introduced "Dirty" Dusty Rhodes—that was my deal, "Dirty" Dusty Rhodes, Joe Blanchard would make me "The Austin, Texas, Wildman"—and I started walking down that aisle. Now, being as charismatic as I am—and it carries over to the fans—instantly as I was walking down that aisle to do my 30 seconds against Grizzly or try to go longer, the people started booing me for no reason. He was over as a babyface. But I thought, "Jesus Christ, there is no reason in the world they are booing me." But it was really raw and I stopped, and that's where I developed that great knack that I got from Johnny Valentine—and also where the Dusty spirit comes in—turning to all sorts of people and having the ability to make them yell, scream, or do whatever I want.

I would take another step in order to look at the people, so if they were booing, I would just stop and look and they would boo louder, and I realized that was the way to turn them up and down.

Charismatically I have that eye contact you need with the people and I knew it … and I didn't know what I was doing. I knew Fritz was back there watching. I can picture him sitting back there with his Pall Mall cigarettes in his hand—he'd smoke a pack or a carton every minute—I get mad visualizing him sitting at his desk. I never crossed anyone who was more over with a hall like he said he was, and made you believe it.

Now I knew he was watching, and I got in the ring and the people were going crazy. The crowd was good and hot, and back then they had these screens so it was physically hot, and man, the atmosphere was great. So the bell rang and I went in and locked up with Tiny, and he took me and just threw me like a piece of rag and shot me off into the corner.

I was preparing myself for the son of a bitch to bear hug me … 45 seconds, grab a Lone Star beer, and I'd be out of here, buddy. I locked up again and nothing was said, and he took me and threw me again. So he threw me off again and picked me up, threw me in, threw me off the ropes, I hit the ropes, I came off, and he gave me a big foot. I said, "Fucker," it was a big shit deal. He nearly knocked my nose off.

He picked me up. The crowd was loud, and I hadn't touched this motherfucker except for getting my ass kicked. The crowd was screaming so loud, booing, I couldn't hear, and I looked at ringside and there was Gary Hart, the manager of all managers, coming down.

CHAPTER THREE

Gary was standing there at ringside screaming at me. "Hey kid, come here. Come here. Come here." Screaming … and finally the spoken word for somebody who never heard it in the ring was spoken.

Pop said, "Go see what he wants." With that, Grizzly shoved me off and I took a big rolling bump, rolled off the ring onto the floor.

People could scream louder because of my association with him. Gary said, "Fritz is watching the monitor—he fucking loves you. I don't know what it is, but go back in there and lock up and tell Grizzly …" Now he was telling me this and I'd never spoken in a ring in my life, "…tell Grizzly…" who I respected and thought he'd kill me any second, "…to keep going and you come back out here in about 20 seconds."

So I rolled in and the action was going on and he was throwing me around and he had me in a headlock, backing me in a corner and I was trying to say, "Mr. Smith … Mr. Smith … Mr. Smith … we have to keep going."

He said, "You don't have to tell me, I know what's going on …" and he shoved me into ropes and I rolled out.

Gary said to me, "Tell him to put you in a bear hug … he bear hugs you by the ropes, I'm going to reach through and trip him with you in the bear hug on top of him … and Danny's going to count one, two, three and you're gonna win."

We were outside and the people were screaming, and I said to Gary, and this is the truth, "You fucking go tell him that."

He knew … Pops knew … I rolled in, Pops threw me into the rope and put me in a bear hug. He was bear hugging, people were going crazy, and he'd been killing people for six weeks like this and he had a death grip on my ass. Then I felt him go out from under me, and bam, I felt myself go on top of him.

As Danny counted one, two, as he went on to three, I said, "No, no, no, no" … to the referee. I was saying this and he never let the bell go. So Danny was laying there and he counted one, two, three; Gary jumped in the ring and raised my hand.

God dang!

That's why Pops, to this day what he did for me … anything that I ever did for him couldn't even pay him back.

The crowd was throwing cups and beer and shit, and I'm saying, "Wow, man, this is great."

"I said to Danny [Plechas], I'm not going to beat this kid. He asked me, 'You see what I see, don't you?' I said, 'I sure do!' There was more there than just getting a win over Dusty. I didn't need to beat him. We went about seven or eight minutes. It was like an electric current was going through him and I could feel him. Watching him and watching the crowd, I knew he had something. I knew he'd make it."

—Grizzly Smith

So I went to the back where Fritz was sitting, and sitting there he always had the claw intact. Fritz always had it up in the air in case you got close, he would put the motherfucking claw on you. He never relaxed. A pencil was never in his hand. He had the claw stationed right over his head. As I walked in, it looked like he was throwing a baseball at me, and when he talked, he talked with the claw. Fritz talked with the claw—he asked, "What's your name?" He didn't even know my name!

Danny came in and said, "This kid's got it. Man, he's got it."

"I first met Dusty in Ft. Worth and I saw a sparkle in him. He was sitting in a corner with a pair of granny glasses on reading a book of poetry. But he had that look. The look was important. He had it. He had it so much you had to not look, not to see it. I saw in Dusty this common guy that could electrify people. That first night with Grizzly, I found out what they originally planned to do and because I had his ear, I told Fritz my feelings on Dusty, to give him an opportunity. I'm proud I saw it in him. I don't know if he was aware that I lobbied for him."

—Gary Hart

I believe Joe Blanchard planned it. I know that they talked, and I know that it just wasn't a spur of the moment thing. They knew exactly what they were doing, because the very next week I was on the double main event, my second match in the history of the fucking business down in Dallas. In the second match I was in the main event against Grizzly and he just slaughtered me in 15 seconds with the bear hug. I was done.

But that set it up for the deal with Thesz and I didn't even know.

I got my booking and I was driving into town, and I nearly shit a blue goose. The marquee said the Spoiler #1 managed by Gary Hart with "Dirty" Dusty Rhodes versus Duke Keomuka and Lou Thesz.

I said, "Whoaaaaa, fuuuuccck. ..."

Thesz had a habit that everybody he didn't like he would not only stretch them, but he would slap the shit out of them. He would back you into the ropes, he would cuff you, he would slap the shit out of you. If you were a rookie, he would slap the shit out of you.

At about this time, I don't know shit, but I'm sitting there thinking, man, God. ...

Gary and Spoiler and I went into the ring to this thunderous roar. Here came Duke Keomuka. Why he was a babyface, I'll never know. Duke was out there in his Japanese stuff and there came Lou Thesz behind him... not with him, behind him.

Spoiler said they were in an angle that I knew nothing about, so he said, "I'll stay in the ring and I'll tag you. Just go ahead and do whatever you want to do until you get tired of it. Gary will tell you, you know what's going on from there. Okay?"

About a minute into the match, I came into the ring with Lou. I said, buddy, I don't know. I said in my mind—and your mind is going like a thousand miles a minute—this is my fucking hero standing here. I saw Duke on the apron and I saw everything in slow motion. The whole world so slow. ...

I had a pretty good lock up, and when we locked up, it was stiff and like bam, he just tied me right into the ropes and I knew there wasn't a thing I could do. He backed me in the ropes and he just reared back to slap me. I was thinking this was a setup, so he reared back to slap me and Plechas, the referee, grabbed his hand and released me. I scrambled like a mother and I tagged Spoiler, and the rest of the night I never touched him.

I got in the ring with Duke and everything, but I never touched Thesz, and I think he would always kind of remember that moment because when I got dressed with him in a lot of different dressing rooms as I was gaining my rise, he always had a kind of smirk on his face.

But he was Lou. He was untouchable to the guys in the dressing room. The respect that is missing nowadays is crazy. When he walked in, you moved. If you were sitting close, you moved. He was the champion of the world and that's the way you looked at it. There's a little mystery there, and I can't even imagine not doing that out of respect.

But all this ties together like I said earlier with paying your dues.

For example, Fritz heard that in San Antonio and Harlingen and the Mexican towns, I was over like a son of a bitch. There was a territorial system in place and he was the Godfather, just like Eddie was in Florida. Not only did Fritz have his own territory booked out of Dallas, but these were his guys. He owned the territory, and they gave booking fees back to Fritz.

My first big payoff came right after the deal with Thesz. It was right after Fritz decided, as the NWA America's Champion, to make two to three trips a year to Houston for Paul Boesch. He'd also make two or three trips for Joe Blanchard and his TV down in San Antonio or Corpus Christi when Fritz wanted to go fishing or dove hunting with the guys. Fritz had a great time when he would come down there.

Anyway, I had only been in San Antonio a few weeks, and already I had almost been knifed … and one time Plechas pushed me out of the way of a whiskey bottle that was coming from the ceiling. "Bulldog" Danny Plechas was kind enough to take it upon himself to look after me in the business; he was a referee and an ex-wrestler and was one of Fritz's lieutenants.

Bulldog had taken care of me on numerous occasions, and the word got back to the office in Dallas that I was really over there. Gary Hart and Grizzly saw me take the area through changes—they were doing the same thing in Dallas but in a little different way—and in San Antonio, Joe's way was a leather strap match. On the card was Pops, Grizzly Smith, versus Gary Hart in what we called a lights-out match after the main event. The main event for the heavyweight title was "Dirty" Dusty Rhodes against Chris Markoff.

I guess I was cockier down there because in five or six weeks I said, "Shit, this is great." I got bit by the ass. …

Fritz came in, and everything was two out of three falls for the title. I can remember trying to make a joke with him, he had his own room of course, and I was a charismatic son of a bitch, and I was just like I am now.

I knew within five weeks that I was the biggest thing. Whether I was or not, it didn't matter. It's what you believe and shall receive, being the biggest thing in the industry.

We sold out, and somebody came through the dressing room saying, "Go tell Fritz how it is," and the guy said they were lined up around the auditorium … they were down the street! I said to myself, "They are down the street!"

Two minutes later Plechas came over and said, "Fritz wants to see you."

"Sure, man."

Going over there I had my boots on and my T-shirt on, but I forgot I had no underwear on. I walked into his office with my dick hanging out.

"What the fuck? Where are your fucking pants? You come in here with your fucking dick hanging out!"

"Ah, shit. I'm sorry. I'll go and get a towel or something, man."

I sat down with my bare ass on a cold seat—it probably had parasites all over it—and there I was with my mess hanging out.

In the match itself, obviously on the first fall Fritz kicked the shit out of me and beat me with the claw, and because they lined up around the building, on the second fall he kicked the shit out of me and beat me with the claw.

Driving to Austin to get back home, I was scared to look at the envelope, because in the envelope you got paid in hard cash, and it was really thick. When I got home, I put it up on the dresser. I was lying in bed, and the phone rang at 7:30 in the morning from Miami, and it was George Wilson who coached the Miami Dolphins, getting ready for football season.

"We got one of your tapes and we want you to come to the Miami Dolphins training camp with us," he said. "We can't offer you anything until you make the team, but if you make the team, then we can make you an offer. Come try out."

During that time, I had never seen over a hundred dollars in my life until that moment. I never had that type of money in my pocket. I looked at the phone, I looked at the money, and I said, "I no longer play professional football," and that was that. And that was my first big payoff.

But it got better.

Harlingen was on the Gulf Coast right down on the border of Mexico, and there was some of the best dove hunting and fishing in the area. The building there was about half the size of the Armory in Tampa, a little auditorium that held about 1,500 to 2,000. The surrounding towns were Kingsville and Raymondville, and Fritz came down there the same week we did the local television show. They also did a live radio hookup that night from Harlingen that was carried back over to Mexico.

They knew me in old Mexico by the description from the radio program and I was the main event there.

Houston also ran on Friday nights and was doing great business with all those guys, Harley Race (my "Dog"), Johnny Valentine, "Flying" Fred Curry.

I wanted to be there, too, because that's where the money was. The money here was from 45 to probably 75 bucks, but the training that Joe Blanchard gave me there on top of the main event, well, you would just want to be there.

Plechas, Fritz's first lieutenant, contacted Joe and said Fritz was coming to Harlingen. There was no air conditioning, it was 185 degrees, and I was sitting with my balls hanging out again because that had become a trademark now for me when I saw Fritz. I would put on my boots and T-shirt, and I would walk around naked.

He came in, and on the first fall I got hold of a chair and busted him with it and got disqualified, so he won that fall and I escaped the claw. The second fall I didn't escape the claw, which he already had cocked and ready, so he took the match.

Afterward, Joe came in with the envelopes and threw one to me. Two hundred eighty dollars; wow! I got my envelope, and Joe put his envelope down, and he and Plechas started messing with a fishing pole and reel that they bought. Joe got up to leave and words were never spoken ... he just walked by, kind of grinning, and threw me his envelope. He threw me his envelope! So I grabbed it but didn't open it up until I got home the next morning. When I did it had five big ones in it—$500! I ended up with $780 ... and that was my biggest payoff to date, but hardly my biggest ever. More would come.

It was just an amazing time. I respected the business, but I knew that I was going to be a star. Joe knew, Fritz knew ... they knew it. They could smell it.

I can look at guys I've broken into the business and guys I brought in, and I can say I knew from the time they walked into the room if they were the deal. However, I cannot walk into a room anywhere in the country where there are independent wrestlers and see one person who tells me they're the real deal. On the independent circuit, I'm walking around and seeing great stuntmen. But hey, independently you can't walk in and just see something that's great and special. There's something missing out of the whole thing. Terry Funk and I talked about it one night on the telephone.

Anyway, I guess I was getting cockier with time, and about the second or third time I wrestled Nick Kozak, I was pretty stiff, very stiff. I went to my room at the Alamo Plaza Hotel in El Paso, and while Jerry Kozak and I were down in old Mexico, Nick and his dad bought a whole sack of potatoes and spread them out in my bed and didn't realize it until I laid down. Nick and Jerry were two brothers I really liked.

I made $17,000 in my rookie year, and it's been a long, hard road since then. But all that would change soon enough. It wouldn't happen for a couple of years yet, but there was going to be an explosion on the wrestling scene in the form of an American Dream.

By the way, remember that little gas station I talked about earlier? Well, later that year I went back to that same gas station and the same guy was there, the same attendant was working; the guy who gave me $9 worth of gas. Now, he didn't remember who the fuck I was, but that didn't matter because I remembered what he did for me. So I gave him $50.

CHAPTER 4

"Dusty Rhodes ... you make me want to puke! You're an apathetic, sympathetic, diabetic, egg-sucking dog."

—TERRY FUNK, FLORIDA TV INTERVIEW, CIRCA 1977

Dusty Rhodes and the Funk family have a tattered history all their own. There was the old man, Dory Funk Sr. and the great technician, Dory Funk Jr. But in my mind, none was better than the consummate athlete, Terry Funk.

For more than 30 years it's been "The American Dream," Dusty Rhodes versus that Texas rattlesnake, Terry Funk; two warriors who are still going strong but grew up together in an industry that kicked lesser men to the curb.

Some people have asked me why that feud continues to be talked about today after so many years. Why has it endured ... survived the test of time when other feuds have long been forgotten?

While others may have their opinions, their ideas, and their take on it, if you will, I have mine. Believability and respect for the business.

Believability and respect are two of the main ingredients in professional wrestling that are sorely missing today.

Believability and respect.

Their whole family was tough. I was 19 years old doing one of my first tours of the Amarillo promotion and I was to meet Dory Funk Sr. for the Western States Heavyweight title on a Thursday night. Holy shit, that was big!

I went out and cut what I thought was a hell of a promo about me kicking his ass and I called him "Old Man Funk." As I passed him in the hallway afterward expecting to hear him say, "Great promo," he said, "Kid, be careful who you call old man, 'cause how are you going to look Thursday night when this old man kicks your ass?"

Well, Thursday night rolled around and sure enough the old man beat "Dirty" Dusty Rhodes in two straight falls. That's promotion!

Dory Jr. was a bit different than either his old man or his brother. His dad and brother were known more as kick-ass wrestlers, brawlers if you will, but guys who could bring it. "Junior," however, was a great NWA World Champion by working the mat. He drew a lot of money working that old-school style with those uppercut forearms and the dreaded spinning toe hold.

Dory and I aren't close these days, but I have all the respect in the world for him. He knows the industry, and if you have a kid who wants to learn about the business, I would make sure that in some way, shape, or form, he passes through Dory's door, because of the knowledge he has.

A lot of people in the business sometimes thought Dory was stupid because of the way he would carry himself or he was softspoken. That's not the case. He is far more intelligent about the business and about life than they gave him credit for. Now if he wants to appear stupid to some people and have someone else do the talking for him, then that's okay ... that's his business. But me knowing him, it's not so. I think that he's just one of those who still lives in the world of believability and respect. And when you have that, it's the real deal, buddy ... you want to be in the business? You will have to battle, claw, scream, holler, and scratch ... whatever it is, it becomes the real deal.

As far as matches between Dory and me, there are not any significant ones that I could pick out. Okay, so a match goes 60 or 90 minutes in Fort Lauderdale, or Miami, or wherever. ... Terry and I got it done in 10 minutes.

Not a knock, because those kind of matches have a place in our business every once in a while. Something like that is more suited for Dory and Jack Brisco.

But that's why Terry was a different story than his brother or even the old man, to me, anyway. And it's not like I'm pulling numbers out of my ass. Dory and I really did 60 minutes in Miami, and the very next night Terry and I did 10 in West Palm Beach.

I honestly cannot tell you what happened in the match with Dory that was different than any other time I wrestled Dory, but I do remember vividly the one with Terry being near riotous.

Terry went and took a handful of wooden coffee stirrers from the concession stand and hid them in his trunks. Throughout the match he would use them, and eventually I was opened up to where my face was a crimson mask from the blood. The people were going crazy as he kept hiding them from the referee. Finally the ref caught him, and the wooden sticks went flying everywhere, up in the air, everywhere. While the referee was distracted picking them up and kicking them out of the ring, Terry had one left on the other side of his trunks and used it on me. It was great psychology.

But still I think that Dory belongs on a list of those who deserve respect and honor … and while I always kidded him, I never defamed him because of who he is and what he's done in the pre-yellow finger era.

Yellow finger?

Before talking more about Terry, let me explain what the yellow finger is.

I always thought there was an invisible line drawn in our business that I refer to as the yellow finger. This line, if you will, divided the pre-merchandise era and the time when they started selling these big number-one foam fingers at the arenas. And who was the biggest yellow finger of them all? Hulk Hogan.

We all set there?

Getting back to Terry, I always looked up to him because he played football at West Texas State and so did I. He and his family ran the wrestling in town that I would go watch; kind of like how yellow finger looked up to me—although he may not admit it—when he would go to the Tampa Armory to see and learn from me before he got into the business. Later on when I was established as "The American Dream," Terry would come to Florida and talk some shit about me quitting the team because I was behind him, but that was just part of the fun.

> *"I always claimed Dusty quit the football team because he was behind me as a second-string guard. That wasn't true. He was a hell of a ballplayer … a hell of an athlete … a good linebacker. People don't know it, but he was a tough, hard-nose, damned good athlete."*
>
> —TERRY FUNK

Terry was always unorthodox. He was one of those workers who really thought he was a hooker and a shooter … like yellow finger, like Hogan. They think they're hookers and shooters, but they have a great wall of imagination. They just had that Dick Murdoch or Wahoo McDaniel mentality—except Wahoo could be mean—that wrestlers should be respected whether they deserved it or not.

Terry has a respect for the business like nobody I have ever met besides myself and a few other people like Dick or Wahoo.

To this day, at 63 years old or however old he really is, Terry believes it's real. Walking out through that curtain when his name is called, it's believable at that point because he does things for his love of the business that people who are younger than him shouldn't even be doing. But that's what he knows and that's how we took care of business. We would feud to the point of real stitches ... 12 or 14 stitches, and ribs really being broken. When he would hit you with a chair, it wasn't like on the flat side. That son of a bitch would either throw it at you or he'd hit you with the jagged part of it. It didn't make a fuck of a difference to him, because in the ring he was always in a barroom fight!

I was on the stage singing at the Imperial Lounge in Tampa one night with my good friend Captain Lewis, and he crawled through the club on his hands and knees, going between people's legs from the back door to the stage to come after me. Earlier that night we had a brutal, brutal match. Once he made it to the stage, he threw a drink in my face. I didn't see it coming and I leaped up and we fought all the way to and out the back door. He just thought that was the greatest thing in the world, and it was funnier than shit because he believed that ... and so that believability carried to the people. And that believability to this day is not carried longer by anybody besides me, the Devil—Kevin Sullivan—and probably Terry, because he's been in it his entire life.

As far as he and I are concerned, I believe it's still a feud that people will pay to see; these two old gunfighters going at it.

Some of the Texas Death Matches we had are still talked about, historic if you will. So you know the feud with him is still going on ... the hatred between us is still strong. We're not shooters, we're not hookers, we're just two sons of bitches who want to kick each other's ass every time we see each other.

Two old warriors beating the fuck out of each other at some independent show in front of hundreds of people going crazy— it doesn't get any better than that. Buddy, there is no gray area here—this is fucking me and him kicking each other's ass in front of hundreds of people and getting the crowd into it. That's a great match!

Longevity is Terry's thing, and I don't know any better way of explaining it than the time he picked up a roll of barbed wire and threw it at me. People know those big rolls weigh about 15 to 20 pounds, and he just threw it at me and hit me in the arm with it—just threw it at me. I was looking the other way and turned around and I was thinking, "This stupid motherfucker!" Well, when shit like that happens, you get so mad you start hitting him fucking hard with whatever you can grab. You're so mad your eyes are shut as you're hitting him and the brutality about it threw us together with great respect for each other.

We have a tremendous amount of respect for each other because we still—and I won't even say the word—we still believe it's real while others don't … that's what makes it great! What you would call an angle or a great feud or whatever, but we can't talk about our ending because it's still going on.

But let me tell you how crazy Terry Funk really is.

He would go down to the airport while I would be there and he would walk behind me without me knowing it. As he was following me, he would scream "Fatso!" then he'd hide behind somebody or in a corner so when I would turn around, I didn't see anybody. I'd walk about five more feet and he would yell as loud as he could, "Fatso!" So I would turn around again and look back and I still didn't see him. But then I would hear him so I would ask him later on, "What were you doing at the fucking airport calling me, 'Fatso?'"

He'd say, "No, I was saying to somebody walking with me, 'Is that so?!'"

"What do you mean, 'Is that so?'"

He'd look right at me and say, "You just took it wrong … that's why we don't like each other." And then he'd walk away.

That was his mentality.

We had a lot of fun together, buddy.

Dr. Jerry Graham was a huge star going all the way back to the 1950s with his tag-team partner Eddie Graham. Their team was legendary and they wrestled as brothers, although they weren't related. But by the time I came in contact with him, he had become a full-fledged out-of-his-mind motherfucker.

What I am about to recount is the God's honest truth. This is the story of one legendary week in the Amarillo territory.

On Sunday, we left Amarillo and headed to Albuquerque early because we had a long haul to show up before the night matches. At that time Terry and I traveled together—running with the boss's son couldn't hurt! As we finished television and went to the show at the Civic Center, Dr. Jerry was already working his magic.

I don't remember who Doc rode with, but he was to manage me as I would be facing the greatest Latin babyface and pro wrestler in the world, Jose Lothario. It was a good house, paid attendance-wise. I think Terry was wrestling some star like Bull Ramos.

Anyway, I got my ass handed to me by Jose, and he got the win, lucky bastard! After the match, as I laid spread out on the mat like a fucking bear rug, Doc jumped in the ring and had me open my mouth. He put three pills down my throat before I could say no. It had happened. He looked at me and said. ...

I didn't know what he said or what the pills were. Shit, those pills could have been LSD or even poison. Well, as I got back to the dressing room I was scared, but I was also pissed at him. To this day I respect the men and women in our industry who kept me from saying anything about it.

Then the real fun began with the drive from Albuquerque to El Paso; a long trip. Terry told Dory Sr. that no one wanted to take him, so the old man said we had to take him. I said, "Let Harley [Race] take him. He was the booker. Shit!"

Harley said it would be fun. Fun?!

We loaded up the green Pontiac Grand Prix and hit the road.

You have to understand that back then there were some back roads we took to get from Albuquerque to El Paso that were right out of the movies: dirt roads, little cantinas, rattlesnakes, bad-ass hombres and federales along the way.

At our first beer stop, Dr. Jerry, who had gotten a $100 draw for the week, said that he would go in and get the beer. He said he needed the money, so we gave him money for a dozen beers. This first cantina we all stopped at had everything but a hose and horse trough standing out front! After about 10 minutes he finally came out and said they didn't serve anything but hard liquor! What the fuck was that about?

Anyway, Jerry jumped back in the backseat and we drove off. We were getting thirsty. We found another cantina about 10 miles down the road. As we pulled in, Dr. Jerry said, "I got it," and without thinking, us dumb fucks gave him money again.

This time I think we waited about 15 minutes before he came out. His arms had no vitality to them. He got in the car and said, "Hard drinks only." Well, as we left, something was adrift because he could barely talk and he was just wobbling as he walked!

We came to a third place and we still weren't even really on the road yet. The lot we pulled into where the cantina was had a big flashing sign saying "Cold Beer!" All right! As I was about to go in, Dr. Jerry had climbed his big fat ass out of the backseat and was on his way in. Terry and I just looked at each other. Okay, something's going on here.

Well, after about five minutes and no sign of him, we both headed in. As we opened the door—I loved it so much, I am thinking about going back to Mexico right now—the scene was right out of a movie. There was the good doctor, a Sidney Greenstreet lookalike, holding court in the corner of the bar.

As he saw us, he quickly came over and said he owed for the beer, and it was getting expensive as me and Funk hit our pockets again. Apparently the son of a bitch was drinking as much of the hard stuff as he could at every stop, spending all our money and coming out with no beer. After about four beers it was time to hit the road. Terry and I laughed a long time about it as our green steed headed through the night. It was on to El Paso and old Mexico ... oh, shit!

It was early Monday morning as we got into town. The Alamo Plaza Hotel was our headquarters for this stay. As we pulled in we could see Harley's big silver Lincoln Continental was already there. Dr. Jerry was out of money so Terry woke Dog—Harley—up and got money to check the big man in. Sleep finally came.

Dog had given him $100. With his $100 from the night before gone, he had hit Terry and me for about $40 and now he had another $100; $240 total by my calculation. Here I only made about $200 for the whole week.

After Dog had got up, he saw Jerry and told him to clean up. Jerry came on the trip with one suit. Yes, one suit; one of those old-time suits with the big shoulder pads in it. He looked like he weighed about 100 pounds in it to the boys.

It was match time, and once again it was "Dirty" Dusty Rhodes versus Jose Lothario, and buddy, this was Jose's town! If it even looked as if you were hurting him, you would have a full-fledged riot on your hands!

Dr. Jerry was to go to the ring with me. The federales hated me. Jerry was nuts, and I was young. But, fuck it, he was my manager. Much like Jim Cornette years later, who carried a tennis raquet, Dr. Jerry Graham carried an umbrella. Unbeknownst to anyone, however, during the day he had gone out and bought an electric cattle prod that fit in his umbrella.

For those of you who don't know, these things take four big "D" cell batteries and are used to move along 2,000-pound bulls and cows. During the match, as I was working over Jose, I saw a fan go flying through the air. The next thing I knew, the ring began to fill up with fans and police as Jerry used his umbrella like Errol Flynn would use a sword as a fight movie unfolded in front of me. As I fought off the fans, the dressing room emptied and all of the wrestlers jumped in to help. A riot with about 60 people was in full swing! No one would get in front of Jerry because he had the weapon, of course, loaded in the umbrella.

The police got us back to the dressing room, and the police captain was out of his mind. He pulled out his gun and started to shake. Man, I thought, "Shit, he is going to shoot me!"

All of a sudden a calming voice filled the room. Of all people, it was Dr. Jerry.

"Sir," he said so calm and straight, "we are sorry. ..."

Doc told the captain that I was young and he would sit me down and talk to me about respect for the El Paso Police Department. The captain bought it.

He put his gun away and left.

I asked myself, "What the fuck is going on?"

As I went for Jerry—I wanted to beat his ass—Terry and Harley jumped in and cut me off.

I told Jerry, "That's it! Find yourself another ride tomorrow."

After the show when everybody calmed down, Terry, Bobby Duncum, and the German, Karl Von Hess, and I headed for old Mexico. Duncum and Von Hess brought the good doctor with them.

We were in this little cantina drinking and talking to the whores, just having fun. The bar had this long sheet of glass that ran behind it; maybe about 20 feet long. Well, I was leaning on the bar when I looked in the mirror and noticed that behind me was Doc. He had a look about him like he was going to throw a whisky bottle into the glass.

As Terry came up to the bar, I said very calmly that the Doc was getting ready to break the glass behind the bar.

Crash!

It happened! The sound of glass breaking filled the air.

The bartender froze. We all put money on the bar and got the hell out of there. By the grace of God we got back over the border and avoided spending time in a Mexican jail!

I got back to my room and to bed I went.

It was the third day of this Texas odyssey, and our next stop was Odessa. If you think you've heard it all, you won't believe the shit that happened next.

We got up early, around 9 a.m., because from El Paso to Odessa you had to drive through Van Horn, Texas, which was like going back in time. You'd drive for forever before you got to Van Horn and the Dairy Queen.

Anyway, we had finished breakfast, and Terry said that Harley would be taking the good doctor to Odessa. As we left the café, we noticed Jerry coming out of his room heading toward the café. He looked funny. He was blue-black.

His suit was wet with a black-dye look. He had bought black dye, put water in his tub, and dyed his suit—with him in it!

Holy shit, this was getting good!

Dog had had his car washed and cleaned. It was spotless. Terry went into the café to talk to Harley as I cut off Jerry. Terry told Dog that Jerry was wet. When Terry came out while Harley was finishing his breakfast, Doc told us to get him a horse blanket from the western store across the street, so he could sit on it. We did and Jerry got in Dog's car. We waited across the street so we could follow them.

Harley came out and went off on the Doc!

Harley drove as if he was in the Indy 500 all the time. We saw that he had put all his windows down so Dr. Jerry could maybe dry off. Dye was flying everywhere! Man, what a scene.

We rode behind them, and I know that Harley tried to throw the good doctor out of the car three or four times going about 110 mph, but it didn't happen.

We all made it to Odessa and somehow we got through the match. Dr. Jerry was partly sick by this time, and Harley said he'd talk to Terry's dad.

The old man told Harley to rent a U-Haul truck and put Doc in the back and bring him to Lubbock and back to Amarillo ... a fucking U-Haul! I loved it!

> *"The Jerry Graham road trip was some of the craziest five days of my life."*
>
> —TERRY FUNK

They were some great times, buddy. And running the road in the old territories was part of the business I miss.

Some people in the business say I'm a son of a bitch fat ass. But, being great in all sports and overcoming adversity, some say I was and am the last "Bull of the Woods."

Back then there were lots of bulls in the woods.

One of them who ran the road with me in pro wrestling was my late partner and friend, Dick Murdoch. As everybody who knows anything about me knows, he was my soulmate in the industry, which is why I dedicated the book to him.

I could truly write an entire book about Hoyt Richard Murdoch, and I might do it one day.

He was so close to me I couldn't even go to his funeral. I am not a funeral guy. Everybody knocked me for that, and that's cool, because I don't care, as you can probably tell by the tone of my writing.

This is the way I feel. I wanted to be able to keep his number in my phone book and I keep it on my cell phone. Some say all this life is only bullshit, so I said if I don't see him for a while, I can always call him. If he doesn't answer, I know he's out somewhere. I didn't want to see him dead, so he's not dead to me. I have his number and every so often I will call him from the road; I just happen not to get him in. That's the way I feel about it.

The first time I saw Hoyt, he was running security at the fairgrounds in Amarillo when they had wrestling on Thursday nights, while I was wasting my life at West Texas State University. He was a big, tall, cotton-headed redneck kid who bleached his hair. I saw him there, and he would help all the bad guys back to the dressing room after the ass-kicking they got. I didn't know at the time that he was Frankie Hill Murdoch's son, one of the wrestling industry's biggest stars of the Amarillo territory. Frankie had passed away a few years earlier.

I didn't see Hoyt again until we actually worked together in Kansas City, Pat O'Connor's territory. I didn't know that he had broken into the business as a wrestler, I believe in Tennessee.

The Kansas City office was in a room of an old hotel. I had short blond hair and was sitting in Bob Geigel's office when he said, "Man, we're going to team you up. Your partner is right next door." He opened the door and that's the first time I met Murdoch, although I recognized him immediately from the Amarillo territory working behind the scenes as probably an 18-year-old.

We hit it off instantly, and for the next three years or so it was as if you put two cowboys in a modern-day setting with a car instead of horses. With all of the whiskey and beer you could drink, the most fun you could have and the most fights you could get into, we had the most notorious legacy as a tag team in the history of our business. We were it buddy, and we were the outlaws … we were the Texas Outlaws.

During that time of learning our trade, I went along with him because he educated me as he was the best plain-ass natural worker in the business, bar none.

There were nights when he used to work and there were nights when he didn't give a shit. When Dick Murdoch wanted to have a match with you, there was nothing he couldn't do, and you knew it.

To this day, in my opinion, one of the greatest televised title matches in the history of free TV was Hoyt against a young Barry Windham on Bill Watts's Mid-South Wrestling promotion TV show.

But I noticed right off about Hoyt that he got a bad reputation. Just like the old gunslinger Jesse James got a reputation about being a bad ass and not liking people, Hoyt had this reputation of not liking black people or any ethnic group.

But he had some great friends who were black. Ernie Ladd—"Big Red" as I called him—and Hoyt were like brothers; they loved each other. So they must have known something that I didn't. And I would think there's got to be something here, because through the years of my traveling with Dick and staying with him 360 out of 365 days a year on the road, in a car, or at a Shady Rest Inn, you know there's more to someone than that so-called reputation.

It was phenomenal times when he would break down and lose that feeling of hatred toward ethnic groups. So, I really knew how he was inside; he had a heart.

There were times when he would say he was not going to go pick this guy up that could have ridden with us, and I'd talk him into taking him and then he would curse the guy all the way there, making the guy feel so bad that he had to do it. But Dick was going to do it anyway. He was going to help out because he had a big heart.

He was funny, he was obnoxious, and his pickup line in the bars was one of the greatest in history. Because he was from Texas, he thought everybody understood what a "flank" was, which was slang for the part of a woman's body right down by their asshole. And his line to these girls would be, "How would you like for me to snort in your flank?"

Well, there's not a flank to be snorted in there.

"My God you know, Hoyt," I'd say, "no wonder you can't get laid."

I went through this whole thing with him, so he would change it and he would say his next line, which was, "Are you married?"

She would say, "No."

"How would you like to be married?" He thought that was the best. "Watch this," he would say, and the girls would look at him like he was fucking stupid with his white cotton hair. He would use those lines continuously.

Years later, after I was established as the Dream, we were outside of New Orleans one night at a bar and he said, "Let's go change bars." So we got in a truck with some guys and we drove down the road right inside of New Orleans and I saw this fire burning. Now this is the '70s and we were driving up the fucking road and they were burning a fucking cross there. It was a fucking Ku Klux Klan rally. Murdoch was taking me to a fucking KKK rally. I am the American Dream. Everybody in this town loves me.

"What the fuck are we doing?" I asked.

He laughed like hell because he really thought this was a funny deal. This fucking belligerent bastard dragged me up there, and I just wanted to hit him in the fucking mouth, the heathen he was.

Sometimes he felt that he had to live up to the reputation he created. But he didn't have to live up to that reputation, because he wasn't really like that. He only did it because of the reputation, and the believability and respect for the business I talked about earlier. There was never a gray area with Hoyt, it was either one way or the other; only black or white.

Dick and the politics of the business didn't mix. He didn't go to West Texas State University when he played on the alumni football team; he became their mascot. He supposedly graduated with a 3.0 grade point average there, but he never went there. He had that knack of getting you to accept him. If you liked him, you were his friend, and he was a precious guy. He truly was. And he was the best babyface worker I've ever seen in his prime. Without a doubt there was nobody there who could compare to him to this day. Not Ricky Steamboat. Nobody. Hoyt was out in fucking Amarillo and he could tell a story. Others could tell a story, too, but Hoyt was in a class all by himself.

In 1969 the two of us set out to work for Jim Barnett in Australia. We would stay 13 weeks; it was Murdoch's second trip, my first. Dick was to get $800 a week and I was to get $700 a week. What's up with that shit? Anyway, it was to be a trip to remember.

Australia was pretty wild back then, and we stayed at the Plaza Hotel on King's Cross! The Cross was the Bourbon Street of Sydney, Australia, the red light district, if you will. The hotel had no air conditioning, small rooms, and a funky smell. The rooms were like small jail cells, and the bathroom was so tiny that when I sat on the toilet, my legs were in the other room. But we were happy, young, and ready to raise some hell.

We pretty much lived in our hotel room, and on our tour were midgets; the little people, both women and men. To this day I have a great deal of respect for them as they worked hard and endured much harassment from people.

We worked hard, too. Jim ran a top wrestling group headed by his booker Mark Lewin; yes, the same Mark Lewin who teamed with Don Curtis earlier in his career and would later become a disciple of Kevin Sullivan as "The Purple Haze." Mark became one of my favorite people.

He taught me a lot about being a pro wrestler from the business side. He was Barnett's right hand, much like Pat Patterson was Vince's right-hand man for many years. Next to Eddie Graham, I learned more about the wrestling business from Jim than anybody else.

I was very fortunate in that I met a lot of great people in the business.

One of the great ones was "Bulldog" Bob Brown from Canada. He billed himself as Canada's greatest athlete. As a matter of fact, every Canadian wrestler I ever met was billed as its greatest athlete. How is that even possible?

Anyway, Murdoch and I had to get from Kansas City, Missouri, to Wichita, Kansas, for a match on Monday night. So we caught a ride with "Bulldog" Bob Brown. He had a new car, one of those big 1969 Oldsmobiles. It was fine.

Hoyt always liked to fuck with Bulldog. He would get him so mad that he would turn red, heart-attack red. After the matches we would get our beer, and Hoyt and I always tried to drink at least a case on the trip back to Kansas City.

As the long trip went on, we were feeling good from the beer, and Hoyt slapped Brown in the back of the head. Man, he was getting pissed!

Bulldog had a blackjack he kept under his seat. Well, he pulled out the blackjack and while driving, he turned and tried to hit Hoyt with it.

Being a smartass, I moved my hand under the armrest and got his .22 (caliber) pistol and slowly removed six bullets onto the floorboard.

As the loud country music, laughter, and talking was at its peak—with Bulldog driving around 90 mph—I quickly put the gun to the side of Bulldog's head. He turned white as a ghost as I pulled the trigger. To make it worse, I began laughing, too.

Then, one of the greatest statements of wrestling road travel was about to come out of my mouth.

"Shit, Bulldog, the gun wasn't even loaded. See!" I put the gun between my legs, aimed at the floorboard, and pulled the trigger.

Blam!

Holy fucking shit! I almost killed the bastard!

The sound turned Canada's greatest athlete into a babbling idiot. As he pulled the car over to the side of the road, the reality set in that these road trips with Hoyt and me were only going to get worse. By all accounts we should have been dead a long time ago!

"Dusty and Dickie always liked to mess with Bulldog. One time on a tour of Australia, they found out that Brown was afraid to fly. So during a flight in one of the little puddle jumpers we took, they convinced him

we weren't going to make it. Bob Brown fell to the floor and began praying."

—GARY HART

When we were together, we were really inseparable. We did some crazy shit.

One night in Edina, Minnesota, we were at this bar and we hadhad a little too much to drink, so we bought a mule off of some guy, but we had no place to keep him, since we lived in this apartment complex. We ended up bringing the mule upstairs to our second floor apartment and he lived there. The mess finally got so bad we just had to get him the hell out of there.

Also when we were working for Verne Gagne up in the AWA territory, just to rib Kosrow Vasiri, the Iron Sheik, we drove from Minneapolis to Fargo, North Dakota, and put him in the back of my pickup truck in freezing 30-degree weather.

There were many, many stories like this and I will tell a few more later on, but it's time to explain why it was my decision to break up one of the greatest tag teams in wrestling history.

After something like 300 days on the road, I'd wake up in the morning and the room would smell like at place where they would slaughter cows and horses and pigs and ducks. On this particular morning I woke up and the smell finally hit me, coming right out of my mouth. After a fifth of whiskey, 37 beers, and all the Slim-Jims and potato chips you could eat, it was horrifying.

I opened my eyes and I looked over to the other bed and there was Hoyt, his big white ass sticking up. His BVDs probably hadn't been washed in days as they were really brown in the back. I got up and I swear to God, washed my face with the cowboy wash; that's where you put your whole head in the sink under the water. I washed my face really good and looked in the mirror and asked myself, "What the hell are you doing?"

After we both got up and had some lunch, I said, "I'm giving my notice tonight to Jack. I'm going to work for Eddie [Graham]."

Jack Cane was the booker for the territory and I said, "I think we need a little time away." I just couldn't get that scene out of my mind right after telling Hoyt ... the brown streak in the back and the yellow stain up front. He thought that was fucking hilarious.

So it was show time in Dayton, Ohio, and I walked in to talk to Jack—who happens to be the stepfather of Billy Bob Thornton—and I saw Hoyt trying to follow me in.

We were a tag team, so he said, "Me, too."

I turned around, "No. Wait. Stop!"

Back then you gave four weeks' notice so the promotion could do what they needed to get things done. If you gave two weeks or less, you found yourself in a world of shit, pile of shit, or whatever other kind of shit you can get into ... because you know what's going to happen to you.

"Just one second ... just one second. ..."

It was hard to say, but I had to.

"Dick, I need to go by myself and you need to go by yourself for a while, know what I mean? We've been on the road 360 days a year with each other and missed a lot. I've got to move on and try to find myself. We're young and we got a shot."

So he kind of said he gave his notice at the same time I gave mine, not knowing what we were going to do and that was pretty much the split.

Sure, we worked with each other in Japan, we saw each other off and on and had a feud with each other, but we never partnered all over the country again like we did those first three years as a tag team.

He went his way and I went mine.

I became whatever I was going to be, but he had a thing about him that he had to live up to, like the thing I mentioned earlier about the racism. Now that I think about it, he probably had to live up to that reputation like I had to live up to the reputation of being the American Dream.

If I wanted a new car, it was important I had one. I was going to be in the hole financially, but it didn't matter as long as I was driving my new car in downtown Tampa, and they—the fans—would see me in it and that would be cool ... that would work because that was part of living the dream as "the Dream."

Like I said ... believability and respect. ...

CHAPTER 5

I've often told people that I feel I was born a black man in a white man's body. I know that probably sounds crazy, but for those of you who are following my story closely, reading between the lines if you will, I'd like to believe that you understand where I am coming from. Perhaps my thinking comes from my childhood, having lived in a mixed neighborhood of whites, African Americans and Mexican Americans. Maybe it comes from the fact that I feel like I've struggled in my life to gain acceptance in my profession, as a black man would struggle for acceptance in his everyday life.

I know it would be impossible for me to really know or understand what my African American brothers and sisters experience every day of their existence in terms of racism, discrimination and exploitation, but in my heart of hearts I know they are the ones who built the foundation for my fan base in order to help me become … and live … the American Dream.

It's hard to explain that the chase for an American Dream is in all of us. For some, just getting up every morning and going to work in order to pay the bills and taking care of business while thinking of a more fulfilling life is an American Dream. For others, just getting up every morning in a free country is an American Dream. For me, right now just writing these words for you to read can be considered an American Dream.

Toward the end of 1973, a different American Dream was about to be realized. At the Landmark Apartments in Tampa, Florida, little did I know that I was about to become "The American Dream" and an American Icon.

The word icon is used in our industry a lot, but most of the time it is bullshit. The territory system had its stars, but on a national level there were only a few who held that star status, and I was about to become one of them … an icon that is.

51

Championship Wrestling from Florida has long been gone, disbanded, but in the eyes of the fans and the stories they still tell, at times it's like I've never left and CWF is still going strong. I love them for that.

While wrestling existed in Florida before 1960, CWF lived from around 1960 and died in February 1987, almost two years to the day after Eddie Graham was found dead in his home, the victim of a self-inflicted gunshot wound. It's still hard for me to talk about Eddie's suicide, probably because he was so close to me, in many ways a second father, and to this day his son Mike is one of my best friends, almost like another younger brother.

Some say the 1980s were not real good to Eddie. With his in-ring career pretty much over, except for the occasional appearance here and there, he concentrated on his promotional and charitable duties, while privately battling personal demons.

While some may scorn me for this, I feel it's not my place to write about his drinking problem, as we all have faults. Eddie unfortunately had a very dark side, and while maybe it is my place to talk and write about the depression that led him to taking his own life, I can't and I won't. I can only talk and write about what he meant to me and the wrestling business.

In our business, Eddie had no equal. Let me repeat that, he had no fucking equal in our business, and I've seen them all. His mind for pro wrestling story telling, ring work, timing, and even advertising and promotional stuff, could not be matched. He was ahead of himself.

A lot of people may not realize it, but the Florida territory did not come easy to Eddie. Florida was originally run by a guy named Clarence "Cowboy" Lutrell. He ran Florida from 1949 to 1971. When he left the business, Eddie took over, but not without controversy. I don't know all the behind-the-scenes dealings here, but from what I understand, "Professor" Boris Malenko thought he was entitled to take over the territory. I don't know if that is true or not, because it was always explained to me by Gordon Solie, Hiro Matsuda, and others that it was Eddie who was the one being groomed by Cowboy to take over. Now I know Malenko drew money in the territory with Eddie, and their feuds are still talked about by some today, but I don't know exactly what happened. All I know is that there was a lot of bad blood, or as we say in the business a lot of "heat" between the two, and they never spoke again.

Every so often a little outlaw promotion would pop up here and there, and just like a Mafioso Godfather, he would say, "Them motherfuckers will pay! You guys go over there and kick their asses." Like I said, he was the Florida Godfather.

Now while Eddie could be a tough son of a bitch, he had a big heart. He was a big supporter of charities and amateur wrestling, which made him a huge asset to the business, by tying his business into the community. He started amateur wrestling camps and was personally responsible for getting amateur wrestling into Florida high schools. He established a $500 wrestling scholarship for the University of Tampa, donated $10,000 in 1978 to the University of Florida to create a wrestling room, and was one of the co-founders of the Florida Sheriff's Boys Ranch, now called the Florida Sheriff's Boys and Girls Ranch. For those who do not think this was genius on his part, you can kiss my ass. He knew exactly how to position himself with the people who would ultimately help his promotion. Remember, in the wrestling business, business is business.

I think it's important to explain just how influential Eddie was back in the 1970s because some of that had to do with the creation of the Dream. Eddie was a much respected promoter within the NWA and was the organization's president from 1976 to 1979. Under his watch, the NWA territories did great business, everyone was making money hand over fist, and he was among those personally responsible for arranging the first ever NWA versus WWWF (World Wide Wrestling Federation) World Title unification match in 1978 between Harley Race and "Superstar" Billy Graham at Miami's Orange Bowl; a card I also happened to be on, defeating Ken Patera.

So CWF really had only three guys the territory was built on—Eddie in the '60s; Jack Brisco, the NWA World Heavyweight Champion in the early '70s; and then me. For each era, each man had his run.

Jack was right in the middle of his run when he passed me the torch, and buddy I lit up the state from Key West to Jacksonville with that torch and it was all so simple.

It was at the Miami Beach Convention Center in 1973, "Dirty" Dusty Rhodes versus Jack Brisco, the handsome Indian from Oklahoma; Florida's golden boy.

In a match that lasted one hour, I saw the fan favorite change to a villain right before my eyes. A very simple move happened, one that Eddie knew would work. At about the 50-minute mark, as the voice of Frank Freeman—Miami's very famous ring announcer—said, "Fifty minutes gone, ten minutes to go," I hit Jack with the big elbow and he flew across the ring.

As Jack landed on his back, the roar of the crowd became deafening. I dropped the big elbow on him, I covered him, and the crowd seemed to know that without a doubt I was about to become World Heavyweight Champion. As I waited for the count, everything seemed to be in slow motion … one, two, as I looked at the ref, he started to get up and stopped fucking counting at two and tapped me on the back to break it up. Could it be over? Was I the champ?

The crowd roared … not with glee, but with anger! The booing from the 6,000 in attendance was beyond belief. I looked down and saw that Jack's leg was draped over the bottom rope—something an outlaw would do to save himself from a hanging … but the World Champion? The match continued and ended after a one-hour draw. Whoa! The crowd was still booing Jack!

As I left the ring, the crowd began to cheer so loud I will never forget it, the icon shit just started to take over. Jack Brisco was still champion, but the world of pro wrestling was about to change.

It was that simple, that easy. No high-risk maneuvers, no stunt bump off a building, just a cover, a foot and leg on the ropes … a champion saving his title.

"Even before putting the leg over the rope, earlier in the match I had Dusty tied up in a corner and when it came time to break, it wasn't a clean break … the fans didn't like that at all."

—JACK BRISCO

Eddie was standing in the door of the dressing room. He looked at me and I'll never forget what he said, "That is the way we do business. That's how simple it is when you are 'over'." But he also had that black and white look on his face—there was no middle ground there, no gray area—"You have to go a little longer before you become a good guy." Business is business. It was business at its best, simple, but good business.

Bill Watts was booking the territory at the time and later that night he, Jack and Eddie talked about me becoming a good guy! For me it was time to become the American Dream.

"It was Eddie's idea to turn him babyface. Dusty had gotten over so hard, it was impossible to keep him heel."

—JACK BRISCO

Eddie had the prime suspect as to who would help me take that final step. In 1974 Pak Song Nam and "Playboy" Gary Hart were the players who not only had a hand in changing the landscape of wrestling, but they were the tools used to build the icon, transforming the interview into the reason so many would attend the event, and most of all to see the Korean Assassin with his manager matched against the son of a plumber from Austin, Texas— "The American Dream" Dusty Rhodes. It does not get any simpler than that. Good versus evil! The emotions would fill the arena and make TV ratings go through the roof! What an era ... what a great time to be a wrestling fan.

There have been a lot of stories of how, when, and where "The American Dream" moniker was first attached to my name. There have also been lots of stories of who came up with "The American Dream" for me.

Let me make it clear. When I first talked about "The American Dream," it really had nothing to do with wrestling.

After I started the turn from being a bad guy or "heel" to a good guy or "babyface," Gordon Solie and I would go to high schools and middle schools in the Tampa Bay area where I would give these little motivational speeches. Part of what I would tell the kids was about me growing up in Texas and working with T.C. Lee as a ditch digger and that he used to tell me, "There's a dream out there ... you oughta get out of this ditch and live it," and so I used to tell that to the kids. When I did, it was like a lightbulb went off over my head.

So we did this little deal on TV with Gary and I where we started arguing over the title shot I had with Jack, and for the first time ever on TV I said, "I'm not doing this for me, I'm doing it for all the black, the yellow, the green, the brown, all the people in the world ... this is the American Dream ... Dusty Rhodes ... you don't like it?" and I threw him against the wall— slam!—and when his head hit, it sounded like it would never come off the wall; it stuck like super glue.

So now during an interview with Gordon Solie on one of the televisions, I was recounting the same story to the people in the audience, about growing up and all and it just came out ... after I said it, about T.C. Lee, I turned to Gordon and said, "I'm 'The American Dream,' Dusty Rhodes." And I remember Gordon saying, "Pak Song Nam, 'The Korean Assassin' versus 'The American Dream' Dusty Rhodes ..." kind of like the exclamation point at the end of a statement.

"The thing that impressed me about Dusty was his incredible charisma. His interviews were awesome ... and the crowd loved his butt wiggles."

—JACK BRISCO

Well, wrestling fans picked right up on it, and that was my new handle. I was now "The American Dream."

And man, it just took off ... whoosh! ... ran rampant across the nation like the fucking hula-hoop. I not only became a big star in Florida, but people knew me all over and I changed people's lives. I was the man and I knew it! Why? Because men could look in the mirror and see their fat stomachs and women could look in the mirror and see their saggy tits and know they didn't have to be perfect to live their dream ... because if this fat black man in a white man's body, with a stupid-looking frizzy white afro hairdo could live the dream, well, so could they. And that's what it's all about ... it ain't the fucking hokey pokey.

Mike Graham was another player who really set the tone for me to turn and become "The Dream." Six-man tags were booked, with me, Mike and Eddie as a team. In the storyline Mike trusted me, but Eddie took the hard line and didn't—remember what he said to me in Miami about turning—as we would face Hart's Army led by Song. This made for great story lines, great television shows and great times in this cosmic world of pro wrestling as The Dream's era began to unfold.

"When Dusty turned it on and became The American Dream, you couldn't turn it off. You still can't turn it off. He's The Dream."

—MIKE GRAHAM

So basically the match with Jack set it up and with one move turned me into the biggest thing in our business. I became the biggest pre-yellow finger commodity and babyface. I respected Jack for that so much because he knew and Eddie knew and everybody knew that they could have put a hook in my act and yanked me right off the stage, but instead I shot out like a cannon.

What a ride that was about to begin for me and my fans!

Simply put, in '74 Song was the baddest motherfucker on the planet. Gary Hart was the ultimate flimflam man; someone who would take money from his own mama! Every Wednesday we shot television at the Florida Sportatorium, a little TV studio at 106 North Albany Avenue in Tampa. Hart would send a fan into the street on Wednesday morning before TV. The fan would bring back a big rock … not one of them brick-breaking fuckers, but a boulder! He would have Song break it into small pieces on TV with his bare hands. Then he took a watermelon and put his foot through it without busting it into a million pieces. The fans knew this was the real deal.

My God, it's the 4th of July in Jacksonville, Florida and it's The American Dream versus the Korean Assassin. Ten thousand people, or no matter how many people it was, it was an amazing scenario. Eddie was a marketing genius and here comes Dusty Rhodes carrying an American flag. It looked like the scene right out of the *Rocky* movie where Stallone has the flag draped over him. The flag that I was going to carry had a broken pole, so I went to the ring wearing it.

> *"When Dusty said he was The American Dream, he really was the American Dream; he became it because he believed it."*
>
> —TERRY FUNK

As the match went on, Pak Song caught me with one of his big hands and before I knew it, I was bleeding profusely … barely holding on for dear life. Then he put the claw on me—he hit me with that fucking claw.

Now we were out on the floor and it was back in the day where they had these little-bitty rails … they didn't have the big barricades they have today—they had the little-bitty rails. The rails were thin and metallic and had a piece that slid underneath it and one that went over the top.

There was a girl in the front row who weighed maybe 110 pounds. Her picture was in the Jacksonville newspaper the next day—an 8-by-10 picture because of what happened and what she did.

You know how some people get strength when their cars turn over and they get the strength to lift the car up? That's what she did … pure adrenaline rush. I didn't know her from Adam but he had the claw on me and she was screaming, so afraid that this was going to hurt me. But the pictures are of her pulling me from under this rail with her body weight being about 110 pounds at the most, soaking wet, pulling me out and he still got the claw on me pulling me his way; he finally broke the grip. I can remember her screaming as loud as she could, "Let him go, let him go, let him go!" and when he finally broke the grip, this hand came up with the blood on her fingernails and my head is in her lap ... that's the picture they got ... and she's crying the biggest tears in her life. The caption read "The American Dream, Dusty Rhodes saved from the Korean Assassin" on the 4th of July.

At that moment I said to myself these motherfuckers are with me. Whatever else is going down, they believe this thing that I'm talking for them ... and she did; she believed. Her story was phenomenal. I remember we battled to the back because the highlight of the story described how I came up from being staggered and she would not let me go to the end. I didn't want to push her aside, but her dress was totally full of blood as I staggered in and I felt this hand on me, this elbow that drew the crowd back to the back.

The Jacksonville police riot squad came, and the cops stood around trying to get us to stop. It was the craziest thing you've ever seen. Song came back and a cop grabbed his arms from the back like you would hold the guy for me to hit just like you see in the movies. I drew back to hit him and he ducked and I hit the cop and broke his nose. As I hit him and broke his noise, Pak Song and I both escaped to the back, but we ended up coming back out.

It was the most talked about day in the history of Jacksonville wrestling. It broke all sorts of records that were set by Eddie and Don Curtis back in the day. It was unbelievable, but I knew then, at that moment, that the picture of that girl was the proof I needed to know that it was really special with the fans that day.

"He had more impact on wrestling than people give him credit for. If there hadn't been a Dusty, there wouldn't have been a Hogan, a Flair, or a Rock. He opened the door."

—GARY HART

For that hour, when the bell rang for the first time with me as a full-fledged babyface, the next two hours belonged to The American Dream and my fans.

CHAPTER 6

The '70s have often been referred to as the "Me Decade" while the '80s were considered to be the MTV Generation, thanks to the expansion of cable television. For Dusty Rhodes, I was ingrained in the two decades as much as you can imagine. I not only rubbed elbows with the beautiful people at Studio 54, walking that thin line between hippies and yuppies, but I was at the forefront of the cable TV explosion, keeping a tight hold on my status as a champion of the people and living the American Dream.

Regardless of where I was and what I was doing, I always remembered my roots and what it took to get there … what it took to get out of that ditch.

Some nights before a match, I would remember those backyard wrestling shows with my brother Larry, and I wondered what my life would have been like if I had made it in pro football or baseball.

What would have happened if I had reported to that training camp when the Miami Dolphins' George Wilson invited me? Football was always my first love, and a career in the NFL would have been sweet. But would it really have been as bittersweet as the thousands of fans who have shown up over the years in arenas and stadiums to get a glimpse of the Dream?

Baseball was my second love, and when I got that scholarship out of high school to play at Sul Ross State University in Alpine, Texas, a school that produced such players as Norm Cash for the Detroit Tigers, I really thought I would follow in the footsteps of my baseball idol, Mickey Mantle; playing in Yankee Stadium one day. But would it have been as satisfying playing in the "House that Ruth Built" as it was when I wrestled in front of thousands, millions for *Starrcade*, the *Great American Bash* or even *WrestleMania VI*?

How different would my life have been if I had stayed on one of those two paths instead of the one that ultimately took me here?

How different would pro wrestling have been without "The American Dream" Dusty Rhodes? How different would it be today?

"To me, he's probably the greatest showman of our time."

—BLACK JACK MULLIGAN

But all of these questions really don't matter. It would all come back to me as it does right now in that I wasn't wrestling my brother anymore in our backyard in Austin, Texas, but I was in Madison Square Garden in New York City, the Cow Palace in San Francisco, the Tampa Armory, or one of a hundred other major arenas I've performed in and I realize that it doesn't matter what could have been, what's important is what was and what is … and good or bad, I was ordained to live the rest of my life as "The American Dream" Dusty Rhodes; something a whole hell of a lot bigger than Virgil Riley Runnels Jr. could ever possibly be. That was my destiny and I thank God for it.

"I think Dusty battled self-esteem issues all his life. His speech impediment and his less than bodybuilder physique, I feel, caused him some anxious moments even as a young kid. I'm not Dr. Phil and I might be wrong, but I think one of the driving forces behind Dream's success for so many years is the fact that he was driven internally to overcome what he perceived as personal liabilities in a very cosmetic industry. He was smart enough to turn what many may have perceived as liabilities into assets because very few wrestlers have ever identified and connected with such a wide spectrum of the wrestling fans as 'The American Dream.' 'Stone Cold' Steve Austin comes to mind on a short list."

—JIM ROSS

When I hit my stride buddy, "The American Dream" was like an out-of-control bucking bronco and there wasn't anybody, anywhere who could tame this wild fucking ride.

Now I've mentioned a lot of ongoing themes so far in this book—rules of engagement if you will—that I consider integral parts of both my life and the wrestling business. I've talked about believability and respect, taking care of family, and business is business. There's another theme that I've touched on a little bit, but in the aftermath of the creation of The American Dream the wrestler, this is another rule that is very clear cut with me and one that I've never taken lightly … everything in wrestling is black and white.

Now, that can mean a lot of things to a lot of people. But the reality of the situation is this: in pro wrestling it's either one way or another, there's no middle ground, no shades of gray. You can't be successful by being wishy-washy. You can't run a successful wrestling promotion by walking down the middle. Unfortunately, some people in the business don't like that notion or don't understand it.

Even though my life outside of the wrestling business might be made up of shades of gray, and that's fine for living a life outside the business, but when it comes to pro wrestling, there can only be black and white.

Here's a perfect example of what I'm talking about … it was during my time at World Championship Wrestling. Sometimes choices are made that wrestlers don't understand and tempers get out of hand and they just don't realize it has nothing to do with anything except business. Business is business!

At well over 400 pounds, his head was so red from rage I thought he was going to have a heart attack. His name was Leon White, Big Van Vader, and at the time my top heel. Vader was pissed, or at least he thought he was. I sat across from him as Eric Bischoff, the newly hired executive producer, sat to the side. It was a conference I've had many times as the head of all wrestling matters, the last of the real one-man booking committees.

Out of the blue he leapt to his feet, looking like a wild rhino charging a hunter. Being only about five feet away, Bischoff fell back in his chair as a horror overcame the room. He was about to either kick my ass or kiss me. Just before the impact came, he stopped right in front of my face and came nose to nose. He leered at me with a rage in his eyes that was thick, man … the breath coming out of his mouth covered my whole head. He spat when he talked. Holy dog fuck, this was intense.

"Dream," he said as he finally broke silence, "that's the trouble with you. There is no gray area; it's always black or white."

And it was. Being able to define the world of wrestling and all its matches was always black or white with me. Some people got it. Some people didn't. It took a wildly tense situation for Vader, one of the best big men in the history of our industry to get it … and to understand why. Think of it this way, Vader was a 400-pound kid who was sent to timeout and he didn't want to go. But when it was all said and done with, he knew he was wrong and he had to take responsibility. He wasn't going to bully his way out of taking his medicine.

But you see, even something that's so apparently black and white can't necessarily stand by itself. Fuck no! Because while it may be black and white in appearance, business is still business ... the people you work with are your family and you've got to take care of them ... and you can't do all that without the respect for the business and the believability that what you're doing is the real deal. It's so important to understand how all these elements are intertwined.

It's also important to understand how this philosophy helped me climb to the top of the pro wrestling industry and overcome those who were either in my way or attempted to knock me back to the bottom rung of the ladder ... and believe me, there were many in the industry who wanted to see Dusty Rhodes fail.

But the more I was over with the fans, the more power I got, and call it ego or whatever, but it got to the point that I became so powerful in Florida, so powerful in the business, that I thought I could do just about whatever I wanted to do, without the fear of suffering any consequences ... and I did ... in a big fucking way.

I realized from an early point in my career that interviews were 75 to 80 percent of the matches, so in order to make my impact and draw a crowd, I knew I had to reach the people; I had to get inside their heads and their hearts. If I didn't know what they wanted to see or hear, there was no way I was going to be successful. Look at the people who draw money, big money in our business, and every one of them could do an interview, or cut a promo as we refer to it in our business. Me, Hogan, Flair, Savage, the Rock ... every one of us sons of bitches could talk just as well as or in some cases better than we could work in the ring.

"The most impressive thing about Dusty was here was a guy that truly had a handicap—he had a speech impediment and a lisp—and at times he was difficult to understand. But when he got in the business, he realized he had to be on TV, so he used it to his advantage. He had to work on it because talk was so important. He had the ability of talking the fans, manipulating them into the arena. He was one of the greatest

talkers in the business and people emulated him—like 'Superstar' Billy Graham and Austin Idol—and they went on to be successful."

—TERRY FUNK

When this big, fat, African American woman fell about ten feet from a balcony at a show in Atlanta at the city auditorium, and they asked her what happened, she said she was trying to get a glimpse of "The American Dream," Dusty Rhodes. Well, right there it tells us why so many people came out to see me. They weren't there to see me do a hurricarana, or a flying drop kick or a flying elbow off the top rope. They were there because during my interview I told them I was going to kick somebody's ass they didn't like, and in the process they knew I would throw the bionic elbow, do the flip, flop and the fly, and shake my ass with as much attitude as I possibly could.

"He was natural ... it wasn't forced. Dusty didn't need to have one bit of wrestling ability; he didn't need to. People came for entertainment. He was showbiz. A performer that had few equals."

—"SUPERSTAR" BILLY GRAHAM

Dick Murdoch was in Jackson, Mississippi, with me one time and he asked me about this whole thing with the people of color and all, asking me how I could go out and act like that and I told him that if not for them, if not for the people of all races, colors and creed, there'd be no "American Dream," Dusty Rhodes. I knew where my bread was buttered.

So Hoyt, what does he do? Here comes "Captain Redneck." Now you've got to remember, before being given that name, Murdoch was the original "Captain Redneck," period. But he understood a lot of things and he knew he could draw money with that persona, because the fans loved to hate him since they knew he was a fucking racist ... even though he really wasn't, as I mentioned earlier. I think everybody's got a little black, a little Indian and a little white in them.

By now I was doing interviews that were so compelling it was almost like I was a reverend delivering a sermon and my parishioners were the fans. One of the guys in the office, I forget who, said I sounded like Jesse Jackson in my delivery, and the people were into it. They bought it, man.

"When Lyndon Johnson died, Dusty gave a eulogy on TV like a minister or something. To this day, it was one of the best interviews I've ever heard."

—REGGIE PARKS

It didn't matter that I borrowed some of the jive from those who were street-smart, and I don't mind saying that, because later on people would borrow from me ... what mattered was that the fans of all colors, black, white, brown, yellow, and red were my people, and I was their hero.

"Did I imitate Dusty? I took a lot from Dusty. I was influenced by him and (Muhammad) Ali. Dusty and I rubbed off on each other. Dusty, Jimmy Valiant and I fed off of each other."

—"SUPERSTAR" BILLY GRAHAM

So you see, I just had this knack. By saying the right thing at the right time, I could talk the people into coming out to the arena. You've got to remember, there are concepts that you have to be sensitive to, and I was always aware of what I was doing. Sure, I had to push the envelope sometimes, but I knew how far I could go, and I knew I had the people in the palm of my hand and so did everyone in the office.

There's no better way to illustrate this than how we set up my match with Bearcat Wright in the world-famous Fort Homer W. Hesterly Armory in Tampa.

Bearcat was one of the first African American heels at a time in the business when others of the same creed and color were considered strictly babyfaces; Sailor Art Thomas and Bobo Brazil out of the Detroit territory are two who come to mind. But Bearcat was different. He was a nasty heel. People did not like him at all. Unlike Ernie "the Big Cat" Ladd, or Big Red as I called him, who had been to Florida and despite being a heel the fans loved—and I want him to know that I loved him too, as he was a great interview—they just hated Bearcat ... he was a sleazy, sleazy guy.

I started to notice at the Armory that there was always a group of black teens who yelled all sorts of shit at him, including the "N" word.

"You're a nigger! You're a real nigger!" they'd yell at him.

Holy shit, I thought, this could be powerful. So I went to Eddie Graham and I told him I was going to say the "N" word during a TV interview.

Remember, my ego told me I could do just about whatever I wanted to do.

So I did. I called Bearcat Wright a nigger during one of my interviews. I said that my black, white, green, yellow, whatever brothers know when somebody's not really true ... we know when somebody's faking. It aired right on WTOG-TV, Channel 44 in the Tampa Bay area.

Then it was his turn, and during his interview to promote the upcoming card at the Armory, he said I wasn't the only one who thought that of him.

"What do they yell at me in the armory?" he asked.

What did they—the fans—call him in the armory on Tuesday nights? Nigger!

With apologies to Kevin Costner and his *Field of Dreams,* I knew that if I said it, they would come. And they did. They came via Interstate-4. They came via Interstate-75. Back then the Tampa police chief would try to keep the African American fans in the balcony. So many fans turned out to the Armory that night to support me, segregation was not going to be possible.

It was a gamble that paid off. If I wasn't as over as I was and I didn't have the power I did, I would never have gotten away with it. If anybody else had even tried to do it, they would have incited a riot. But then again, nobody else was "The American Dream."

But that wasn't the only time we were able to talk people into the arena. When we ran the Bayfront Center in St. Petersburg, we usually opened the doors at two o'clock for an eight o'clock show because the building always had a low proportionate attendance as it was a lot bigger than the Armory ... but not for this show. Terry Funk and I talked all kinds of shit back and forth to build it up. When the doors opened at 2 p.m., there were 2,000 people waiting outside.

Just before the show started, an announcement was made: "Ladies and gentlemen, we have just set a new attendance record here at the Bayfront Center."

The new record broke the previous one set by *The Lawrence Welk Show.* That's right, Lawrence fucking Welk. He always had a big show in the building ... we held the new indoor record ... un-fucking-believable.

I remember asking Duke Keomuka who was part of the office, "How is it?"

He looked at me and said, "Not bad."

Not bad? Horseshit! This fucking announcement stated we broke a record and the office shrugs it off, trying to make it less than what it was; that would be their mentality, though. They always protected the office.

I said, "Duke, you set a fucking record."

That night Andy Hardy, the local TV news guy and a good friend of Gordon Solie, had a helicopter shot of the Bayfront Center on the six o'clock news and it looked like 10,000 people had been turned away from the show instead of 2,000. From the sky, the building looked like it was the Super Bowl.

"Give Dusty a minimal amount of TV time and he can create a promotion."

—BLACK JACK MULLIGAN

If that ain't having power, buddy, I don't know what is.

It's the stuff like this that irks me nowadays sometimes when I see these guys who write for the Internet and they've only come on board from yellow finger until now and even afterward during the stunt wrestling era and they know nothing about what happened before … they haven't got a clue as to who really had power in the business and most importantly, why. They've not really studied their so-called profession.

The industry of pro wrestling is not what they think. The ones who believe they are on the inside are really just standing on the banks of some raging river, looking across it … and that my friends, is risky business.

So all these guys think the power and icon shit started with yellow finger. Bull fuck. It's been around a hell of a lot longer than Hogan, or any of us for that matter. In Texas, Fritz von Erich had it. In New York, Bruno Sammartino had it. In Detroit, the Sheik had it. In Minneapolis, Verne Gagne had it. Going back to when I was a kid, I know Lou Thesz had it. Before him, I'm sure "Strangler" Lewis had it. And if you go back far enough, I'm sure George Hackenschmidt had it. The fact he was the world champion like 100 years ago and we even know his name today, proves that he had it, because 100 years from now people will still know the name "The American Dream," Dusty Rhodes. Power, respect, believability, longevity … what the fuck is so hard to understand?

It's very simple. When you have power in pro wrestling, when you are so over with the fans, they become your people, and once they are yours, the promoters can't do anything but let you do whatever the hell it is you want to do. This is all part of what made me who I became during the "Me Decade" … "The American Dream Decade" … and in a way it carries right on through to today.

It happened at the Atlanta airport recently. One of the skycaps who has been there for about 30 years said to me, "What happened to you, man? You're getting too old to make a comeback." He was talking about the fact that I had started working with TNA and being on their *Impact* TV show.

He said he saw this deal on TV where Ron "The Truth" Killings went out and got hit with a guitar by Jeff Jarrett. Well, he didn't like that at all.

So on the very next TNA *Impact* show, I was sitting at the announcer's table, and this time I had the guitar wrapped around my neck by Jarrett, and "The Truth" came out to save me.

So when I went back to the airport and asked him, "How was that? Was that okay for you?" he said he thought it was cool that a brother saved me, but added that I "needed to get him," meaning I needed to kick Jarrett's ass because of what he did to me.

This was one of my fans who remembered … respected me … and believed.

If there ever was a John Wayne of pro wrestling, I'm him.

"When Dusty got into an angle, you believed everything that came out of his mouth. He had the lisp going … he was a great worker and he had great psychology."

—"STONE COLD" STEVE AUSTIN

Throughout the '70s and '80s not only did I meet many great wrestlers who came through Florida, but I met many in my travels and many were those whose names the modern-day fans may have either forgotten, or never even heard of. Kind of like an eight-track player, it was hot when it was new, but now…

This was a time when pro wrestling was starting to mold itself into what was about to become sports entertainment and the stunt wrestling of today.

Some of the guys I worked and drew money with or who just stand out in my mind came in all shapes and sizes. These were men like "Superstar" Billy Graham, Bugsy McGraw, "The Canadian Freight Train" Jos LeDuc, Ox Baker, Wahoo McDaniel, Buddy Colt, and Ray Stevens just to name a few.

While I probably won't get into detail about all of these guys, there have been some over the years who stand out more than others as they have been associated with me most through our feuds. They are in no particular order, Terry Funk, Kevin Sullivan, Harley Race, Abdullah the Butcher and the Four Horsemen of Tully Blanchard with Baby Doll, Ole Anderson, Arn Anderson, and Ric Flair.

Throughout the years I've had my own personal favorites for a variety of reasons, and a little bit later in the book I'm going to get into some details about some of these people when I lay out my Starrcade Prime fantasy card for you.

But for right now, two of the people who set the standard for being the ultimate babyface and heel in the business were both out of Detroit; Mark Lewin and Ed Farhat, better know as The Sheik.

Mark, who I mentioned earlier when I talked about going to Australia for the first time, as a worker was unbelievable, and he is who I patterned myself after when I made the switch to babyface. You were drawn to his in-ring presence. His command of the squared circle as a ring general was phenomenal. His timing was immaculate and his connection to the people, the way he "sold" being hurt, the way he made his comeback to fight the villain was brilliant. He was brutally handsome and he could make people cry or draw any emotion out of them he wanted just by the way he looked at the crowd. Jose Lothario was a very close second. So I studied Mark and I added to his style. Another person I saw a lot of Lewin in was Hogan, whether yellow finger realized it or not. When he sold 75 or 80 percent of his matches to guys like Roddy Piper or Paul Orndorff and built them up, and then he'd start making that Superman comeback, in a lot of ways it was like Lewin. The shake of the head, the glance to the crowd and then boom, he'd explode and fire back on the heel and draw that emotion from the crowd so he could whip the guy into the ropes, put his boot to their face and drop his leg on them for the one, two, three … ring the bell. Just like my flip, flop and the fly, and I'd drop the big elbow instead of a leg.

"Dusty is like an onion, he has many different layers … if you meet him and get a chance to have a conversation with him, you can't not like him. He's charming in a hillbilly sort of way. He really is a common man, and I've never seen anybody relate to people like he does. He has the ability

to connect with the people and a lot of people do not have that talent. He
relates to the people and maybe more importantly, they relate to him."

—Sir Oliver Humperdink

Then on the other side of the coin there was The Sheik. Not to be confused with Kosrow Vasiri, who was the Iron Sheik, with this guy there was nothing made up. He could make a large crowd of people scamper away simply by making a motion like he was going to attack them. All of his credit cards had "A Sheik" on them; they didn't say Ed Farhat or whatever, they read "A Sheik" because in Detroit he was a Sheik ... he was The Sheik. He was the one you were afraid of even as an adult. You were scared to death of him as a guy in the business, too ... you were scared of him because he was the ultimate heel. You'd think, boy this guy's fucking crazy. He carried himself like that all the time, never out of character.

A couple of guys who patterned themselves in the style of The Sheik were my old nemesis Kevin Sullivan and The Sheik's real-life nephew, Sabu. While Sabu never got the exposure he probably should have gotten because of his uncle's political stature in the business, Sullivan, like The Sheik, was a master of living his gimmick 24/7, and to this day is never out of character.

In our era, there is nobody who can compare with Mark Lewin or The Sheik in their prime ... nobody ... none ... zero.

Now from a pure wrestling perspective, one of, if not the best, wrestler had to be Jack Brisco. As I stated before, he was a real hero of mine. When he was the NWA champion and would come back for his monthly tour of Florida, we would ride around the Tampa Bay area after the matches, drink beer and listen to the newest outlaw albums. He didn't know it, but he taught me a lot about being a student of the game. He was great and a lot smarter about the wrestling business than most people gave him credit for. He was a guiding hand in the building of "The American Dream" and a friend. If you're too young to remember Jack wrestle and have not seen him in a match, get yourself a tape and see what your punk ass missed by not being around in the '70s.

And then there was Andre.

Next to Dick Murdoch and Terry Funk, the one guy I probably had the most fun being around during this era was the man who rivaled me in notoriety and maybe even in popularity—Andre the Giant.

Born Andre Rene Roussimoff in Grenoble, France, Andre started his career in his home country wrestling under the ring name "Monster Eiffel Tower" when he was discovered by "The Flying Frenchman" Edouard Carpentier. Before long he was wrestling in Canada for the Grand Prix promotion under the name Jean Ferre, and he eventually found his way to New York working for Vince McMahon Sr., who changed his moniker to Andre the Giant and billed him as the "Eighth Wonder of the World."

I think the reason we got so close was because while he was booked by Vince Sr., I was booked by Eddie and Jim Barnett, and many times we would find ourselves booked in different territories together. Just like Sam Muchnick, the NWA president back then booked the World Champion—Harley or whoever—Andre and I would also be booked. I'd always end up back in Florida, but every so often I needed a break and would go to work for Bill Watts, Jim Crockett, or whoever.

Anyway, one time Andre and I were at the Playboy Club in New York after a Garden show. There was a fat woman singing like Kate Smith and we were sitting at a table right up front and you could literally put your elbows on the stage. She was singing at the piano and Andre was so big that his head came up to where her leg was. She must have weighed about 500 pounds, and he started laughing one of those uncontrollable ones where you try not to laugh but instead you just keep going ... then I started and this went on for about 30 minutes. We finally went outside and as the club was closing, with virtually nobody on the street, we somehow managed to rent these two horse-drawn carriages that go through Central Park. Well, I rented one and he rented the other one and instead of going through the park, we decided to race them back to the hotel.

Andre always had money on him like there was no end and before I could get my money out, he just threw a hundred dollars to the driver of my carriage, and they took off. So there we were racing down the street. If the carriages would have been hot rods, flames would have been shooting out the back. Andre was leaning over because he was so big and his dark afro and my big white afro were flapping in the wind, and the drivers were these two black guys with these big top hats. What a sight that must have been.

I was so drunk, I told my driver to get close enough to Andre's carriage so I could jump from mine to his and go in between the horses like they do in the western movies ... where the stuntman rides between two buckboard

CHAPTER SIX

or stage coach horses and pulls on them to get them to stop. Well, that's what I wanted to do, anyway.

We were driving and people were coming out and they were looking at us like, "What the fuck ..." and it was just things like that I remember about him ... laughing so hard during the fun times. You enjoyed being around him, because we would have so much fun.

Toward the end, unfortunately, he became hateful and bitter toward people; he didn't want them around. I think he was just worn out as they got everything they could possibly get out of him. In the beginning, people were kissing his ass, but not anymore. Seldom do people care as much about you when you can't do anything for them.

But, like I said, when he was at his peak, and I was at mine, we had a lot of fun together. The one thing was, however, he always had a unique way of reminding me that even the most powerful people in our business can be fucked with every so often, and there's not a thing you can do about it except laugh.

The Giant was my friend and he loved playing ribs on people, and most of all he loved to play them on me. Whenever we were in New Orleans we would always head down to Bourbon Street after the shows to raise some hell.

And so the story goes. ...

On this particular night the weather was fucking bad; it was raining, lightning, and the wind was howling. It must have been the wind that brought us to Andre's favorite place on the street, the out-of-the-way home of some ugly French whores—well maybe not all of them were French—but they were all ugly whores!

She loved talking about her girls. She loved talking about New Orleans. But most of all she loved talking to him; him being seven feet, five inches and 500 pounds of giant ... Andre the Giant. She was from Montreal, Canada, and spoke French. He loved going to see her as I think it made him feel close to home. God knows it wasn't her girls, because like I said, she had the worst stable of butt-ass ugly whores in all of New Orleans.

We walked up to the top of the stairs and stopped. His eyes met hers and then lightning struck the roof of the fucking bordello and all the lights went out. After about 30 seconds I felt warm water running down the side of my pant leg. Ah shit, the rain. A slow, low laughter came from the Giant's head—next came uncontrollable laughter... what I thought was rain from the roof was nothing more than him pissing on my leg. The fucking Giant had just pissed on "The American Dream" in a French bordello in New Orleans, Louisiana!

As the lights came back on, the look on his face was priceless ... he always smiled big at something funny, and his mouth looked like it had about 290 teeth in it; what a head! It was a great rib; a rib on me and the whole rest of the night I walked down Bourbon Street smelling of Giant piss.

CHAPTER 7

n April 2003, one of my agents, Mike "Arli$$" O'Brien, got me an independent booking in Lynhurst, New Jersey, not far from Giants Stadium.

He picked me up to go to the small town, and as we drove there I couldn't help but get this funky feeling inside and remember my guided tour of the Big Apple more than 25 years earlier, when Vince McMahon Sr. surprised me and "Superstar" Billy Graham with a tour of the city that never sleeps.

Anyway, we arrived at the Knights of Columbus Hall and I was scheduled to fight Steve Corino; a little more on him later. The building held a couple of hundred people. The dressing area was a ten-by-ten room with 20-plus wrestlers changing in it. There was no rest room. No shower. Mike felt bad, but the guy paid us on our arrival. I had to piss in a popcorn box and throw it out the window, which I did several times that night. Every time I went to that window I could see the city—New York—off in the distance, across the river.

Manhattan. The Garden. Cops on horse back. My first Garden sellout. "The American Dream," Dusty Rhodes versus "Superstar" Billy Graham— Knights of Columbus Hall. "The Dream" versus a young star who was chasing his dream, also sold out; standing room only. What a fucking difference. What a wild ride on this lighting bolt!

During the '70s and '80s, I had an incredibly large Southern fan base, and by the time I reached New York City I had already reached legendary status in Florida and Georgia. But this was it, man. Madison Square Garden. Wrestling's Mecca, if you will.

Thanks to the wrestling magazines, the Florida TV shows being seen in New York on WNJU-TV a Spanish station out of Newark, New Jersey, and

Ted Turner's WTCG-TV Channel 17 out of Atlanta (which would later become TBS) now being beamed across America, people in the Northeast were already starting to catch on with who "The American Dream" was.

It was 1976 and here I was headlining the Garden. ... I finally understood what all the hype was about. To play the Garden as a pro wrestler was and is equivalent to playing in Yankee Stadium as a baseball player. And headlining is like ... well, it's like something else.

"The deal with Dusty in the Garden was no one ever heard anyone cut a promo like that or heard anyone as equally entertaining as I was. He literally took New York by storm. This guy came in and when he was making his comeback, he would make this stroll while I was down and selling and people would jump. Putting Bruno [Sammartino] aside, no one got a reaction in the Garden like Dusty got. He was the ultimate in entertainment. Not one technical move between us except the basics. It wasn't necessary. It was all me getting heat on Dusty and him making a comeback ... a simple formula. The New York market never saw anything like us together. It was pure magic."

—"SUPERSTAR" BILLY GRAHAM

I remember looking down from the ring and there they were; a virtual who's who of the Greenwich Village "in crowd." Right there at ringside were Andy Warhol, whose career included paintings, films such as Outer and Inner Space, drawings, music production, sculpture, commercial art and pop art masterpieces such as his portraits of "Marilyn," "Liz," "Elvis," "Campbell's Soup Cans," "Brillo Boxes" and "Flowers"; Omar Sharif, the actor best known for his lead role in the movie Dr. Zhivago; Cheryl Tiegs, the top supermodel at the time who appeared on the cover of Sports Illustrated among other magazines; and Peter Hill Beard, one of the world's most prolific photographers whose works include "Longing for Darkness—Kamante's Tale from Out of Africa" and "End of the Game" of which I proudly have an autographed copy ... one of my prized possessions ... where he wrote:

*Dear [a drawing of a deer instead of the word] Dusty [a drawing
of a star follows my name],*
   Warmest regards and many thanks for the ringside epic raved by all!
   Regards and admiration,
   Peter Beard

The signature was followed by a drawing of an elephant symbolizing much of his work in Africa and his thumb print. It was very cool.

After the show we all piled into a limousine and made our rounds to all of Manhattan's hot spots. That's all it took. I won't say I was star struck, because I was a star in my own right. But from that point forward I knew that there was a crossover between what we were doing in wrestling and what they were doing in the so-called mainstream entertainment mediums. Before I knew it, "The American Dream," Dusty Rhodes would have another nickname; Stardust. A star named Dusty … it was that simple.

And as hard as it is for me to say this, a lot of what drove me back then was ego. Not all of it was ego, but a lot of it was.

But, here's the thing … everybody who gets into the wrestling business, has been in the wrestling business, or is thinking of getting into the wrestling business is driven by an ego; a big ego. Some of us may just show it a little bit more than others, but without pulling any punches, anybody who is in this business and says they don't have an ego is just full of shit. If in their own head they don't think they're the star, they're full of shit … and for those who didn't or don't make it big, I bet you can't find one guy who doesn't blame someone else, whether me in the past or someone in a position of power today, who they blame for their failure to reach their dream. Why? Because their ego tells them they were a star, but because of so and so, they never got the notoriety, the star power, the push into the spotlight or whatever.

While I'm sure some of you cannot believe what an egotistical son of a bitch I must be or how full of myself I am, well, that's no different than what my wife, Michelle, thinks of me when it comes to my "American Dream" persona.

But I'm really not the egomaniac people think I am. It may be how I come across sometimes, but that's just how I carry myself. Some people come across insecure, some people come across cocky, some people come across bitter. I happen to come across as having this big fucking ego because of the way I carry myself and how I present myself. I think people get confused between ego and confidence.

My philosophy of the business says you are who you make yourself to be and you make it to the top and stay there because you've got that much more talent or charisma than the rest of those who are chasing their dreams. It's that presence and perception, that confidence and believability of walking through the curtain or down the runway and carrying yourself like a star because you really believe you're a star.

Now most people, except for those who are very close to me, can't tell where Dusty Rhodes the celebrity ends and Dusty Rhodes the individual begins or vice versa. The line is very thin and even some who are close to me can't really tell the difference. Well, say what you will about me, but the one thing I stood for, if I went out for a match or an interview, was when the fans left the building, they knew they definitely got their money's worth. I may have been known as a common man to them for my chosen style of dress, including jeans, T-shirts and cowboy boots instead of Armani suits, but I've had my share of limo rides and dressing to the nines. I didn't mind eating at McDonald's or somewhere like that most of the time so my children had health, happiness, and financial security, but I've eaten at the Russian Tea Room, Club 21, and Christine's. That's the real Dusty Rhodes.

Of course my heart will always belong to Texas and specifically to Austin, but I could have easily made New York City my home. I love the city and I love the people in it. The diversity is unbelievable. Sure, my friendships with Willie Nelson and David Allan Coe are legendary, but I've also partied at Studio 54, sang on stage at New York's Lonestar Café with John Belushi, and hung out with people like Bobby "D" ... or as you know him better, Bob Dylan ... as well as people like Roy "Halston" Frowick, the famous designer for people like Jackie O and Liza Minnelli. As a matter of fact, the New York Times ran a story one time on Andy Warhol and his "three hundred pound wrestling friend," alluding that we were more than just friends if you catch what I'm saying! Whoa! We were close, but not that close!

Isn't that what the American Dream is really all about? Living life to its fullest and doing the best you possibly can with the hand you've been dealt? Some people use the analogy of taking lemons and making lemonade. I say take the lemons, but try to go out and grab some apples, oranges, bananas, or whatever and make fruit punch.

So is this really all about someone with an inflated ego? Or is this just me talking about someone who took responsibility for providing for themselves and their family? You make up your own mind, because I've already made up mine.

It's like those stories in the wrestling magazines we all read as kids. I used to read them and think they were real. I didn't realize until I got into the business that Bill Apter, George Napolitano, and some of the other guys used to make those stories up. Some of those guys were real dipshits, but not Bill or George. I read an old magazine recently that said I was studying in my den in Montana. ... I never had a home in Montana, let alone a den. I couldn't help laughing because my home was on the road and my den was in the ring. If fans would have been given the chance to read the real stories about "The American Dream," Dusty Rhodes, they'd have a whole different perspective of me. They wouldn't have to read a book like this to understand who I really am. And no offense to those magazine writers, but the real stories about the people in the business are a hell of a lot more interesting than the ones made up.

"The purpose of the wrestling magazines, like the wrestling business, was to sell. There were a handful of people who we knew we could put on the cover to turn that issue to gold. Dusty was one of those people."
—BILL APTER

The thing about Bill, or "Wonderful Willie" as I call him, was that he was always very respectful of me, and as a matter of fact, to this day he thinks he can imitate me better than anyone else on the planet and does so every chance he gets. If you call his answering machine, it's him trying to sound like me. George was also very respectful and gave me lots of press.

One of the things I was always thankful for when I finally reached that celebrity status was the crowd of people I ran with that I fondly refer to, even to this day, as my posse. While some members of the posse have changed over the years, these are the people who were and are my second family. These are the people who probably know me better than anybody. And unlike in other entertainment circles where some people try to sponge off you because you are famous, these people didn't hang with me because I was Dusty Rhodes, this wrestling celebrity or any of that bullshit ... these people hung with me because I was Dusty Rhodes their friend.

Some of the stories and experiences we shared are pretty wild. So, in the words of my brother and posse member David Allan Coe, "If that ain't country, I'll kiss your ass."

First and foremost there's Jerry Allen Lewis, better known to those in the Tampa Bay area as "Captain" Lewis of Captain Lewis and the Gator Tail Band. A regular performer at the Imperial Lounge in Tampa during my heyday, the good Captain could play a mean keyboard as well as the sax, having grown up in Detroit with such musicians as Bob Seger and Ted Nugent.

Along with the Captain, two other members of his band were part of my posse; they included the late guitarist Phil Swain and a big, bald, tattooed guy, who made my buddy David Allan Coe look clean by the name of Jim Binns, also known as the Great Binnsinni. The Great Binnsinni not only played the spoons, but was a somewhat famous—or should I say infamous— tattoo artist, having put his work on Tanya Tucker and Jimmy Buffet among other celebrities.

While these three guys were part of my Florida posse, they were also my Detroit posse. I say this because I was wrestling The Sheik at Cobo Hall in Detroit one night and these guys not only showed up at the airport to pick me up in a limousine to take me to the building, but after a near riot broke out right after our match, they got me the hell out of there unharmed by driving the limo right into the hall and escorting me out of there like Mafia bodyguards.

To this day the Captain is still one of my closest friends as he is the man who kind of introduced me to one of my favorite musicians and now good friend, Willie Nelson.

I was wrestling in Atlanta at the Omni on a Friday night—a sell-out— and the very next night Willie Nelson was scheduled to be in concert at the building, so Captain Lewis, Greg Troupe, another close friend who I'll talk about in a moment, Michelle and I all decided to go to the concert. Before the show, however, the Captain, who knew one of Willie's band members, made arrangements for us to meet. Well, when I was backstage, making my way around, we kind of just came across each other and began talking. The Captain, being the character he is, said, "Hey Willie, this is Dusty." ... He said this as after we'd already introduced ourselves to each other and were already talking! Anyway, I don't know who was more excited to meet who, but as it turned out we were both big fans of each other and we just hit it off.

CHAPTER SEVEN

You gotta love the Captain.

So, not only did he "introduce" me to Willie, but he was also with me the night I decided to propose to Michelle.

> *"Dusty and I were out drinking one night and he told me to make sure that no matter what happened that he should not call Michelle, because if he did, he was going to propose to her and he had already been married and divorced once. So every time he went to the pay phone to call her, I'd cut him off and make sure he didn't. Well, eventually I had to go to the bathroom and by the time I came back out, it was too late. He had called and proposed."*
>
> —CAPTAIN LEWIS

To this day I think he believes I actually proposed to her by telephone, but I didn't. I did call her to tell her how much I loved her though, and that hasn't changed. How could I not love a woman who has put up with me and my shit for more than 25 years?

Anyway, aside from the Captain, Swain, and Binnsinni, Greg Troupe, who I mentioned before, was also a member of the posse. Greg was and is a real cowboy. I ain't talking about an urban cowboy that you see up on a movie screen, I'm talking a flat-out Florida cracker cowboy … a real tough son of a bitch who spent some time on the rodeo circuit.

Greg was around me during some crazy times, and this one night he brought this other cowboy friend of his along with us for a road trip from Tampa to Jacksonville. I figured this guy must be a tough son of a bitch like Greg, because why else would he bring him along? Now, there was a little bar that was also a barber shop, not too far from the Jacksonville Coliseum, where I always stopped to get my beer after the matches. This place was in a rough neighborhood, which kind of reminded me a little of where I grew up. Well, when they'd see me pulling into their parking lot, they would always party it up and they would go fucking crazy. So this one night, we stopped the vehicle and I said to Troupe, "This other guy doesn't get out of the truck. I ain't kidding. I ain't got five minutes or I'll be shooting you."

So I went in and come back out in a few minutes, get in the truck, and Willie Nelson is blaring on the fucking radio. As I got in and slammed the door, I looked over to the right and the same door that I just came out of, one guy comes out fighting with this woman and another guy comes up from behind her. I knew there might be some bad shit going down, so we took off.

As we drove off, we thought we heard a gunshot. It could have been a car backfiring, but we talked ourselves into thinking it was a gunshot.

So this cowboy, who's never been around me and who came with Greg to go to the matches, didn't say anything the whole 210-mile drive back home except, "I can't believe that shit. I can't fucking believe it." He didn't say anything else. Nothing! We didn't see anything going down, but we could only imagine. Buddy, he was white as a ghost ... scared to fucking death. For Greg, he was used to shit like that; just another night on the road.

"The night Dusty met Willie Nelson, after we left the concert, he, Michelle, Captain Lewis and I went back to the hotel room and getting drunk on Jack Daniels, decided to give the Captain an earring by using a paperclip to make the hole. I haven't seen the Captain in years, but the last time I did, he still had the earring."

—GREG TROUPE

Rounding out the non-wrestling side of my posse was Danny Ellis, another cowboy and local Tampa rodeo guy, John "Sugar Bear" Berg, a local Tampa dirt track racer who did some time recently for trafficking, and of course later on, my buddy David Allan Coe.

David Allan was a notorious country outlaw musician. As many of you may remember, he played at many of the "Great American Bash" shows, which are what they were all about, wrestling and country music. I always thought his music was a lot like my wrestling. He not only wrote for Elvis Presley, George Jones, Waylon Jennings, Willie Nelson, and more recently Kid Rock, but he wrote "Take This Job and Shove It" for Johnny Paycheck, "Would You Lay With Me (In a Field of Stone)?" for Tanya Tucker and had his own hits like "Longhaired Redneck," "Jack Daniels If You Please," and "Willie, Waylon and Me." He even billed himself as "Davey Coe, the Mysterious Rhinestone Cowboy" performing in a mask and driving a hearse, which in a way was a lot like my Midnight Rider or Uvalde Slim personas.

When I won the NWA World title from Ric Flair in the steel cage at the 1986 "Great American Bash" show in Greensboro, North Carolina, David Allan was the first one to hit the ring to congratulate me, even before "Magnum T.A." Terry Allen.

CHAPTER SEVEN

"I was a big fan of Dusty's long before we went on tour together. Being in his posse was no different than when I was with Elvis, except there they called us the 'Memphis Mafia.' We've been friends for about 30 years now. When you're always on the road, it's not unusual to be around those types of people and to be in those situations. It's a way of life."

—DAVID ALLAN COE

From the wrestling side, there was Banny Rooster (Mike Graham), Barry Windham, Bobby "Black Jack" Mulligan, who was like my lieutenant, Dick Slater, and later on, Magnum. We had some crazy fucking times.

At one point it seemed like the center of the wrestling universe, or at least my universe, was a little place called Yeehaw Junction, Florida, located on Highway 60 about midway between Tampa and West Palm Beach. I think more funny shit went down in Yeehaw Junction than anywhere else I can remember.

One night, Black Jack, Barry, and I were heading home and just outside Yeehaw Junction, this guy had this shed on a field that had these donkeys. So, being drunker than shit, I got the brilliant idea that we should try to ride them. Well, they had a little too much in them too, and so they were all for it. So, here we go trying to get over or through the fence and I caught my balls right on the fence wire. Anyway, we got through the fence and onto the field. What a fucking picture that must have been. Can you imagine me, Barry and Black Jack late at night chasing after these mules in a field and trying to ride them?

"The donkey kicked me in the chest and knocked me down, almost knocking me out. And then the guy that owned the place comes out and starts shooting a shotgun. We started running away, and as we're going through the fence, Dusty catches his balls on the fence again; the look on his face was funny as hell."

—BLACK JACK MULLIGAN

As funny as that was, it was really tame compared to some of the other shit that happened out there. One of the wildest stories out there involved Dick Slater, Louie Tillet, Paul LeDuc, Jos LeDuc, and me.

This one night Slater was driving in my car and the other guys were following us in another car; it was pretty normal in the business for one car to follow another from town to town. Anyway, we were far enough in front of them that we pulled over to the side of the road and I took a small can of gasoline and poured it in a line right across the two-lane highway. We had our lights off and when they got close enough, I lit the gasoline and woosh … up went the flames right across the highway.

Well, their car swerved, doing donuts and shit, going right past us and finally coming to a stop, dust flying up in the air, dirt being kicked everywhere. Well, like in the old west, we came driving up to the car real slowly alongside them and we were just laughing so fucking hard … Jos LeDuc jumped out of their car and he was so fucking scared and shaking so bad that he almost looked like a pale white … anyway I had the window down and had a wine bottle in my lap. Well, you know how things happen by instinct? There were no bad intentions or anything, but he just reached inside my window and slapped me in the face. It was like we were getting ready to fight. We were laughing and he slapped me in the face. So I took the wine bottle and I hit him right across the forehead with the fucking thing. When it hit him, he staggered to the front of the car and he was so mad, he jumped on the fucking hood.

When he jumped on the hood, Slater took off, as in he hit the gas! So now we were driving down the fucking road … we were going about 30 miles an hour … and the "Canadian Freight Train," Jos LeDuc, one of the strongest son of a bitches anywhere, was on the hood of our car looking right in at us. He had his hands where the hood comes up to meet the windshield and he had a death grip on it. Pretty soon though, Slater was going 60 … he was going 70 … we were going 70 fucking miles an hour with Jos LeDuc on the hood of the car looking in at us and his lips were now pressing against the windshield like one of those stick-on "Garfield" dolls and his eyes looked like a fish … he was all puckered up.

We were laughing so fucking hard we finally came to a stop and when we did he rolled off the hood and into a ditch. Now here came the other car in behind us and Paul LeDuc and Tillet jumped out and ran over to Jos to pick him up, and by the time they got him up, man, he started laughing so hard, realizing what we all just did. But it was the funniest thing to see big Jos LeDuc on the hood like that.

Highway 60 was notorious for shit like that. We always had our guns with us, and if we saw a guy who was taking a piss on the side of the car when coming back from a trip, we would come by and shoot the gun in the air …

boom, boom, boom … to scare the shit out of them so they'd piss all over themselves. Well, this one time we came along and Banny had a bunch of the guys pulled off there, down by the ranch road. They were all naked and were going to moon us. Well I came back holding my gun out the window like I was gonna shoot and Banny was holding a beer bottle and daring me to fire. …

"… and I said go ahead and see if you can shoot the fucking bottle from my hand. Well, Dusty points the gun and pulls the trigger and shoots into the air, but all the other guys hear the shot and take off into the field thinking he's really shooting at us."

—MIKE GRAHAM

Through the years the posse has changed quite a bit. The original posse was Murdoch and me, which was more of a pussy posse if you catch what I'm saying. There were also some people who wanted to be in the posse or thought they were in the posse, like "Beezer" Brian Blair and Steve Keirn, but they really weren't. Even Flair to a degree wanted to be in the original posse with me and Hoyt.

Back when Ric first started and weighed about 300 pounds, he was driving down the road with me, driving my car as I gave him a ride to the next town. He looked over at me and said, "I want to ask you a question … a big favor of you … I got my wrestling name, and if it's okay with you I want to be a cousin. I want to be 'Rambling' Ricky Rhodes."

I said to him, "No! Make your own name. Be your own self. Make something of yourself in your own likeness of what you see … not 'Rambling' Ricky Rhodes."

Could you imagine if Flair would have been "Rambling" Ricky Rhodes all these fucking years … Jesus Christ!

Thinking back, I don't know when I had more fun than when I was on the road and hanging with my boys.

"In Tampa, there's a big bar called the Dallas Bull and in the early '80s when the movie Urban Cowboy came out, they were going to put these mechanical bulls in the place. Well, one night Dusty convinced the owner to let the wrestlers ride that thing before anybody else did. It was outside in the back of the place and these fucking things were still wrapped

in the plastic they came shipped in. None of the boys were successful riding that thing; it threw everybody off and into the dirt."

—SIR OLIVER HUMPERDINK

Sometimes memorable shit just happened without the posse being around or even involved, like this one time down in Key West. After one of the shows, all the boys went downtown with half the guys ending up in Captain Tony's and the other half ending up in Sloppy Joe's. All the babyfaces hung together and all the heels hung together. Well at one point in the evening we all came face to face right in front of Sloppy Joe's. All the boys were right there, and so I drew a line with my foot on Duval Street and dared the heels to cross it. As somebody put it, we were way past sobriety at that point, and for about 30 minutes we had a Mexican standoff right in the middle of town. All sorts of people were in the street to see if this big-ass brawl would break out. Back then, that was great publicity for us. Think of how many people went home and told their family and friends, "You ain't gonna believe the shit I saw on Duval Street last night." Man, shit like that just doesn't happen anymore, and if it did, nobody would believe it.

Sometimes, however, it's not all fun and crazy shit when it comes to the posse or the business in general. Sometimes it's harsh reality; the kind that feels like a bull just gored you in the pit of your stomach. One of the hardest things I've ever had to endure in the business is when Magnum had his auto accident. To see that happen to my brother was ... gut wrenching.

The call came in the morning. It was from his wife and she was crying. I dressed and headed to the hospital. As I arrived, I found that the world of Jim Crockett Promotions, the NWA and pro wrestling would be changed forever. The Golden Boy ... the heir to the throne ... had been paralyzed in an auto accident.

Terry and I were very close. He became a member of the posse when I took him under my wing, because here was a kid who had it all from the good looks to the ability to that natural charisma, the one thing you can't teach. He had been fucked by Buzz Sawyer, hard, and breaking into the business cost his family something like $60,000. Financially, it almost broke his family.

Florida Championship Wrestling is where he really learned his skills and was where he'd begin to claim his piece of wrestling history. Then he went to go to work for Bill Watts and the UWF in Oklahoma, the old Mid-South promotion. That's where he became a star, but they knew it was my job to make him a bigger star. We at JCP were getting ready to get on an unbelievable roll and he was to be the centerpiece.

But in the blink of an eye all that shit didn't matter, because it all came crashing down. Plans had to change literally overnight because business was still business, but it ate me inside to see a young lion like Magnum in that condition.

> *"Dusty pushed me harder than I'd ever been pushed before. We watched the thing grow from 2,000 and 3,000 people a night in small towns to 10,000 people jamming those same arenas ... we were on a rocket ride. We went from flying on commercial airlines to flying on private jets... it was right there on the teeter-totter edge just before pay-per-views. The week of Starrcarde 1985 I made the most money I had ever made in a week—$13,000. My future was just getting ready to take off. But that all changed on October 14, 1986, when I had the accident. They took care of me while I was in the hospital and I made about $185,000 that year. I probably would have made $225,000 if I hadn't been injured. Who knows how much I would have made with pay-per-views. I watched the landscape of wrestling change from a hospital bed."*
>
> —"MAGNUM T.A." TERRY ALLEN

I remember standing with the doctor, his wife, and his mom and dad when the doctors told him he would have a million-to-one chance to ever move from the head down—Fuck it I thought. ... Fuck it! His story of strength and will is a book in and of itself. Magnum walked out of that hospital and is walking today.

Shit happens, they say, but some of it is shittier than others.

> *"When Magnum got hurt and we used to go visit him, I thought it was great Dusty stood by the guy like that. Dusty told him, 'You'll always have a place with us' when Magnum was worried about how he was going to pay his bills and make ends meet."*
>
> —DAVID ALLAN COE

These days the posse consists more of refined and established businessmen than wild outlaws and wrestling people, although there will always be people in the business as part of my gang.

A couple of the new generation posse members down in Florida include Smoothie Kane and "Big Tilly" James Tilquist. Many moons ago Tilly worked as an enhancement talent for WCW. He also worked in Florida on the independent circuit as part of a tag team called Phi Delta Slam. Two super nice guys who take care of me when I'm down in the Orlando area, but two guys who never really made it in the business and they're okay with that which is really a cool attitude for them to have because as I said earlier, not everyone can be the star of the show.

Then there's David Qualls. Not only is he a member of my posse, but David is one of my business partners with Turnbuckle Entertainment, Black and Blue division. David is a high-level executive in the casino resort industry as a property developer and manager. We met over the telephone when he just picked up the phone and called me one day and have been friends ever since.

> "Dusty was my idol growing up because he didn't have the body of a Greek god, but rather a Hindu one … Buddha. His euphemisms and body language were hilarious without making him into a buffoon. But the thing that most impressed me about him, was when we had a show in Miami, Oklahoma. He sat everybody down and said, 'We're going to give the fans a show tonight … no extreme crap.' He told everybody to have a good time, but to give the people what they're looking for."
>
> —DAVID QUALLS

Another member of my posse is Jerry "J.D." Douthit. I've known J.D. for about eight years and I met him when he started coaching my daughter Teil's softball team when she was about 14. A couple of years later he and I were assistant coaches together at the school where my son Cody played football along with his son Jeremy and we just remained friends.

When Turnbuckle was getting off the ground, he helped out with some sponsorships, but that's not why we remained friends … it was the bond through our kids and after they finished school, we just remained friends.

"He's a real man. You've got to look beyond the celebrity to see he's a real person. I helped him when he needed it and he helped me when I needed it. When I lost my father in October 2003, Dusty was right there for me. He came by to see if I needed anything and it was quite a blessing for him to be there."

—J.D. DOUTHIT

And finally there's former Georgia Senator Richard Green. Senator Green and I have been next-door neighbors for the better part of 18 years, and like J.D., he and I became friends through our children, when Teil went to his daughter Stephanie's Halloween party many years ago. But that friendship isn't like one of those "Can I borrow your lawnmower?" friendships. This was one of those friendships that stuck and these days the senator is my main hunting buddy, especially for deer and turkey.

"Dusty's idea of hunting and my idea of hunting are much different. He's a gentlemen's hunter. I take it more seriously. This one time I shot an eight-point buck and I said to Dusty, 'Let me get your picture with it.' The next thing I know, Dusty put the picture up and claimed it as his own."

—RICHARD GREEN, GEORGIA STATE SENATOR

But our friendship goes even beyond that. Through the years, the good times and bad times, he was right there for me. And when I lost my mom, he was right there for me again; one of those unselfish people who would do anything that needed to be done. I'm grateful for that type of friendship, because someone like that doesn't walk into your life every day.

"Dusty is one of the nicest, kindest, gentlest people I've ever known. People who don't know him don't realize how caring he is. When I went through the loss of my mother in August 2004 and my father-in-law six months earlier, Dusty would call just to see if I was okay. You don't have many friends who genuinely care. Dusty genuinely cared."

—RICHARD GREEN, GEORGIA STATE SENATOR

CHAPTER 8

Without a doubt, pro wrestling is the greatest business in the world to be working in. Like I've said before, it has given me everything I have, and for that I am forever grateful. But for every bright spot in our business, for every positive thing that happens, there is the dark side to it too, and there have been far too many prices that had to be paid along the way.

It is within this one aspect of the business that the Mafia blueprint comes into crystal-clear focus. It is here where people jockey for positions of power, say one thing to your face and something else behind your back, make you promises they cannot or do not intend to keep, and congratulate you with one hand while stabbing you in the back with the other. Welcome to the cutthroat world of pro wrestling politics.

The politics of the business were here long before I was born, and will most likely continue long after I am in a field somewhere in Texas pushing up daisies. But in my 30-plus years of being in the business, I have seen more shit go down than one can imagine. Sometimes I was played like Nero's fiddle and just kept doing what I was doing while Rome burned around me. At other times it was I who had to play the political game just to keep my position.

Before I go any further, I want to be perfectly clear here about something. Despite what you may read in other wrestling books and biographies, do not expect me to sit here and bury people who I feel have done me wrong or who I may not like personally. If that's what you're expecting to read because someone else said something bad about me in their book, then you're wasting your time and you might as well close the book now and stop reading because it's not going to happen.

Coming into this thing I made a decision that I was going to tell my story the way I saw and lived it. I was not going to grind any axes. I was not going to come across like some bitter old man. I made the decision to tell my story like it is, and if some people are soiled in the process, well then, that's an unfortunate side effect of the story.

It is my deep belief that the people who live in a glass-house industry like ours should not throw stones. Believe me, I can sit here and fill ten books with all the dirt I know on people, but too much of it would be inappropriate—does it really matter who was sleeping with who, or cheating on their wives? Does it really matter which wrestlers were gay? Only when it directly affected business did it ever matter. Otherwise, a lot of that shit is personal between the people who lived it ... stories like that can ruin people's lives even after so many years and I'm not about to do that. I have too much respect for this business and myself to stoop to that level.

That said, on to business.

Jim Barnett, Eddie Graham, and Vince McMahon Sr. were the men who, in my opinion, ran the world of professional wrestling in the '70s and early '80s.

Eddie, being my mentor, was always in constant contact with the other two. As I explained in a previous chapter, TBS had helped make me the first Golden Boy of Cable TV and the Florida show was on TV in New York City, so I was an instant draw. The Dream and Gordon ... Muhammad Ali and Howard Cosell ... take your pick as our careers ran parallel to each other.

Jim Barnett ran Georgia Championship Wrestling and like I also explained previously, he was my booker when I would be lent to other territories. Vince Sr. did the same with Andre, which is why the Giant and I were on the road many times together.

But Barnett was more than just my booker or the guy who ran Georgia. He was a flamboyant, creative businessman with a master's degree in business. He often dressed to match his personality, wearing flashy three-piece suits. When he talked to you, there was no mistaking that nasal Midwestern drawl, "Dusty, my booooy ..." he would say. A lot of people thought he was a character, and in many ways he was, but he was a great, great friend.

Barnett got started in the business with the old Chicago territory, helping its promoter, Fred Kohler, get on the old Dumont Television Network. In the mid-'50s he helped revolutionize our business by creating studio wrestling, something regional promoters in the country benefited from, as it was now affordable for them to do television and reach more fans. In the early '60s, while still promoting here in the States, he opened up the virgin Australian territory. Like many of the great ones in our business, he had a vision and an amazing sense of our industry.

A lot of people knocked Barnett or didn't like him because of his personal lifestyle or the way he did business, but he was successful, and because of cable and TBS, he became Ted Turner's closest confidante in wrestling … and one of the most powerful promoters in the NWA (if not the most powerful) at one point.

Even though he was in the wrestling business, Barnett also had a lot of Hollywood contacts throughout the years … people who were considered the movers and shakers of the entertainment industry back then and that was crucial, because when Vince Jr. decided to make his big move, Jim Barnett would end up playing an important role in that whole scenario.

It meant nothing to the other promoters at the time, but "Junior" wanted to be the only one in charge. He was very much into his dad's business … the family business. Behind the scenes, however, he was in the process of taking over the wrestling world, which he eventually did. The NWA … we thought the territories were too strong and it would never happen.

To me, Vince Sr. was the classiest guy in our industry I had ever met. When I talked about how Lou Thesz was perceived to be when he walked into a territory's dressing room you knew he was the World Champion.

Vince Sr. was the promoter of promoters and he ran the empire of empires. He was the Godfather of the East as Eddie was the Godfather down South. Vince Sr. was a classy guy, and you could tell from your first meeting with him that he took care of the people around him. He had a little entourage and he was always really pleasant and respectful, but he was the type of person who demanded respect.

The first time I actually got the opportunity to spend some one-on-one time with him was at one of the old NWA conventions. Even though he was the owner of the WWWF at that time and he ran New York City and had his whole thing going, he still made sure to attend the meetings as he was still part of that group of promoters from around the world that I talked about earlier. Anyway, I had cocktails with him and just being around him … he just had that presence about him.

Once I became a so-called star and became somebody who drew a lot of money and became more and more involved with him, I understood Vince Sr. a little more. Even in the Garden he had a way about him. I used to watch him … and I think if you want to be a student of the game, you should watch everything that happens … and on the night of the Garden shows, Vince Sr. would run all his old cronies in—all the old promoters who worked for him—and all these old guys would come there for their payoffs. They wouldn't get paid off like with an envelope or anything, Vince Sr. would walk down the hall and every time he shook hands with one of these guys, he would give them money. He took care of them; gave them their payoff, whatever it was. I thought it was the coolest thing that he not only ran New York City while living down in Palm Beach, but he took care of all these guys … in many ways these were his lieutenants. This was something that you would read about in a book or see in a movie. But anyway, you knew he had a really good sense of loyalty and respect about him.

The best example I can think of that illustrates Vince Sr.'s loyalty had to be around the time we had the second "Superstar" Billy Graham-Dusty Rhodes match at the Garden. Vince told me that he had given his word to Bob Backlund that for a certain amount of time he would have a title run. Eddie Graham was once again involved in this as Bob started down in Florida with us and we had some great times with him—and I like the shit out of Bob—but anyway, Vince knew that if Bob was going to carry the WWWF title, he was going to need charisma, he was going to need someone around who was a hard-working guy to work with him.

Me and "Superstar" were in a very hot feud, and Vince and I flew from Tampa to Philadelphia to go do this television shoot in Hamburg. We sat next to each other on the plane, and then we caught a cab to go to the town. This was right before one of his TV tapings, and Vince asked me, systematically, "Man, how do you get this guy charisma?"

I said, "Vince, you can't! You're either born with it or you have it … or you got to put stuff around him and whatever it is until he gets over. It might take a long time."

Eddie understood that and I'm pretty sure Vince did too, but I guess he wanted someone to give him confirmation.

"Well, I gave my word," he said. "So it's not going to change."

If Vince Sr. said that, it meant to me if the guy was drawing 5,000 people in a 21,000-seat building it was going to be like that for the next few years

... 5,000 people in a 21,000-seat building ... because he gave his word and that's the way he was.

But he was obviously also smart enough to know that a "Prince" in his first ever title defense match at the Garden had to be protected. So he put Billy Graham on the show so when Backlund defended his title for the first time, he insured himself of a sell out and the perception of Backlund looking great; the perception of "this is my champion, champion of the world, and he drew a sell-out crowd."

The reality, however, is that it was "Superstar" generating the house, but that was just an old tool that promoters used when they wanted to get somebody over or to drive them to bigger things.

Bottom line is he was a classy guy and his wife was a classy lady and it was a great era to me, because all those territorial guys, all those regional Godfathers, ran together. They would call each other, counsel each other and there was just an unbreakable bond ... or at least we thought it was unbreakable.

While Vince Sr. demanded respect by the way he walked around, at the time Junior—Vincent Kennedy McMahon—was the guy who did the television interviews and whatever else he did behind the scenes.

So when you talk about Junior, he came from that era when if you wanted respect you had to earn it, and because of who he was, he eventually did.

The second-generation guys in the industry are all alike in that they're the most talented people. You wonder why they are the most talented or why they know the industry like they do, it's because they grew up in the family-run business.

Anyway, I remember how VKM was so energetic. We were around the same age ... him, me and "Superstar" ... and he was into body building and would read "Superstar" parts of this health book about eating right and all these things. He would always have his TV and so there was a special closeness with him and "Superstar" Billy Graham and a different kind of closeness with me. We had some great interviews and I know he enjoyed doing them—I could see that—but I could also see he had a real eye for power.

At the time Vince Jr. was involved in a lot of stuff at the Garden and a lot we didn't know of that was going on behind the scenes. I was a little bit aware that Vince Sr. was not feeling well and Eddie had talked to me about that. We talked about it and discussed if it was going to be one of those black and white situations if Junior took over or if it was going to be one of those gray areas … if it's gonna be a positive thing or not. I think in the back of our minds we knew what was coming, but we were too caught up in the old ways to think anything would really change.

Since I was already going up to New York, I figured I could keep an eye on things. But I wasn't looking too closely, as I was living the life of limousines and enjoying it, even though back then we paid for those things ourselves because that was the perception of headlining the Garden. If I was the main event, it didn't matter to me that I was gonna pay four, five, six hundred dollars a night for a limo because I wanted the perception of who I was to be seen, which like I explained earlier, is what I learned from Lou Thesz.

So anyway, "Superstar" and I sold out the Garden and Vince Jr. came to us and said, "I'm going to do this movie."

He already had visions in his head of the thing he wanted to do. But this wasn't the first time he had grandiose plans. Sometime earlier he had an idea for an album for me to make and a concept for a movie; he already had this movement going—that was phenomenal.

Now my attorney, Henry Gonzalez from Tampa, planned to go with me to Ed Germano's Hit Factory, which was a major place you made music in New York City at the time. Henry was a very good friend (and is to this day), but at the time he was a noted attorney on the Patty Hearst case and he defended some really heavy people in high-profile cases.

Anyway, after one of the Garden shows at about midnight, after driving around in the limousine, we went in to cut this song. As a matter of fact, Hall and Oates were in the next studio doing their thing. While the session went well, I wasn't prepared for it. I didn't really understand what we were trying to do there as I was more into country. What they set me up with was actually a rap record called "Let's Get Funky" with seven or eight black chicks on the track singing backup and everybody getting … well, getting funky. Just like that, there I was with a mama in the kitchen that night and I was just kind of messing around with the whole thing, not knowing the seriousness of it all. I had practiced all week on a country song by Willie Nelson as I thought that's kind of what it was going to be about; a wrestling song with a country twist.

After we cut the song, me and Henry went and sat down with Vince and Ed Germano right there at the Hit Factory and they had what looked to me like one of those 950-page contracts that Vince uses to this day. It's like the more paper you use, the more serious you think it is when it really could be done in one line … you're going to get this, I'm going to get that and don't do this or it will cost you that. I know it's necessary and all that shit, but sometimes it's just so stupid.

Anyway, it came around to money and I could tell Vince was uneasy with Henry because I had enough brains to not go in there by myself, which he was not used to. He was always dealing directly with the wrestlers, never representatives, and being one for all these years, there were many times where I tried to make deals by myself and it rarely works out. That's why everybody hates my agent now—Michael O'Brien —because he makes deals for me. He makes it easy for me and I don't have to do anything. This way I stay the babyface and he becomes the hero. Anyway, nobody would dare bring an attorney into a meeting with Vince at that point in time, but I did, and so that deal didn't look real good when we got in the limo. Vince was pretty perturbed with it as he had that "nobody stands up to me" attitude. But, hell, I was "The American Dream," Dusty Rhodes, and still am.

Here comes my ego again, but I know I'm on a level with him mentally or what I think I know about the industry … what I know about my business. I'm not talking about marketing and going out and selling T-shirts, I'm talking about the wrestling end of our business. I don't think anybody knows more about the wrestling industry than I do—whether I do or not— and surely not him.

After that was done he tried the movie thing with Superstar and me. We would be there doing about 100 interviews or whatever it is each week and at the interview segments, afterwards he would have people tape Superstar and me and tape an interview with me almost like a documentary; he was trying to put this thing together. So the big blow off came in New York City at the Warwick Hotel where they always stayed. We went up there to VKM's room at about three in the morning, and he was sitting at a desk writing stuff down. The room looked really dimly lit and he had these producers, directors, or whoever they were, sitting in the room with us.

Well, Superstar and I sat down and Vince said, "We're going to do this movie about you two guys…" but it was about ex-wrestlers or whatever was the storyline… and we would be cops in New York running around like Starsky and Hutch and all that type of stuff.

It sounded good so I said, "Man this is going to be good," 'cause I could handle that. Superstar didn't say a lot at this point.

Then I asked Vince, "That sounds great ... what's the financial?"

This came up again, but this time he said, "You get a Garden payoff."

Well a Garden payoff at that time was three grand ... $3,000 ... that's what you got. You got $250 to be on all the other matches and you got $3,000 to be in the Garden main event whether it was sold out or not, because that's where you wanted to be—and that was a lot of money back then, but it was only $3,000 for a movie?

So, I was drunk now too, and I'm sure Vince was drunk or whatever, as he was pretty well there too, and I said, "That ain't gonna get it." Just like that.

Defiant once again.

"Oh no," he said. He couldn't believe that shit so he left and went into the bedroom. When he came back out he broke the pencil in half and said, "The deal's off."

Uh oh, shit! Jesus Christ ... so that deal never came about.

The next thing that happened after that—and at the time I had just come off a bout of phlebitis in my legs where I had to go on a diet and was down to about 255 pounds so I looked pretty good—was that it was actually played for me to be in the Hogan spot.

Now I know you're gonna say, "Oh, that egoistical motherfucker! That's not true!" But the next thing you know, Hogan was there. Hogan was the one who came in and he jumped right into that spot. He must not have brought his attorney. ...

Anyway, he's being his attorney now, that's for damn sure. But he went right into that spot and he was getting ready to do that whole big thing with them; rock and wrestling, celebrities, all that shit we started.

So Vince Jr. and I always had that kind of back-and-forth respect relationship. He knows I know the business and I respect the shit out of him. But shortly after that the territories started to get bought up. VKM decided to take over the world. The territorial system was on the verge of being killed as we knew it, and the Evil Empire was about to take over.

Like I alluded to earlier, when that started to happen, we were very comfortable in Florida, and I was very comfortable with it because of the office's ties with the "Wrestling Mafia" in New York ... Eddie's ties with Vince Sr. But it was around this time that Vince Sr. was starting to get very sick and Eddie was always in a depressed mood, not knowing what was going to happen.

After one of the shows at the Garden I thought I really needed to find out where the Florida office stood. After every Garden show Vince would have all his people—his cronies, his posse, his crew—whatever you want to call them, they would all go over to Jimmy Weston's restaurant and they would have a big, long table and they would eat dinner. If you got invited to dinner, that was a big deal, because it was a real fancy renowned supper club that had live music, mostly jazz; not your typical kind of place for a wrestling crowd.

I always liked the fact that I was invited, and if you were on top, whether you were invited or not, you would be sure to go by and pay your respects and rightfully so; that was kind of an unwritten protocol.

This one particular night Michele wasn't with me like she usually was and I rode around in the limo, went down to the Lone Star Café, had a few drinks and then headed back over to where everybody else was to pay my respects. I knew Barnett was in town since he was still booking me at the time with Florida and another territory he owned—Georgia Championship Wrestling—and Eddie and he were part of that group of guys that could not be broken up.

So I went over there, got out of the limo and walked in to see this long table with Vince Sr. down at one end and Vince Jr. and Barnett down at the other end. The table was like one of those tables you see in a "Knights of the Long Table" movie or something—not round table—but there were people sitting everywhere. So I went around the table and paid my respects to all the important people.

Barnett and VKM were at the end of the table and by this time they were pretty high. And when I mean high, I mean *high*. When Jim Barnett drank he would get giggly … girlish … girlishly giggly … and he was really fun to be around and I loved being around him. I loved the guy. So I went and sat down right across from Vince Jr. and next to my booker and friend Jim Barnett. Well Barnett was smiley faced and he was always smiley faced when he was either drunk, had money, or he'd come into money … that was something that he did. Or he had just met someone he really liked and the guy was younger than him. Not a knock. That was just how Jim Barnett was. Everyone knew Jim was gay and after many drinks he was an unbelievable guy.

Vince Jr. looked like he was feeling real good and when Barnett got up to go to the bathroom for a white powder break, Vince Jr. leaned across the table, looked me right in the eye and said, "I own Jim Barnett, Dusty, and you work for me."

I thought, "Holy shit, what does this mean?"

He glanced down the table toward where his dad was sitting and then looked back at me and said, "They all work for me."

Well, I knew the shit had hit the fan. I knew there was something going down bigger than just running the Garden and this move was being made. Barnett came back and when he did I think he was kind of ready to go and I noticed he had this paper in the lapel of his coat.

At the time we were staying at the InterContinental Barclay Hotel, so I put him in the limo and I was taking him back. As the limo eased through the streets of Gotham, he leaned over and showed me. It was a contract; the contract that I found out later was the first big sellout to Vince Jr. So now every time the limo driver turned a corner, Jim would lean toward me. ... I thought he was drunk enough so I kept trying to grab the contract out of his coat lapel so I could read at least the fine print of what was going on. I wouldn't let that go. ... I was determined to read that thing.

We got out of the limo, walked into the hotel and we sat down in the middle of the hotel where a little bar was. We got a couple more glasses of brandy—he loved brandy—which was like 20 times more expensive than Schlitz beer. So I figured I'll give him a couple more of these and I'll lean towards him, reach over for his lapel, grab the contract, read it and then drop it on the floor or something. But I could never get it, so I was really confused about what was going on.

When I got back to Florida, of course, Eddie had said that Vince Jr. had bought out another one of the great territories of all time—Georgia Championship Wrestling—and Jim Barnett.

"God damn!" I said, "It's some big shit going down here!"

Not long after that happened, I'll never forget a very, very sad day.

Vince Sr.'s health had taken a turn for the worse and he was in the hospital. I used to call him on the phone to see how he was doing. Well, he called me back at home and I asked him how he was doing, he said, "Not well." Then I talked to his wife and she said he's not doing well and I felt bad and he got back on the phone and said to me, "Don't let this happen. You have the power to not let this happen!"

He never came right out and said it, but to this day what I think he was talking about was his son's plan to take over the business, because we all knew what was happening. He knew that it would change wrestling history forever.

At the time I had a tremendous amount of power. People don't understand or don't realize just how much power that I had through Eddie and through being the top babyface in the industry. I was the top money producer and I had a knowledge Eddie had given me about running the business—about the wrestling business—that other people didn't have. It came very easy to me and I had a lot of power and I had a lot of say with all the members of the NWA, and that was because of Eddie.

I think Vince Sr. was not necessarily worried about his family as I'm sure everything was taken care of there, but I think he was really concerned about who was going to take care of all his cronies. Did he come right out and say, "You have the ability to stop my son from doing this"? No. But like I said, I interpreted it that way because we knew what was happening as it already had begun to take shape. I can't say for him and I want to make sure that everybody knows this is only my opinion … and my opinion is that those guys he took care of, Senior was concerned with who was going to take care of them now? Who was going to take care of the business the way it was as a territorial system?

I think if you could ask any promoter of the time, they always wanted to consider themselves as one of the Godfathers like Eddie. Even Jerry Jarrett was in that mold, and all those fucking guys ran our business … and here was the head honcho saying, "Man, you got some power to stop this." That's pretty strong to say and what can I do? Do I take a shot? Do I keep the status quo and say I'm not going to do it?

It's like when I got a call one time from Wahoo McDaniel, my bud, and he said we had to go to Hawaii to wrestle to build the territory up a little more with the AWA stuff. He said, "You're the champion of Hawaii," which I was, and so I had to go. At that particular time we were working in Winnipeg and I got to work with Crusher, and I made a lot of money with him. Well, he almost missed the last flight and we just decided not to go. If you leave us, we won't go. Now these are all veterans trying to fuck this young Dusty Rhodes. All of those guys told me that, so what did I do? I didn't go to the show. I was the champion and it was the only show that I'd ever missed like that, so I didn't go and they all went … those motherfuckers all went … and I thought Crusher and I were going to have a fucking fistfight over it, even though he knew that's the most fucking money I'd ever made in my life, I learned a great lesson because of it, and that is go with your instincts, go with your gut.

And so my gut, my instincts, told me that's what Vince Sr. was trying to tell me; that I had the ability through business to stop Vince Jr. from doing this to the industry.

Anyway, I wish I would have talked to him a little bit more about what I needed to do to stop it from happening … but if it never would have happened, we never would have had this big, tremendous financial windfall for the top guys that we had. We would never have had this humongous television stuff going on with wrestling. I think in that aspect of it, VKM took it to a different level … but he killed the territorial system, which killed wrestling for a number of very talented guys—it's the double-edged sword with this thing.

Shortly after that happened, Eddie committed suicide. Gone was my mentor, my close friend, and a father figure. There was a lot that happened in our business during this time that was dramatic, sad and just crazy … but Vince, no longer referred to as Junior, took no prisoners, no matter who they were. He made sure that swagger his dad had when walking down the corridors of Madison Square Garden became his own. He became the "Prince" of the "Evil Empire" and pretty soon he was the "King" of the "Evil Empire."

That just kind of gives you an idea of what went on and how things were done back then. They were done in secrecy and it was done where only a few people knew what was going on without any thought of who it was going to hurt or who it's not going to hurt, and it was done only for "What's it going to do for me." Unfortunately, I think that goes without saying in any walk of life for any business.

Anyway, that's what I thought of Vince Sr. and the respect that I had for him and the way he did his business.

Business is business.

CHAPTER 9

While Vince was on his crusade to capture the world of pro wrestling, we were busy trying to fight his "Evil Empire" from an office in Charlotte, North Carolina; an office that would eventually lose the battle due to mismanagement and miscommunication.

Since its demise, there have been people throughout the years who claim that I was solely responsible for the downfall of Jim Crockett Promotions. This issue needs to be laid to rest once and for all, because quite simply, that's just bullshit.

I've often said that the Crockett era was the sweetest era and it could never be matched again. Mid-Atlantic Championship Wrestling was a special place in our history. The guys who worked there—Ric Flair, Arn Anderson, Tully Blanchard, Ronnie Garvin, Magnum T.A., Nikita Koloff and others— were all stars because of TBS ... and because I was the guy in charge, like the captain of a ship. Before Eddie had died, I had a chance to make a tremendous amount of money running Jim Crockett Promotions.

Facts are facts. Wrestling-wise, I went in and ran his company the way I saw fit. I had already gained power before arriving there, as I explained earlier, even helping them book their territory while still in Florida. But once I got there, I garnered so much power that I was able to do, with just a word, things that were just unheard of; things that revolutionized our industry, like Starrcade, The Great American Bash, The Crockett Cup, Clash of the Champions and War Games, to name a few.

"'The American Dream,' Dusty Rhodes identified his physical liabilities and turned them into positives on his way to becoming one of the most famous wrestlers of any era. The son of a plumber from Austin,

Texas, had a Texas-sized helping of charisma, passion and the overwhelming will to be the best in his chosen field. No athlete—and 'The Dream' was a very underrated athlete—in their prime better connected with the fans than Dusty Rhodes. Dusty gets a bad rap from some of his peers because of his in-ring prominence when he was the man in charge behind the curtain. But my guess is that not one of them would have positioned themselves any differently if given the opportunity. Dusty Rhodes is a Hall of Famer in my eyes."

—JIM ROSS

But while we were revolutionizing the industry, in the shadows of the greatest promotion in history was a guy named Dave Johnson, a bookkeeper ... an accounting person ... a tax guy ... who oversaw all the books there.

To me the Crocketts were the North Carolina version of the Kennedys. They owned property. They owned baseball teams. They were a powerful southern family ... phenomenal. And on the wrestling side, Jimmy Crockett paid unbelievably, but for a good reason.

The arena business was unmatched in our era. The amount of business we were doing was unheard of thanks to some of the most talented workers in the history of the business who busted their asses seven days a week and twice on Sunday. I was fortunate to be at the helm, steering the ship, and couldn't have been more proud of our crew.

Right around that time, this thing the wrestlers called "the sheets" started coming out, and all of a sudden there was a guy who had never been in our business, with opinions about our business, who catered to a small group of fans. Over time that small group has swelled into many, many fans, but at that point for the first time the business started to be unwound a little bit, it started to be exposed a little bit, it started to become, "This is what I think. ..." It was almost like a reviewer of a movie and while others let these "sheets" influence their actions, I would never let the opinion of people who were not in our business sway what I believed.

"Although I thought at the time Dusty could have helped some of us underneath guys make it to the next level or be more than just curtain jerkers, at least he gave me the opportunity to wrestle in order to make ends meet, and for that I was grateful. While some workers might be bitter at Dusty because they might feel he didn't give them a shot, I'm not one of

them. ... I still regard him as a Superstar and one of the greatest creative minds in the business today. A lot of people owe him because he put money in their pocket. I think he takes a lot of undue criticism."

—RIKKI NELSON, WRESTLER

Meanwhile, there came a time when we thought we were spending too much money on transportation to get the guys from one city to another and so we decided we needed to get some type of plane like any corporation doing a lot of travel would have.

But we didn't just get one plane, we got two, and from that point forward we lived like rock stars. The jet was the elite plane of the two and it would go across the country to places like Los Angeles or wherever else it was needed to go. One thing we didn't need to do was stop in Las Vegas. But Jimmy always wanted to stop there. So if we were on a California swing, we would base the tour out of Sin City, flying back and forth every day. Like I said, we lived like rock stars in an unbelievable era.

"When Dusty was the booker in Charlotte, I was there with Al Perez. As we were getting ready to get on one of the two planes, here comes Dusty driving up in his red Mercedes convertible. He started unloading a Haliburton, a Louis Vuitton and a Gucci bag to put on the plane. I looked at him and said, 'Is all this necessary? Or are you really that busy?'"

—PLAYBOY GARY HART

Even the parking lot at Jim Crockett Promotions looked like a parking lot for the rich and famous. It was an auto collector's wet dream from Magnum's Porsche to his white Harley to Flair's Mercedes to my Mercedes to the different trucks ... everybody had a new set of wheels. Arn Anderson, who like me came from humble beginnings where he hardly had anything in his life that he didn't earn, was driving a new Mercedes.

"There was never a time that I wasn't grateful for the opportunity to work for him. I'd call Dusty every Monday morning to thank him because that payday meant I could make my house payment. After a while he'd tell me, 'I know you're thankful, but you don't have to call me every day to tell me.'"

—GEORGE SOUTH, WRESTLER

All of this happened over a relatively quick period of time. Why? Because stars like Nickla Roberts, better known as Baby Doll, became bigger stars that would all of a sudden be in magazines like *The Wrestler* or *Pro Wrestling Illustrated.* What a phenomenal run it was, and that was my job, to make people into larger than life stars.

> *"You can't disrespect anything about Dusty. I'm thankful that we were able to do something for the good of the company, him and me, year after year. He was in charge when the tidal wave came, and the one thing Dusty should know is in my opinion he grossly underestimated the ability of himself and some of us. We had the right players. If he would have played it a little differently, maybe the result would have been different."*
>
> —TULLY BLANCHARD

My job was not to sit in there with Dave Johnson and tell Jimmy Crockett you're five million dollars in debt. Like anybody in my position, I thought he would let us know if we could afford things or not financially. At the very least, he should have told the owner of the company. But Johnson waited one year to tell Jimmy. One fucking year … and back then Crockett knew five million dollars for a company as big as we were, was a big fucking hole to be in.

While he got a hell of a deal from Turner at that time, Jimmy Crockett came to me and said, "I want out of Charlotte. I want us to move this office"—a big beautiful office—"to Dallas." *He* said that.

I said, "Okay, I'll go with you," because that's home for me.

It was not me who said we needed to move our operations to Dallas. Deep down I really believe he wanted to get away from the family thing. So he made that decision. Every financial decision that was made, he made. When it came time that what we were doing wasn't drawing as much and our business was down a little bit, the bills were bigger, because now we were sitting in Dallas while the office was still open in Charlotte.

Jimmy Crockett had a great vision of all this, but he was stuck with Mid-Atlantic Championship Wrestling people and their regional mentality. He had no young people. He didn't have the people who just came out of Harvard or Yale who went to work for Vince, who were marketing geniuses. We missed so much on that. We were just in the arena wrestling business.

We had no yellow fingers. The company remained very small-minded, even though both of us remained very big minded.

So as far as I'm concerned, the fall of Jim Crockett Promotions was partly due to the way Jimmy handled the innerworkings of his family business and the way he financially mismanaged the office; we didn't need the three secretaries who had been there forever.

The one guy I felt bad for during this time was Sandy Scott, who was very loyal to me once we got to know each other. He could tell me whether a house was going to do 50 or 60 grand by the advance, and he would come in and say to me, "You're doing the right thing," or "You're doing the wrong thing" … he's the only one who could talk to me like that, because I knew he knew what he was talking about and I really cared about what he thought; he became my confidant there. Even more than Jimmy, it made me feel good when we'd draw a house to where I told Sandy this would draw or this would happen.

There's no denying that my mind was focused on running the 120 people—our family—in his company like a ball team, because that's what it was like. Jimmy should have been concentrating on the other end, running the innerworkings of his company instead of driving down the road with me, drinking martinis and celebrating over big houses … because as big as the houses were, we were still going into the hole because of several moves that he had made outside of the industry.

Like I said, the move to Dallas was his idea without a doubt, and he knows it to this day. As I understand it, he's still there with his family, he's very happy there, and I'm glad for him.

But the Crocketts, as we knew them, kind of like how the Kennedys fell from grace, eventually came crumbling down like the burning of Crockett Park.

It was a St. Patrick's Day weekend in 1985 and I remember Klondike Bill, who was our ring guy, coming in and telling Jimmy at a show in Greensboro that a call just came in from the office to say Crockett Park was burning. Crockett Park was the stadium in Charlotte that the family owned along with the Charlotte Orioles, the minor league affiliate to the Baltimore Orioles, who played there. We had just done a big house in Charlotte and we had hired a limousine to go to Greensboro … a limousine to go 60 fucking miles instead of driving to the town ourselves … to drive back before the main event went on.

It was like watching *Gone with the Wind* when Atlanta was burning. The sky was lit up. We could see it for miles driving back. We drove into the yellow taped-off section where you normally can't even get in and the park was burning, smoldering. Jimmy opened the moon roof of the limousine and stood up. When he did, he looked like Napoleon looking out and over a battlefield as this wooden stadium was burning ... and I jokingly said to Klondike Bill, "How much gas did you use on the park?" It was funny at the time, because obviously I didn't mean it like that, but we had that feeling that we could do no wrong. Oddly enough, investigators later determined the cause of the three-alarm blaze was arson, and the fire was set by a small group of juveniles.

So when they talk about the fall of Jim Crockett Promotions, it definitely doesn't lie on my shoulders, because all of the time that I was there, there was money and planes and booze, enough of everything to go around for everybody. Everybody had a new car. Everybody had a big bankroll. I take as much blame as anybody as far as the wrestling part of it, but we lost a lot of guys to the WWF, and despite that we kept fighting and fighting and we were on par with them for a long time.

But Magnum going down on the wrestling side cost a lot too, because I think he was that strong of a talent. He was the heir to the throne. He was the one who was chosen to lead us, and at the time Hogan was Vince's choice as the two went head to head. I remember magazine covers with their pictures on them, the two fighters going head to head just like the two big companies were going against each other. When the Lord intervened and fate happened, the company went to shits; not just because of what happened to Magnum, but because of everything together that was going on at that time.

So I think the real downfall was in the everyday operation of the company, the innerworkings, by this same little crew of people that was running this huge business. But it was no longer, "Let's go run Charleston, West Virginia, let's run Hickory, North Carolina" ... it was now "Let's run the Forum in Los Angeles where the Lakers play, let's run the Cow Palace in San Francisco." We were in the big arenas all over the country, and that was my job. Even with that said, I really believe that if Jimmy hadn't sold the company, we could have turned it around. I remember saying to him we could get the five million dollars back, but I think he really wanted to sell it at that point in time.

When we were in Dallas, Jimmy had given me a new Mercedes for doing the first million-dollar night for him, which back then was unheard of. That's what he promised me and he got it for me. As the fall of the company happened, his sister Frances had the title and she had the car reclaimed. Because it was given to me by Jimmy and for what that car represented, I loved it so much, so before I let that happen, I paid the remaining portion of what was owed on it. I wasn't going to let them take the Mercedes that Jimmy had given me; that I had earned.

He was powerful, being the president of the company and the guy in charge, but small thinking on their part was what cost them in the long run. They can take a look back and actually pinpoint what happened to the NWA, Jim Crockett Promotions, and it surely wasn't Dusty Rhodes. Where do you put the blame? I don't know, but it surely wasn't me. My part was done. My part is documented history. It's on tapes. It's on videos. You can see my work all over the world. It's on ideas that Vince even took, and that's okay too, because I would take some ideas from him. I think Jimmy's vision was huge, but mine was bigger. I created some unbelievable stuff that still holds up to this day. It was an amazing triumph for me.

"Dusty was a great leader and he instilled pride in the workers."
—"Magnum T.A." Terry Allen

I was very hurt that Jimmy did not want to give a statement for this book if for no other reason than to help put this issue to rest. But I feel good about my era there and all the guys should be thankful that the Crockett era came along during that time, because there was nothing like it before and nothing like that will ever come again.

So that's that. A great time in our business that belongs to history.

Then came the Turner era. And when people ask me about Turner, I tell them just what I think.

I loved them … Ike and Tina Turner were the hottest group I can remember, Jack, and she had the longest legs, it was unbelievable! When she would do that little jumping up and down thing where her legs are moving and shit … *"rollin', rollin', rollin' on the river. …"* I loved them. I didn't like Ike, but I loved Tina, man. Tina was so hot … Tina was during my era. When "The American Dream" was hot, she was hot. Tina was a hot black chick … Tina Turner, man. …

Okay, seriously, let's talk about Turner—Ted Turner.

My history with Turner didn't start when Crockett sold to him. We'd have to roll the clock back a bit, for as things heated up at Championship Wrestling from Florida, my career was also heating up. WTBS in Atlanta was cabled across the country, and as I explained earlier, I was its biggest star as I was in demand all over the country.

Ted Turner was a self-made man. He was very strong and powerful and made his business in the independent television industry when others were only thinking about it. He had a vision of doing it and he did it; a maker of dreams coming true. Success was at his hands, as he took no defeat lying down.

I say to this day that wrestling made TBS—Turner Broadcasting. Without a doubt, wrestling was one of the things, if not the single thing, that made his company nationally known. He could put around it all the blue and gray and civil war stories he wanted to make that didn't draw any numbers, but he did them because he liked them and luckily he liked wrestling, realizing we also drew large numbers.

In the early days he was a great friend to the business. He used to come down to the old studio and watch us put it all together. He knew it had viewers tuning in, and many times we'd be on right before the Atlanta Braves games, a strong lead in to his team, which became "America's Team." He gave me the opportunity to be his first "Golden Boy" as I mentioned previously, and it was really cool ... and I thought he was cool, because he was a no-bullshit guy.

Only when America Online came in to buy Turner Broadcasting, and in the process WCW, did I see Ted kind of move down a little bit and not stand up. I don't think he wanted to sell the company, but that doesn't change the way I feel about him any. I was bitter because of the wrestling portion of it. Like I said, wrestling was used to build his empire and now it was being treated like the redheaded stepchild, the bastard division of the Turner family that nobody wanted to acknowledge.

Then Turner South came along, not Ted's per se, but he was instrumental in getting it off the ground, and David Rudolph, a 26-year-old executive with Turner who came up with the idea of the new network in the shower one morning, was appointed as one of the youngest company presidents. And what did producer and director John Perry do the first thing off the bat? All in the mold of the original TBS, almost like Ted saying, "Hey you want to get this off the ground?" … it was Atlanta Braves baseball, *The Andy Griffith Show* and a wrestling show starring "The American Dream," Dusty Rhodes, called *WCW Classics*. It was the same formula, and the show that put Turner South on the cable map. Of course like they did through the early days, they dropped me when Vince came in and bought the wrestling company away from Turner, but the network continued to use me on different shows. So there it was, Turner South was created in Turner's image and probably would have folded within a year if it hadn't had been for wrestling … and of course being the egomaniac everybody believes me to be, if not for "The American Dream" Dusty Rhodes hosting the hottest show on the network.

But Ted was amazing. He not only had this vision … and I always considered myself having a vision of seeing things happen or doing things … not only did he have that, but he made it happen.

TBS, Gordon Solie, Dusty Rhodes, it was kind of like the Cosell-Ali thing that I mentioned earlier, and we were so hot around the country cable-wise, it was amazing. 6:05, every Saturday night … then as the years passed I became WCW's executive producer. They called it "booker" back then—I think some still try to call the guys who do wrestling bookers—but there are no more bookers, because that term was used when a person in the business was booking a territory. The more appropriate term for the independent promotions today would be "match-maker" and if you're heading up television, executive producer. Anyway, I became executive producer of everything that happened on the TV, and Turner gave me that opportunity. We did numbers for TBS.

Ted's a man's man. The one story I remember vividly is about going to his office. Jim Barnett set up a meeting with Ted and me at the old studio on Techwood Drive. I was so hot on his television and he had just had his photo on the cover of *Sports Illustrated*. I was going into the meeting with the man the media dubbed "Captain Courageous."

I suppose being around all of those stars in New York for so long and having the discussions with Vince about movies and records, that I had this vision of doing television commercials, especially now with me being the hot commodity on cable that I was. This of course was before I got the Mellow Yellow gig, before it was fashionable for wrestlers to be in commercials, and I was thinking of something a little more elaborate than spots for the local car lot … "Hey, come on down to Yellow Bob's and let's buy a car." The stuff

I do today with Bill Butler down in Warner Robbins and Macon, Georgia, I've been with him ten years, and he has other holdings all over the area, so it's not just a mom and pop thing down there, but it is in a way, and that's what makes it great. I've been with him a long time with Chrysler and all that, even though I drive a Ford.

Anyway, it was 2 p.m. and the receptionist said, "Mr. Turner will see you."

As I walked up the stairs I couldn't help but remember the Saturday mornings Ted would come sit with us as we got dressed for wrestling in the makeshift dressing room in the very lobby I was waiting in for my appointment.

Turner was sitting there behind the desk when I walked in, and for some reason I had worn a suit. I kind of looked like Willie Nelson in the suit, completely out of place. But I wore it because Barnett thought that was the way I should go in there.

Contrary to what people believe, I had suits. I owned suits. I got rid of them. I had $1,500 - $ 2,000 suits that I got rid of a few years ago and Michelle looked at me like I was crazy because I went to the closet and took them all out and went down to Goodwill and gave them away because I wear jeans and boots, or I go barefooted and I wear T-shirts with my belly sticking out. It does not matter, that's the way I am. But I can dress up if I need to. This particular time, however, I wore this blue polyester suit I had made for me in Japan when I toured there with Dick Murdoch.

So Ted was sitting behind the desk. His baseball team was as about as bad as you can get by putting nine guys out on the field. He even became a coach that year for one game. They had a slugger named Bob Horner, and everybody would mistake him for me. If he went out to eat —this is how hot we were—they would call him Dusty Rhodes ... their third baseman who hit four home runs in one game. And he said, "They [the Braves] don't have any charisma. They can't put people in the stands."

I thought, "Winning puts them in the stands." I didn't want to say it to him at that point, because we got winners and losers, not business. So I said seats are 17 inches, now they're a little bit wider, but I said you want to put an asshole every 17 inches, that's the bottom line. And we agreed on that, so we knew where we were going.

But I went in there to ask him to get me commercials. Which I thought—this is how we were—I didn't know how powerful he was. I thought he did the marketing too. I wanted him to get me commercials and be my agent.

This is fucking Ted Turner, right?

So he looks at me and he said to me, of all people, "You ever been on the cover of *Sports Illustrated*?"

I said, "No, sir." So, without even blinking an eye, I said, "Have you ever been on the cover of *Pro Wrestling Illustrated*?"

He said, "No." Then he said, just like that, "Fuck, I'm looking for commercials. I want to do commercials. You're in here wanting me to get you fucking commercials."

So I kind of figured out what was going on at this point and there was nothing going to happen out of this conversation.

Ten, 15 years later he bought Jim Crockett Promotions, which at that time controlled the NWA, because really they were the only ones left aside from one or two other promoters. On the cover of *Pro Wrestling Illustrated* is a picture of Ted Turner. All this time had passed—that's how I knew he was a no-bullshit guy because he remembers conversations—that's what makes him good … he walked all the way across the atrium at CNN center, walked across it like a common fan with a wrestling magazine in his hand to stick it in my face.

In 2002, in *Sports Illustrated*, there was a picture and a quote and a paragraph on Dusty Rhodes, "The American Dream." It was a Q&A session. I went to Tallahassee, Florida, looking for the motherfucker because I was going to show him this fucking picture. As luck would have it, two of his kids were on the plane with me. These days he's down in Tallahassee and a lot of people don't know that, so his kids say, "We're going out to Dad's, do you want to go?"

I said, "Take this *Sports Illustrated* and right at the appropriate time, show him this picture."

It's funny how things transpire. Visions different men have. … Turner is the greatest visionary of our lifetime. No one can compare to him. Without him we would have been shit as far as the wrestling industry in the South.

And I can always remember, "Hi, I'm Tommy Rich, and I'll be in Carrollton tonight. …" and it would be packed. Ted Turner gave us that opportunity. I'll always thank him for that.

But I wish he would have been my manager like I wanted him to be the day I walked into his office. Ted was a cool guy. He sold out, but I don't think he sold out as much as the company's board of directors sold out.

The only thing was Ted sent Bill Shaw in to be the president of WCW, a guy who did not know jack shit about wrestling. I believe he was in charge of human resources before coming to WCW. That's almost as funny as Bill Bush. I liked Bill Shaw, and Eric Bischoff should kiss his ass every time he sees him, because Bill Shaw put Eric in power because he knew he couldn't handle the job himself. But that's the way Ted hired. He had somebody overseeing and regulating what we were doing.

The only thing I got hot at Turner about was that he sent Bill Shaw to oversee all of his land holdings and buffalo out west. Hell, that would have been a perfect job for me. All he had to do was give me a pick-up truck and a million a year like Bill Shaw was getting and send me out to fucking Montana and I'd have been gone, nobody'd even hear from me —it'd been cool.

So Shaw hired Eric, who was a visionary in his own right, and he turned WCW into something very special.

But before he hired Eric, there was Jim Herd, a marketing guy or something like that who came from Pizza Hut, who was the blooming idiot of corporate America. Now I know I said I wasn't going to bury people who I feel have done me wrong or who I may not like personally, but this guy was never really in the wrestling business, so he is fair game. That said, he was the most untalented motherfucker in the history of the world, whether you were running pizza, whether you were running a road race, or whether you were running to the fucking bathroom. He had the least talent of any human being that I had ever been around in my life; he had no gamesmanship and no skills at all as far as employees went. I say that a lot, but I liked him outside of the business when he wasn't drinking with Jim Ross after each day was over, where they would have their cocktails and Jim was pointing him on the floor because he knew how to play Herd like a fiddle. We know Jim's pretty smart, and to this day JR is a cool guy as all he wanted was my job, and what's wrong with that? He made no bones about it, and I respected him for that. Since then I think JR's fallen from grace a little bit.

I don't think any announcer stands up to him. We used to say Gordon was the best and he was the king, but JR is the best man to get if I was going to get someone to call a world's title match and everybody was equal, age-wise, at the same time, Jim Ross would be my chosen guy to go to war with.

So I had nine bosses when I went back to being the corporate cowboy, and each of them were bosses who came from the other floor that knew nothing about the industry.

Kip Frye was probably my favorite, as I understand he's become a millionaire out in Los Angeles in the video business, but at the time he was well ... an unusual choice.

They got rid of Herd. Bill Watts blew into town with both six guns blazing and they got rid of him, and I think Ole Anderson was there one time earlier, and then there was Bill Bush, who was an income tax guy who was running our business, who made J.J. Dillon and Gary Juster his big buddies ... and if I was running the Montana stuff, I would've put all three of them shoveling shit out there during that point in time. There was also Bob Dhue who ran the Omni. He'd book the Omni for us like, "Hello, I'd like to book the Omni," and they'd say, "Okay, sure!" That's what he did. But getting back to Kip Frye, they went over to the 12 floor on other side of the complex, the north tower where all the big wigs with Turner were, and Jack Petrick, I believe, one of the big lieutenants for Turner all of those years—respected by Ted because he knew how to delegate and what he had to do in his own frame, but another person who knew nothing of the wrestling business—they're passing a room and Jack says, "Hey what's your name?" As he looks in this room, Kip Frye is putting videotapes in sleeves to ship out. "Are you interested in wrestling?"

"Yeah, sure."

"Okay, you're the president of WCW. Get your shit together and go over to the office." And they brought him over. "Ladies and gentlemen, I would like to introduce the new president of WCW, Kip Frye." That's exactly how Kip Frye became the president of WCW.

The first thing he did was change the show that had been the legendary cornerstone of TBS at 6:05 p.m. for forever. Jim Ross hated it, and the only reason I went along with Kip Frye was because Ross hated it so bad ... he made it *WCW Saturday Night*, like the Saturday night show and half of the two hours was a talk-show format with Jim Ross interviewing people like the group Alabama or whoever would be there, nothing to do with wrestling whatsoever. He had a vision and went on to make that happen, but he was out of place, he didn't know, and that's the kind of people who were being hired. It was boss after boss after boss, and you never knew where the head of this corporate jackass was as you always got to talk to the ass.

"Jack Petrick was looking for someone to come in to run WCW. Dusty was the booker when they called me to come in to talk. The Braves were in the World Series, so I brought Jeff with me for the meeting. Jack took Jeff and me to the ball game. Dusty was sitting in the same section, but up in the cheap seats. Every time I'd come back from the restroom or concession stands, Dusty would be in Jack's ear. After talking throughout the game about wrestling, I told Jack that his wrestling company would fail unless he made radical changes in management conditions. I also told him that his best bet was to keep Dusty Rhodes. Of course Dusty thought I was coming in to take his job. He didn't realize that I wanted his boss' job, so he wore a trail out to Jack's ear. When I left before the game ended, I stopped and whispered in his ear, 'Dusty, you're the only person alive that has a chance to make this go. God bless you.' I then kissed him on the cheek. Dusty thought I gave him the Mafia 'Kiss of Death.'"

—JERRY JARRETT

It goes back to why Vince McMahon is so successful, and that is because even though they are a publicly traded company, it's still a family-run business. When their business is down like it is right now as I write this, they go back home and on Sundays they sit down and they think about their business. This is our livelihood. How do we make this business work? It's like Vince stepping out into other things like bodybuilding, falling on his ass … XFL, falling on his ass … but he had a vision and he went ahead and did it even though he was out of his element. He thought he could make football players into wrestlers as far as marketing was concerned.

WCW kind of went like that. There were some down times and good times, and it was hard work, but somebody was always trying to screw somebody else and the biggest problem was they went to the contract system to where Hogan was making more money than Greg Maddux. That's a for instance. And they looked at it like that. It's a team over here; Hogan's making more money than Greg Maddux. They spent a lot of money—not on Hogan because he was well worth the price of admission to anything he ever did—but a lot of guys went through that company, got their money and there was nothing put back into the company, and the business started to change.

Although he really wasn't a part of it anymore during that time, Turner would always ask about wrestling. He knew when it was doing well and when it wasn't. The story of the things that happened there … the intrigue of what went on daily I think needs to be a book on its own as it would be an amazing read to uncover all the bodies that are buried there.

CHAPTER 10

While many people will remember my time at Jim Crockett
Promotions or World Championship Wrestling as being perhaps
my most successful in the business, in between my several stops
there, I always returned to Florida—my home away from home—because I
knew I could make a living there. After all, the Sunshine State was where I
had some of my biggest runs with men like Harley Race, Terry Funk, and
Kevin Sullivan.

There was also a time in between my WCW stops that I sucked up my
pride, got a little humbled, and went to work for VKM's "Evil Empire,"
wearing those damn polka dots.

I know this keeps coming up over and over, but the "business is business"
statement that Eddie Graham first taught me is not only a statement that
rings true in so many aspects of the wrestling business, but really in life, too.
Like in other jobs, you often have to put your personal feelings aside for the
sake of business. You don't have to like someone to do business with them—
you just have to respect them for their abilities. It's kind of like the family
member who you love, but you just don't like.

At one point I went back to Florida and joined this group called the
PWF, Pro Wrestling Federation. I had just finished one of my runs with
WCW and it was right before the polka dot era. While I of course wanted
the PWF to be successful, in the back of my mind I always looked at it and
my other brief stops back in Florida like they were a hiatus between the
movies I made; with the movie scripts being my big wrestling creations. The
fact of the matter is by the time I got there the company was already in deep
financial debt and none of the partners—Mike Graham, Steve Keirn, or

Gordon Solie—really had any serious money to reinvest back into the company, and that really disenchanted me with the whole thing.

I brought a friend of mine by the name of Randy Roberts in with me who had a strong business background in casino management with Caesar's Tahoe and corporate startups; with the hope that we could turn Florida back around. But we just couldn't do it. We didn't fail for lack of trying, however. We ran the office and television right back out of the old CWF office at 106 North Albany in Tampa, home of the famous and sometimes infamous Sportatorium. We were on the air all over the state —Tampa, Jacksonville, Miami, Orlando—and we ran the towns weekly like we did in the heyday, trying to recapture the old lightning in a bottle. Everybody involved busted their ass to make that venture work, but the bolt never struck.

> *"One thing about Dusty that everyone would probably agree with me is he is an extremely creative person. He has a great imagination. He has a great perceptual view of things and their outcomes and he has great vision because of that … and he also took that to a business standpoint and he would recommend something if it looked like it was going to be a good business deal or not. Along with that creativity, from a business standpoint, he also had a very keen awareness of what was good business, what would work well and what wouldn't work well."*
>
> —RANDY ROBERTS, FORMER BUSINESS PARTNER

At one point I really believe Vince was scared of what we were trying to do because he thought we had big money behind us and that we were going to break out with something really special. He even sent Bobby Heenan up to the office one day to snoop around.

"Hey, I was just in town and wanted to know how you are doing. …"

I like Bobby a lot, but in all the times he'd come to Tampa, it was the only time he came by to see how we were doing. It was definitely one of those sniff around things, and Vince would do that to me like I was stupid. I only told Bobby what I wanted him to hear, though, knowing he would go back to Vince and repeat what I had said. Not a knock on Bobby, as he knew where his bread was buttered, but it was really like a big chess game between me and Vince, and I kept my king and queen well hidden.

That's when the next movie script came in for me to go back to work for Vince, but without thinking I said, "No." He even said he would pay me for the territory and I said it wasn't worth it, but again I wasn't thinking. It was actually worth more money than he was offering. Looking back on the offer, I should have taken it. I was an idiot.

"Dusty has a passion for the business and an obsession to be successful. 'The Dream' always treated me respectfully and fairly and I don't recall ever having a harsh word with him even though we did not always agree on creative direction. What can you expect? He's a Longhorn and I'm a Sooner."

—JIM ROSS

But I eventually left Florida when we couldn't make the PWF work, went to New York and for a year and a half "The American Dream" was put on hold as "The Common Man," Dusty Rhodes, took center stage in my life.

Vince always had his own vision of things, and if you look at his company and the characterizations of people throughout the years, you'd see that he had such a great marketing group that they figured out before anyone else that they could make more money per night on marketing T-shirts and dolls and yellow fingers than they could make at the box office, which on some summer nights they proved.

So in his mind everybody had to have a place, and I couldn't be "The American Dream," Dusty Rhodes, because he didn't think of that characterization, and he was like me in the sense that if he didn't think of it, he would change it; which was why I was very, very surprised that he used *The Great American Bash* in 2004, which actually really pissed me off because that was one of my creations along with *Starrcade*, *The Crockett Cup* and others. These were my shows. I created them before the pay-per-view era, and if you look at it this way, they were my movies, and I don't like my movies to be butchered or fucked with. You don't take a movie classic like *Psycho* from a master like Alfred Hitchcock and colorize it. Okay so he bought all of those creations of mine when he bought WCW, but he didn't even send me any money for it and he should have, because it's like me being a songwriter and selling a song for $50 because I really needed the money at the time and all of a sudden you sell about a hundred million records ... so it pisses me off. He could've been good about it and thrown me two or three hundred grand and I would have been happy. I would have kept quiet about it, but he didn't, so now it's in the book.

So anyway, getting back on track here, if he didn't think of it, you didn't exist, even though your new character might be just like your old persona.

Really, I shouldn't have been surprised that he would do that, because all of those other guys who had had gotten there before me like the Funks and Harley, their histories were cast aside, too. For God's sake, Vince turned Dory Funk Jr. into "Hoss Funk" and created a third Funk brother named "Jimmy Jack" who was actually former Florida champion Jesse Barr in a fucking Lone Ranger mask. What the fuck were they thinking there? So it stood to reason that if they would do that to those guys, "The American Dream" wasn't going to see the light of day in the "Evil Empire."

But when Vince had Bruce Pritchard produce a series of mini-videos for TV to show me working in different jobs like a coal miner in Pittsburgh and being "The Common Man," all that kept going through my mind was this is "The American Dream" with a new name. I realized this was all designed to prove to the world that he could take a guy who was the biggest star in the country, and just make him into whatever he wanted to.

Although we were good friends and were the same age, growing up together in the business with our dreams being similar in many ways, knowing how talented I was, this was going to be his way of saying, "I run the show." But being like I am, he didn't realize how strong I really was with the public.

So there I was doing these videos like being a plumber, which in a way was a tribute to my dad, and being a meat cutter, which I thought was a cute skit. But the pizza delivery guy was done because Jim Herd, over at WCW, was hired from a pizza company as I explained previously, so that was a rib on him.

And up there, ribs like that were pretty common, and a lot of them were pointed at me. Ted DiBiase's black chauffeur, Mike Jones, who they called "Virgil," was meant as a rib, but that backfired because that's how he got over. Later on when Mike came to WCW they called him "Vincent." Another one was One Man Gang, who they called "The African Dream" Akeem, who I loved. While that character was meant as a rib, if it had been around when I was booking the old Florida territory, they'd still be standing in line at the Tampa Armory to see him and me go one on one. Then there was Ray Traylor, who had been a bodyguard character in the NWA called "Big Bubba Rogers" running around in a Cobb County prison guard outfit as a bad guy now called "Big Bossman." Well, Cobb County, Georgia, was

DUSTY

REFLECTIONS OF AN AMERICAN DREAM

Some early photos of my family and me. I truly was the son of a plumber.
My brother Larry, sister Connie and I had some great times growing up.

DUSTY

Top and middle photos: Blowing off steam with wrestling buddies. From left to right is Hiro Matsuda, me, David Crockett, Dick Murdoch and Pat O'Connor. From left to right below is me, Murdoch's first wife and Richard Hoyt.

Baseball was one of my first loves. In fact, my wrestling name is the same as my dad's favorite baseball player of all time. That's me on the bottom left.

One of my favorite opponents over the years was Harley Race.

Photo by Dr. Mike Lano, wrealano@aol.com.

Bullrope (vs. Tiger Jeet Singh), barbed-wire (vs. Terry Funk), steel cage—the stipulations didn't matter—The American Dream was ready to go.

It was always a big show when Kevin Sullivan and I clashed.

Working over the arm of another former NWA World Champion, Dory Funk Jr.

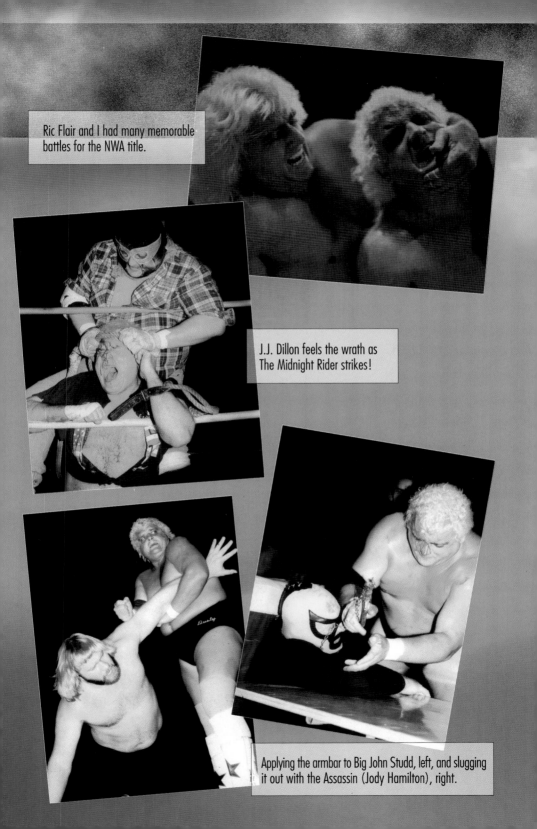

Ric Flair and I had many memorable battles for the NWA title.

J.J. Dillon feels the wrath as The Midnight Rider strikes!

Applying the armbar to Big John Studd, left, and slugging it out with the Assassin (Jody Hamilton), right.

DUSTY

AMERICAN DREAM

Winning the Crockett Cup with Nikita Koloff.

I had three successful NWA World Title reigns.

Dropping the bionic elbow on Cowboy Ron Bass.

Dustin and I jamming with Willie Nelson.

Cody was a two-time state champion in amateur wrestling.

My grandchildren Dakota (right) and Dalton.

DUSTY

REFLECTIONS OF AN AMERICAN DREAM

Michelle and me.

My children, Dustin (above) and Teil, Kristin, and Cody (left to right in photo on right).

where I lived, and I was considered the bad guy "boss" of the opposition; a prison of sorts if you will. So there were a few ribs on me, but all of those characters got over.

Anyway, they were trying to decide what I would wear to the ring and they had me wearing every kind of outfit you could imagine. Well, a few years earlier the polka dot was big on the fashion scene, and it seemed every trendy magazine like *Vogue* and *Glamour* had featured them. It wasn't just a crazy marketing scheme where they said, "You've got to wear this or you can't work here." It was never done that way. It was more Pat Patterson and me laughing about it one night out back.

Pat, who I love dearly, and his life partner, Louie—who has since passed away, rest his soul—were talking to me about it and Pat brought up the marketing aspect of it. Well, after listening to him, we had to fucking do it, because it just made sense. So then he says, let's put a common woman with the common man and the idea was to have a hooker off the street; tall and skinny in a red dress who kind of looked like a female version of Slick, who was one of the WWF managers back then.

Terry Garvin, who was one of the road agents for Vince for many years, knew Juanita Wright as somebody who drove the wrestlers back and forth between the airport and the building in St. Louis. She was a big fan who loved the business and would do anything she could for the boys. I believe she was 50-something years old back then, and Vince agreed to bring her in and—this is the good side of Vince where he has a heart—it made her more money than she ever made in her whole fucking life. When she came in and I saw her, I said, "Oh my God!" because I just knew it would click.

In a way I kind of felt it was Vince saying that this guy—me—is getting old, so let's make him this goofy, mediocre character. But when I was riding in the car one time with Pat and an African American clerk who said to me completely out of left field, "You are the only one who can pull it off for us black guys," talking about Juanita and me, who would now have the character name Sapphire, I knew I got one step up on them. As soon as he said that I just knew, because even in this ridiculous fucking getup I was still connecting with the people and I thought it would be fun to turn that around on them. So it backfired on him when I got over, but he took full credit and it ended up with me being there a year and a half making one of my biggest years financially without the headache and stress of being the boss.

I had three great programs while there. The first one was with Bossman, and that was easy because I had given Ray, rest his soul, his first big break in the business. Then I had a program with "The Million-Dollar Man" Ted DiBiase, which was interesting because he was the guy who along with Vince came up with the "Virgil" rib, but we were professionals and did good business together, plus he was a second-generation guy and knew how this business worked. And then there was the big program with "Macho Man" Randy Savage. "Mach" made me a lot of money when I was up there—I loved the guy. "Mach" and I also had that before-yellow finger respect because he was another second-generation guy, his dad being Angelo Poffo, so "Mach" respected the business roots. Looking back, I consider it like they asked me to be in this huge blockbuster movie and paid me a shit load of money to play this character.

Don't get me wrong now. There were times that I wanted to go in and tell Vince to shove it up his ass, but Pat was always my voice of reason up there. He'd say to me, "Take a step back. Just relax here. Take it easy." And really, he was right, as it was the most relaxing time for me in the business. For whatever the reason was, we all came out smelling like roses, and I remember putting my head in my hands and saying, "From here down, shoot me because from the neck up, that's the real me. 'The American Dream' is still up here." But deep down I was busting. I needed a creative outlet. I had the urge to get the hell out of there to settle some unfinished business.

"While we were in New York (WWF) together, he was upset about being in the polka dots. We were in Hershey, Pennsylvania, and he said, 'I can't do this anymore. I'm going to talk to Vince.' Well, all the boys used to line up to have their five minutes or so with Vince, and Dusty comes out about ten minutes after going in and says, 'He got me. He's the best ... I sat down and told him my whole life ... I told him how I felt. Vince said, 'I know. But who else can pull it off except 'The American Dream,' Dusty Rhodes?' I got up and left. What could I fucking say? I was the only man who can pull it off. I knew it was a bunch of bullshit, but how do you argue with that?'"

—JIMMY HART

I think one of the things that frustrated me the most at the WWF was that they had writers trying to put words in my mouth, saying things I would never say. The first time there, Vince had me trying to read off of a teleprompter. Here I was, one of the greatest interviews in all of our industry and they were trying to put words in my mouth that I would never say. It took one of their writers nine times trying to write and rewrite what they wanted me to say until finally Vince had them just bullet point what they wanted so I could say it my way. I had noticed that when Hogan would cut his promos, they would have his bullet points and he would never use a teleprompter to read, so why was there a different standard for Dusty Rhodes?

When it came time for me to leave the "Evil Empire" and go back to being "The American Dream," I remember Pat asking me if I was going to be okay. I told him, "Don't worry about me. Just take care of Juanita."

Juanita was a sweet lady, and she would hold all her checks because she never made that kind of money before. She didn't know what to do with it. When I would see her she would ask me, "What should I do with these checks?"

I'd say, "Cash those fucking checks. Cash them and put the money in a bank, in your icebox or a dress shop or something. Just cash them."

She made a lot of money, and of course she made huge money when she did the WrestleMania there with me. I was sad when I heard she passed away.

When I went back to WCW as their booker, which back then it wasn't quite the full-blown executive producer role just yet; at first it was really cool. But it wasn't long before the politics of the business started in again, some of which I talked about a little earlier.

"Dusty gave me the insight that somebody has got to draw the money. My dad always said that a night of wrestling is kind of like the Ringling Brothers Circus. If you looked at the Ringling Brothers Circus and there were ten high-wire acts, you wouldn't draw the money. You've got to have the clowns, you've got to have the midgets, you've got to have the jugglers, you've got to have the tumblers, you've got to have lion tamers, you've got to have that whole show every night of a wrestling event ... and Dusty was the high-wire act or the lion tamer, or whatever you wanted to say. But the lion tamer or the high-wire act also had to have the jugglers and the clowns and everything else to make the show complete. Just a good main event isn't going to do it. You need the whole package to make a

wrestling show, so the people will come back week after week after week ... and Dusty understood that better than anybody."

—MIKE GRAHAM

There were just a few guys who said about me, "Man, what an asshole this guy is." But when they really stop and think about it, they had no talent. I remember this one guy who used to badmouth me at WCW all the time was in all honesty booked because Jim Barnett called me in to his office and said please keep this guy here. Obviously that was the only reason the guy was there.

You talk about behind-the-scene politics? That is the worst, when you get called in to an office and are told to make sure so and so stays in the territory and keeps his job. Barnett would tell me I didn't have to do shit with these guys, but that's the reason why they were there. Certain members of the wrestling crew were kept on not because they were talented, but because Jim Barnett, one of the most powerful men in all of wrestling at the time, wanted them to stay on.

Now you've got to remember, I respected Barnett. My admiration for him was unreal, and I hope that has been apparent in what I have written about him thus far. He was my friend, booker, one of my mentors, and next to Eddie, the man I learned more from about this business than perhaps anyone else. But that is a part of the politics that you have to keep in mind. Because just like Andre would rib me to keep me grounded so I could keep things in perspective, Barnett would pull those type of power moves that sort of said, "You don't have that much power just yet ... you will, but you don't have enough power just yet to tell me we can't keep this guy here."

And it didn't just happen at WCW, it happened in other territories too, and I've seen it my whole career. There were always guys who were kept on in a territory because someone wanted them to stay in that territory, whether it was the owner, the booker, or the top draw. Whoever had the power would leverage that clout and use it frequently. And some guys were given titles, even World titles, again not because of their talent, but because they were kept around for a particular purpose, and I'm sure if you use your imagination, you can guess what that purpose was. So these guys were going to be made stars no matter what the consequences were to the territory. Like I said before, I never cared who was fucking who in the ass, except when it directly affected our business. So as reluctant as I was to discuss this, this is something that had to be told, because sometimes it did affect our business, and it was and is a part of the business that is just wrong, but it nevertheless is a part of this business, the dark side of this business.

On the positive side of that double-edged blade, however, if you were like me and always put business first, then that political influence meant you could not only book wrestlers who you knew had talent, but who you could trust and who you knew would draw. To me, that balance was important in order for both the office and me to be successful. So the thing is, a lot of people say this booker or that booker brings in their friends and sometimes that's true, but if the booker or executive producer wants to keep his job, he sure as shit better bring in those friends who can draw. Because friends or no friends, if they don't pull their own weight at the gate or through PPV buys, then you're looking for a new job and somebody else is booking or executive producing.

> *"When Dusty left to go to New York (WWF), I ended up without a job because the suits at WCW didn't know me. I went two years with no insurance and I was completely upside down. When Dusty got the call from Turner to go back as a booker, he took the job with the understanding that I would be his assistant and he brought me in and gave me an opportunity to make a living – he didn't have to do that, but he did. While it was more physically demanding than I could really handle, Dusty opened a door for me when I had nothing in my life going for me."*
>
> —"Magnum T.A." Terry Allen

So a lot of times when you see a booker or executive producer with a successful track record bring in certain people, while at first you may think he's just bringing in his friends, the odds are he's bringing in people who he can trust and who can help him accomplish his goals. After all, friendship is friendship, but "business is business."

> *"A lot of people have knocked Dusty's booking. But when you've been a booker for as long as he has, he probably booked a thousand workers ... so he's got five hundred workers who liked him and five hundred workers who thought he was the shits, because in every match somebody has to win*

and somebody has to lose. He did a lot of wonderful things ... he worked with a lot of wonderful people ... he did a lot of wonderful angles."

—TERRY FUNK

CHAPTER 11

I f you were to ask 20 wrestlers, "What the most important aspect of their industry is ... the most important thing they can do?" what would you say their answer should be? If they've got any sense for the business in them whatsoever, they'll give you one answer and one answer only—draw a house ... or in today's world of PPVs, generate a high buy rate.

That right there is what our business is really all about. It ain't about the politics, although the politics do exist. It ain't about pleasing internet and sheet writers with fancy stunt wrestling moves, although all of those guys may have their own opinions on the business. It's all about giving the majority of the fans a show that is so entertaining it draws them back to the next show so you can do it all over again.

You don't need to be a fucking rocket scientist to understand that drawing a house is the backbone of our industry. You don't need to know why $E=mc^2$. But to be successful in the wrestling industry, you should know how to get from point A to point B, and understand that the shortest way to get there is a straight line.

How do you do that? You create storylines that have some believability in them. You have feuds that settle scores. You have angles that hit close to home. You look closely at pop culture and try to imitate what's going on in the world around you. You use formulas that have worked in the business for 100 years and will work for the next 100 years. Do you really think "Stone Cold" Steve Austin was the first guy to drive a truck into a building and drink beers? Hell, I did that in '75-'76, right in the Tampa Armory, only difference is I didn't do it on TV. The thing is, though, if you do it right, if you carry out your plan correctly, people will remember those storylines, those feuds and those angles for years to come, no matter how many other people come after you and copy what you've done.

I've been one of the fortunate ones in the business who has been able to do some of those things correctly, and so with that in mind, in this chapter I'm gonna talk about some of my famous feuds, some of my favorite storylines, some of my favorite angles, and some of the people who were involved in them with me. I'm also gonna talk a little bit about some of the guys who I've met during my career, and finally, I'm gonna talk about the one thing that everybody seems to want to talk about with me—the so-called "Dusty Finish."

There have been so many people who I have worked with over the years from the early days right up to the independents and TNA. It's hard enough to stuff my 30-plus-year career into a few hundred pages, let alone a few paragraphs ... it's kind of like trying to fit into your favorite size 42 Levis even though you're a size 46; while most of you is in there nice and snug, some of you just ain't fitting in.

Anyway, there are so many guys who I can talk about, like Don Muraco. His nickname was "Magnificent," and for a damn good reason. Don Muraco was the first really clean-ass natural best worker in the business, bar none. His background was surfing off the North Shore of Oahu in Hawaii—Sunset Beach—so he had unbelievable balance. There were nights when he used to work and when he was on, holy fuck he really was "Magnificent"! Unfortunately, however, there were also nights when he didn't give a shit when he was at work, and in those cases it was like a fucking train wreck. Muraco first came to prominence on TBS in the angle that turned Roddy Piper from a heel to a babyface, when it looked like Don was going to attack Gordon Solie. Piper jumped in, and like they say, the rest is history. Some of Don's matches in the Fed with "Superfly" Jimmy Snuka were classic, and in the Yellow Finger era he went from being "Magnificent" to being called "The Rock" and doing those God-awful videos like "Fuji Vice."

Another of those guys was Jos LeDuc. Although he didn't call himself Canada's greatest athlete like Gene Kiniski or "Bulldog" Bob Brown did, LeDuc was known as "The Canadian Freight Train" and drew so much fucking money in the South and in Florida, it is unbelievable. But people today would ask, "Who's Jos LeDuc?" These fuckers wouldn't know Jos LeDuc from a douche or a dirt rag. But LeDuc was one of the toughest motherfuckers there was. In the days before video promos were real popular,

LeDuc did one where his back was against a wall and he held a truck at bay, which was revving its engine, with just the power of his legs. That little video right there put asses in the seats because just like Pak Song broke rocks with his bare hands like I talked about earlier, and that was legit. LeDuc held that truck back with his legs and that was legit, too.

Ox Baker is another guy who comes to mind. Ox drew a lot of money in his day, and while he had a hard time walking and chewing gum at the same time, he did an interview that was phenomenal. He had that look and that conviction in his voice that whatever he said, you would believe. If he said he was gonna kick somebody's ass, you believed somebody's ass was gonna be kicked. Ox was also one of those guys who used the business to get into other things and even had a role in the John Carpenter movie *Escape from New York*, playing this wild, scary-looking fucker. But that was Ox; he was a scary-looking fucker just walking around the dressing room.

Speaking of phenomenal interviews, arguably one of the greatest heel interviews I ever heard was from Curtis Iaukea, "King" Curtis. A lot of fans might say Ric Flair was the best, and I'm gonna get to Ric in a bit, but while he was good, I always thought he was repetitious in his interviews. Tully Blanchard was excellent in his own way because he spoke from the heart in that scary calm manner, kind of like that character out of *Cape Fear*. And Arn was good too, because when he did an interview, he always kept things in perspective. But Curtis was just unreal in that he said thought-provoking things and he was always a little different each time. Even years later when he did the thing on WCW playing Kevin Sullivan's "father" and in that gruff, commanding voice would say, "Sullivan my son …" you just listened, because you knew he was going to say something powerful. He was just one of those guys who knew how to manipulate the audience with what he said, and his interviews were always spot on.

Other guys who come to mind for giving great interviews or promos are "Playboy" Gary Hart and Sir Oliver Humperdink, who I will talk about a little later on in the book; Kevin Sullivan who, like Flair, I'll get to in a bit; "Superstar" Billy Graham who I spoke about earlier and who was just unbelievable with the gift of gab—*"I am so strong, they can smell me in the TV studio six blocks away!"*—and Killer Karl Kox. Like Jos LeDuc, many people today wouldn't know Karl from shit, but Triple K was just one of those guys who could bring it during an interview. Karl was unique in that he was like one of the first guys I can remember fucking with an announcer during an interview, like they were the only two people there and the audience was just eavesdropping in on their conversation or something; a style some guys in the WWF borrowed later on when working with Gene Okerlund. Karl also created the mythical "Alex" character, this unseen entity who would tell him what to do, thus putting into the audience's mind that this guy was really off his fucking rocker, and we all know there ain't anybody who's more dangerous than some crazy bastard who talks to people who ain't there. Years later when Rick Steiner was doing the "Varsity Club" gimmick in WCW, Sullivan suggested he borrow "Alex" to help him establish that he too was a little unbalanced. It worked.

"The greatest promo Dusty ever cut was for nobody. It's 1986, Atlanta TV at the old studio, and another Midnight Express squash match— Bobby [Eaton] and Dennis [Condrey] against somebody, I can't remember and this five foot six, 185 maybe, jacked-up little kid, going bald, and he came from Florida with these two big bodybuilders and he wanted to call himself Blue Thunder because he had these pretty blue tights. But Dusty saw him and said, 'No, we're gonna call him Wee Willie Wilkins.' So he was hot already going into the fucking match. In the old Midnight Express job matches, they'd whack him, boom, boom, boom, toss him out on the floor. He jumps right back up, jumps up on the apron, jumps in over the top rope. He ain't gonna sell shit and he's a pretty good little worker, but he's nobody. So he's not selling … he'll take the bump or whatever, but he'll pop right back up and the other guy, blah, blah, blah. Well, finally they're taking the finish on old Blue Thunder, Wee Willie … so powerslam, rocket launcher, boom, one, two, three … and Bobby and Dennis get up and as Bobby raises his hands, he's got his back turned to the guy. The guy's laying on his back and he lifts his leg, the only thing that moves on his body, and doesn't even kick, just taps Eaton on the ass. Bobby turns around like 'What the fuck?' and working stomps the guy and then turns back around. The guy scoots over on his ass and sideways kind of kicks Bobby in the ass again. Well, I was starting to walk away and Dennis was too, and we turn around and saw this and Bobby went over and now Bobby and Dennis are starting to kick the shit out of the guy for real, they're putting the boots to him. I can't remember who his partner was, but he got so fucking freaked out he wanted to run, but ended up running toward Bobby and Bobby just pickled him right between the eyes. Now

they're kicking the shit out of Wee Willie and I'm coming back to the ring as I'm already on the floor. He's rolling for the ropes as fast as he can and as he comes over that bottom rope, I see his leg and I fucking—whap!— knee-chop him with the edge of the tennis racket. He lands on the floor and scurries off. We're like 'What the fuck?' so Bobby and Dennis are hot and we're storming backstage. Meanwhile back in the control room, there's J.J. (Dillon) sitting in front where he always did and Dusty sitting at the executive producer's desk, and I think it was J.J. who asked, 'What did he just do?' and Dusty said, 'I think he just kicked Bobby in the ass.' When he did it again, now Dusty's saying 'What the fuck?' and now he's hot. So as we're coming around to the dressing room, the guy is already back there and his two jacked-up bodybuilder friends have come along ... we're coming around the corner and Dusty's in front of us. We're going to get the guy but we slow up a little bit because Dusty walks up to them, doesn't even look at the two jacked-up guys, looks down at the guy and has his finger pointed right at his nose, looking down at him going, 'Motherfucker, you want to make a comeback on someone? Make a comeback on me! What the fuck do you think you're doing? Get your fucking ass out of my building right now,' and he kicked him and his friends out of the building. They grabbed their bags; they didn't even stop to change, never to be seen again. But the guy thought he was going to get over on Atlanta TV and sure enough he did, because 18 years later he's in Dusty Rhodes' book as the biggest fucking asswipe in the history of the wrestling business!"

—JIM CORNETTE

Two guys people ask me about all the time are Bruiser Brody and Stan Hansen. Brody, known better to me as Frank Goodish, was someone I went to school with at West Texas State and I liked him before he got into the business ... but I don't know who broke him in. I have no clue how he got into the business and how he became this legendary cult guy. Aside from his runs in World Class for Fritz and the Kansas City territory for Bob Geigel, Frank was a big star in Japan and that was it. He was a big star there, but he really wasn't a big star in the United States. Like I said he had a cult following of people and I liked the shit out of him when we were roommates in college, but it's like when Stan—who I really liked too—went to Japan and I didn't see him any more. Stan had a little run with WCW in the late '80s early '90s, but was most famous for his feud in New York with Bruno Sammartino in the early '70s when he supposedly broke Bruno's neck. But that was really it with him. Fans here don't know what happened to them, even though I know they were huge over there in Japan and that's where they made their living. Stan probably could have been huge here too, because of the way he was, but he chose a different career path than say me or Terry Funk. As for Brody, I know promoters would say he was hard to handle, that he was this badass troublemaker or whatever, but he was always just my West Texas State football buddy … that's the way I looked at it. No real thoughts or nothing. … I didn't look at him with no prejudice or anything and I can't put him in either DT time or YT time—"Dusty Time" or "Yellow Finger Time"—I don't know which he'd belong in, but I do know in the end it was very disturbing to me what happened to him, being stabbed in the shower in Puerto Rico like that, because I really liked him outside the business. He was just one of the guys I didn't pay a lot of attention to. Yeah, there were a few times I was too drawn up in being "The American Dream" Dusty Rhodes while he was over there in Japan and maybe I should have paid more attention, I don't know. I can't put a finger on him, but there are a lot of people who were stars outside the U.S. I can't put a finger on as to why they made it big there and not here.

Two guys who were big stars here in the States, but most prominently, though, in the Northeast, were Pedro Morales and the man who I just mentioned, Bruno. Pedro and I got along great; I guess it was because I've always gotten along with Latinos from my upbringing and all. I always thought he was underrated as the WWWF champion, that he somehow was looked down upon by the fans, and that was wrong because he had some great runs there. He had the Puerto Rican fans on fire in New York. I guess the argument was outside of New York and maybe Philadelphia, that the Puerto Rican population wasn't strong enough to support a minority champion. As for Bruno, the Italians in New York, Boston, Philly, loved him, and I wish I could say the same in that we got along great, but we didn't.

Before going to New York, Bruno was the one guy I really wanted to meet, because let's face it, he owned the Garden. Madison Square Garden was his Yankee Stadium and he was Babe Ruth. Just like the Armory in Tampa was my Yankee Stadium and I was Ruth there, he was Ruth in the Garden. Bruno's reputation preceded him and he had that aura about him that all the greats had. Well, since I really got to New York after his long run there was over, it came time for me to meet him, and at first everything was cool. But then I went with Pedro to this club in the City called The Savoy one night after the matches. Well, this crowd of people was around Bruno getting autographs, and when we pulled up in our limo, and I got out, the crowd ran, literally ran from Bruno to me, and I could tell he was pissed. He probably shouldn't have been upset because the fans had probably gotten his autograph a hundred times, and I was the new kid on the block up there. But professional jealousy is pretty commonplace in sports and entertainment. If the roles were reversed, I probably would have been pissed, too. But that's what happened and I can't change that.

Anyway, after that happened our relationship was a little strained. It was nothing like "fuck you" or anything, but you could tell there was some tension there. As a matter of fact, this one time Bill Apter wanted to take a picture of Bruno and me and neither one of us wanted to go to the other one to pose; sort of like playing this game of who's gonna blink first. "If you want our picture, let him come here. ..." I'm sure he said the same thing to Bill. But Apter finally got that photo he wanted. Bruno and I were passing each other in the hall and Willie said, "Can I get that photo now?" We stopped. We posed. He snapped the picture. I guess neither one of us blinked. What bullshit, huh?

My favorite person of all-time in the business was Dick Murdoch. I know I've written a lot about him so far and probably said some of this already, but that's okay, that's why I dedicated this book to him. Like me, he was partly true, partly fiction. But one thing with him that was always true, when he wanted to wrestle, not Flair, not Ricky Steamboat, none of the so-called great professionals were better than Hoyt. He had the greatest timing ever in our business and had no equal when he was "on." He was a lifetime partner and road companion, and then one day they said he died. I don't know if that's true, that's why I did not go to his funeral. Like I said early on in the book, I hate funerals and I am not sure he's dead. Terry Funk deep down is still pissed because I did not attend the festivities in Hoyt Richard Murdoch's name. By not fucking attending, I could keep his phone number in my book and mind and dial it whenever I needed to talk to him. If he doesn't answer, I just tell myself he isn't home. Call you later, Hoyt! He would actually fart on the young performers today with all their stunts, with no story, no emotions, no real passion for our business; our business of pro wrestling. He would fart at the schools that say come and learn to wrestle, run by men who never drew a fucking dime in the business. It's like you can't sing the blues if you haven't had them. He is pissing on them from wherever he is! I do love you, Hoyt!

Another one of my favorite people is Terry Funk. I could write an entire book about Terry, but I guess he already wrote one himself and with the same damn publisher that I have. I know I probably wrote too much about him already in this book, but because we are still beating the shit out of each other on the Indy circuit, and him being 60 and me being five years younger than him, it is very hard to keep carrying him! I love his wife, Vicky, and deep down I love him. I enjoy being around him a lot! His matches against Shane Douglas, Sabu, and Mick Foley while he was in his 50s with ECW are classics. His acting in movies was almost as good as mine. He played Johnny the Thumper in *Paradise Alley* and had a role in *Over the Top* with Sylvester Stallone, while I played Deputy Johnny Morton in *Paradise Park* and also had roles in *Gold Raiders* and *It's My Turn* among some others.

Like I said before, I will not retire until he does. I looked up to him when I was at West Texas State. Throughout the years he played the game the way it was supposed to be played, and as the business changed, we had to change a little too, but the Indies gives us that opportunity to apply our trade. Terry and I are the last of a dying breed, truly the last of the outlaws, riding a long road, night to night, town to town, never knowing when the end will come.

Then there's the "King of the Ring" himself, Harley Race. To me Harley was the greatest NWA champion of all time, and we made a lot of money together, buddy. "Mad Dog" or Dog as I called him earlier, was also a tough son of a bitch in the ring. I remember one night at the Bayfront Center in St. Petersburg, Florida, standing in the middle of the ring. He noticed that I put an earring in my ear and he said, loud as fuck, "What kind of a man would put an earring in his ear?" and then tried his best to rip it out. Only my great speed kept him at bay! Great memories of hour-long matches and of course my favorite match with him at "Last Tango in Tampa." He was a great champion when the NWA belt meant something.

"It falls back to the charisma. He could take and back up 90 percent of what he said. Dusty was as good as anyone playing the role of Dusty Rhodes. With me, Dusty always kept his word. If a guy never lies to you, you don't have a problem doing anything he may want to do in the ring. Our business worked off trust. Of all the thousands of matches we had,

most of the stuff we did went 60 minutes. Dusty could go at a pretty damned good pace. You knew you could trust him. He was a guy who knew what he could do in the ring and would go to the peak of what he could do."

—HARLEY RACE

Of course, there's also the guy who many fans consider to be the greatest NWA champion of all time, Ric Flair. Now that's one hell of a statement if they've seen guys like Lou Thesz, Buddy Rogers, Gene Kiniski, Dory Funk, Jr., Jack Brisco, and Terry Funk in their primes. From day one of our meeting, "The Nature Boy" had that outgoing, charismatic attitude. He looked up to Murdoch and me for some of the wrong reasons—beer and raising hell was I think what he looked up to, but in my case, I think that the swagger I had made him want to be like me. "Rambling" Ricky Rhodes. Like I mentioned earlier, "Be yourself. Be the first Ric Flair," I said to him, and he did. Much is said about our relationship—partly true, partly fiction—but one thing is sure, in my mind the good outweighed the bad. Day after day, night after night, when you spend that much time with one very talented athlete such as Flair, you become very close; close enough to know how insecure he is, but he didn't have to be, he was too talented. His lack of trust in me as his booker was really unjust. Even though I got some thick skin, it hurt me as all of his friends or so-called friends only told him what he wanted to hear. Only Arn I think, was really close to him, the rest were just hangers-on. It made him bitter about who and what brought him to the dance. Sometimes his shit was purely flimflam! Most of the time he blamed it on me. I was able to stand it then, and I can still handle it! I will not write about my parties with him, because anybody who really knows Ric has seen him naked; the matches with him, because we had so many good bouts, but only to say he was good. Not the best, but good. I'll enjoy my good memories of us together, and if truth be told, I was his fucking closest friend!

There were some hot angles I did with Flair, but most of the really hot stuff was with all of the Four Horsemen as a whole, like the famous video we shot of them breaking my arm in the Jim Crockett Promotions parking lot in Charlotte. That was pretty brutal for back then, completely fucking violent and about as hardcore as you could get.

But the one angle that everybody asks me about, even the guys on road, the wrestlers themselves—it ain't my best matches with Flair, it ain't the tag-team matches against Arn—the one thing everybody asks me about to this day is my feud with Tully Blanchard and the night Baby Doll, Nickla Roberts, brought out this envelope in the Greensboro Coliseum. Everybody asks, "What was in the envelope?"

I'll get to the envelope in a bit. The deal with Tully was that when I was booking, he was always my "go-to" feud. We knew that if business was down, he and I could always do something to lift business back up a little. I think the thing that made that feud so great was that the fans really saw our real personalities out there. It was as real as you could get. We didn't necessarily like each other—we didn't hate each other, either—but we respected the hell out of each other and we did business.

> "When I was a kid I'd watch TV and I thought Dusty Rhodes was a cool name. I appreciated a big guy who could work his ass off and go an hour Broadway [draw]. Dusty's charisma was over the top. I remember a TV match with Dusty and Ronnie Garvin against Ric Flair and Arn Anderson with Baby Doll. It was a big influence. During the match Dusty reached over and kissed Baby Doll. I remember the way it lit up the crowd."
>
> —"STONE COLD" STEVE AUSTIN

Okay, the envelope ...

In our industry really it's about a very simple angle that I had thought up and shot that really was just a thing that I put in to generate something for television. I couldn't come up with anything else and it turned out to this day to be one of the most asked questions besides "Who was the Midnight Rider?" and of course they smile after asking that question. So what was in the envelope that Baby Doll handed me in the Greensboro Coliseum?

They say the dramatic look on my face even to this day was priceless because that was the only time somebody was able to get "The American Dream," Dusty Rhodes to shut up. Right in the middle of my interview I clammed up tighter than John Kerry at a Swift Boat Vets reunion. It was probably one of the last true shoots in our industry where people believed what they saw was real, and they should believe it because it was the most heartless thing that anybody had ever done to me ... it was unbelievable. It was unplanned. Tully put her up to it, I believe, and it was an unmerciful cowardly act by them.

I remember it like it was yesterday, when she came out and handed the envelope to me on the interview, I thought it was like a rib but really couldn't sell it like that, so I said to myself, "Okay, let me open up this and look inside. ..." the picture that I saw was the most phenomenal thing. ... Until this day even the boys ask me what was in that envelope. So knowing all that and what it means to everybody, I think to keep them on a good square level knowing what can really happen if the things are done right, I don't think anybody will ever know what was in that envelope unless Baby Doll tells you ... and I don't see that happening.

"I still have the envelope ... the angle was going to be over a couple of weeks. I was going to reveal pictures that would expose him. Now Dusty was married and was faithful, the whole nine yards and all that, but the premise of it was that I busted him in a hotel room with another woman. And every week I was going to show a little more and a little more, like the hotel and all that. They even thought of having a video of me walking through a hotel room with maybe hearing giggling and laughing in the background and then seeing Dusty's legs intertwined with another woman's legs. And then it was going to be a little more pictures, a little more pictures, but to add even more to it, it was supposed to be a black woman. Every week it was supposed to be a little more. Maybe clothes thrown on the floor, jeans up on the couch or something, and then I'd bust him and his wife would bust him and it would be quite a soap opera. It turned out they didn't like it, because my husband at the time, Sam Houston, was working for the WWF and I was working for Turner and they felt it was too much of a conflict of interest, because on my days off I would fly out to be with him and they wanted me to be very exclusive. Dusty always wanted me portrayed as this Marilyn Monroe figure, very single, very available, and being married didn't fit in with that. So what I ended up having in the envelope were some really goofy pictures of him. There's a picture of him copping a feel in a hotel lobby on a Venus de Milo statue with this goofy look on his face, then there was a photo of Dusty and either a security guard or a policewoman where it looks like he's giving her a bribe. Then there's one of him with this rainbow clown wig on with Groucho Marx glasses and nose. They're just these goofy pictures.

It was my idea to deliver the envelope and I took it upon myself to do it because I always liked that little bit of mystery of was it a work or was it real."

—NICKLA ROBERTS, AKA "BABY DOLL"

So when I got into the back and away from the camera, I laughed my ass off, because that's exactly what it really was, a fucking rib that was played on me. But to this day it played like a shoot, because in my mind that's how I had to play it. Back then you never broke *kayfabe*, ever, no matter what. You learned how to roll with the flow and that's how we took a rib and made it into an angle that was talked about for more than 20 years. And I can guarantee you that some of the people who were there, some of the wrestlers who saw it, will read this and still think we are working them on this, because it really was that good.

"What was interesting about the whole thing with Baby Doll, is that originally it wasn't supposed to be Nickla, it was supposed to be Sunshine, who worked with me out in Texas. She was supposed to be the perfect 10, but looking back that never would have worked as well. We were lucky we couldn't find her and ended up with Nickla, because she was the only person who could have pulled all that off the way it was."

—TULLY BLANCHARD

Speaking of working, the man we called the devil, Kevin Sullivan, is the type of person who after being in the wrestling business all these years thinks everything is a work. We drew more money in a time when the house you drew was the thing that drove our business. His mind in the world of pro wrestling was tremendous. We had our run-ins both in and out of the ring, but I really enjoy him now. Over the years he had some Sheik-type ideas and we fed off of each other. There was nothing more exciting than the ref being knocked out and the devil reaching into his box and pulling out the golden spike, driving it deep into my chest area, as I went down. The crowd in that white, cold, silent heat is a memory that still wakes me up screaming in a cold sweat and looking into the fucking darkness, and after a while I smile. I think, whoa! It's show time. He might have been the best. He was a devil and I was "The American Dream." He was the antichrist and I was the savior. It was good versus evil at its very core.

CHAPTER ELEVEN

"When I came to Florida, Dusty had no intentions of working with me. I went out and cut an interview that there was no 'American Dream.' People were in gas lines, there were hostages in Iran and interest rates were high. I said there was no such thing as 'The American Dream' and that Dusty's hoodwinking the people. I said you can't afford the B.S. he's giving you. I thought of that promo for two weeks. Dusty blew right by me and proceeded to give a rebuttal. He booked it. That Sunday we had a good house and it went from there."

—KEVIN SULLIVAN

Kevin was a weird guy. He was not big in stature but he was a tough fucker and he always had a group of people with him, an entourage—snakes, and belly dancers, fire-eating dragons and shit—and Abudadein. He had all these fucking people around that I could kick their ass but I could never kick his ass, kind of like the super villain who would always get away at the end of the movie, even though all of the other bad guys had been caught or killed. And he had a cult following of these people who would follow him from town to town sometimes. When he would do an interview, Eddie would get close but not too close and would be concerned with what he said on that interview because he believed Kevin was the devil. But when he would say it I would tell Eddie it's okay because I had a rebuttal and I would make them know that he's just saying that ... but maybe he is.

In Orlando, Sullivan had a group of ten to 15 people, mystics, who came down from Casadega, Florida, who would follow him—as they would follow Jim Jones who gave the people Kool-Aid to drink and they all fucking died—that's the way these people followed Kevin. They had a van with his name on it and all the peace signs, crosses and other stuff, and they would drive to this place they parked on the Fairgrounds inside a big fence, and once you had it parked, you couldn't get out. Now of course, the local cowboys and Indians, the blacks and the browns, the amigos were my people in Florida. I was the pickup truck guy who the cowboys thought was the second coming of John Wayne. They didn't give a fuck, so the devil was the only guy that on Christmas night turned Santa Claus into a heel at the Bayfront Center in St. Petersburg. When I left the building that night, people were standing what looked like two, three thousand deep, screaming to hang Santa Claus! It was Christmas night and they had the kids with them who just got presents that morning, and they wanted to kill Santa Claus.

As part of the promotion, Eddie had five or six Santa Clauses during the night for the kids circulating through the building. Well the fans soon found out that one of the Santa Clauses was actually one of Kevin's disciples. Jake Roberts had dressed in a Santa suit and, passing the security guards, he knocked me on my ass to help Kevin beat "The American Dream" on Christmas night; starting the biggest feud in the history of our business in Florida that's still going on today. But on that night it was like a riot. It was a bad Saint Nick that people wanted … they wanted somebody to kick that shit out of old Saint Nick!

> *"When we did the loser leaves town match in Orlando and I beat Dusty on Christmas, he came back as the Midnight Rider and beat me … and then I came back under a mask as Lucifer and we did that for a while. Dusty understood good versus evil. Years later when the Sheik was 59 years old, we did a Starrcade in Detroit and we made a bet that we could do a double switch during the tag-team match between Dusty and the Sheik versus me and Dick Murdoch to where the Sheik would turn heel and Murdoch would turn babyface. We pulled it off."*
>
> —KEVIN SULLIVAN

So Sullivan had a knack for doing stuff like that and he was also the only guy I beat in a bull rope match that didn't go off his feet! It's hard to pin that little bastard, that little stiff fucker, when he won't come out of the corner. So you had to put yourself in a position to be creative. I had the referee count the turnbuckle! I crawled up in the corner and cross-bodied him like I would cover him on the mat and the referee went one, two, three.

> *"All this B.S. about Dusty being an egomaniac … he did a job in the middle of the ring for me. He knew when to do it. When it made sense."*
>
> —KEVIN SULLIVAN

Anyway, that Santa Claus thing in St. Pete really ignited the feud, and so getting back to that group in Orlando, one night we had drawn a big house and I was showering and I heard fire trucks and there's only a one-lane road getting out of there. There were people running, screaming and shit, about to fall over each other. These cowboys who came to Orlando knew every week where these guys from Casadega would park their van, and so they torched it after the match, they lit it up! They burned it to the ground in the parking lot while these goofs stood around it in a semi-circle as if watching a cross burn. Burned it to the fucking ground, buddy. They believed it was real.

And this is all after Kevin, Molokai, and Demetrius had won. But where were these fucking people he named? They beat the fuck out of me, stretching me out and laying out Black Jack Mulligan, too. Molokai of course was Gene Lewis, but Kevin would change their names to go with his gimmick, to go with his character; that's how Mark Lewin became the Purple Haze, how Bob Roop became Mayhar Singh, how Nancy Sullivan became the Fallen Angel, and how Angel Vachon became Luna.

This was a perfect example of something that I talked about earlier in the book where there were no shades of gray, because on that night for two and a half hours after the bell rung, it was all black and white for you to get excited about.

I remember this other night in Orlando when I was in the ring with Molokai. During my match Kevin and Black Jack started fighting in the back, fought their way through the crowd, fought at ringside, fought in the ring, fought out on the other side of the ring, and fought right out the front door of the building. One week later, I was in the ring again with Molokai in a return match, the front opened and here came Kevin and Bobby Jack fighting into the arena. This old guy sitting at ringside said, "Goddamn, they've been fighting a whole fucking week!"

That feud obviously was classic, and Sullivan became a very good booker out of it. Like the Sheik, he lived his gimmick. He had a great vision. He had great ideas, and I really felt proud because I believe he learned a lot from me, and I, in turn, learned a lot from him. But he watched me closely earlier on in my career and he became a heel who drew money. That's what manipulating people and things and territories is all about. God, we had a big feud, and given the opportunity, it would still be going on today.

"I've never thanked Dusty. I wouldn't have had a career like I had or have everything I have without Dusty giving me the opportunity to wrestle him, and because of the track record to get the rub with Hulk. I wouldn't have done the things with Abby and the Sheik. I thank him!"

—KEVIN SULLIVAN

A guy who was similar to Kevin in a lot of ways was Larry Shreve, better known as Abdullah the Butcher. Abdullah was a guy everyone was scared to death of and they still are today. If you ever watch the History Channel about the Haitians, they have these Voodoo dancers who go into trances and they pass out and fall down and they just go crazy. Well, one night as we fought in the West Palm Beach Auditorium, we fought out to the back of the building. There would be a lot of Haitians who came to the matches there, and a group of them were out in the back and they were the kind of Haitians who were worshipers. Well, Abdullah got away from me and he ran up on this group of people and they threw themselves into a fit just like you see on the History Channel and they got in a circle around him and they started doing all this shit. I was watching this unfold in front of me and they started passing out on the fucking floor. They just started laying out doing these weird gyrations and shit. As a heel, he had that kind of power over people. He had that knack like the Sheik, like Sullivan, that you believed this fucking guy was a bad motherfucker and still is. And heavy—Jesus—he must weigh 900 pounds! Today, while he still wrestles, he's a successful businessman in Atlanta with "Abdullah's House of Chinese Food and Ribs," but there's only one Abdullah the Butcher, and our feuds in Atlanta were … shit it's one of them if you want to sell out, that's what you booked before Yellow Finger— you booked Abdullah and Dusty in Georgia. The mysterious person you see is who he was, and almost like the Sheik, he lived the gimmick. The only time I saw him out of character was down at the Underground nightclub one night. They told me Abdullah went down to this club after I wrestled him in the Auditorium. That was the night the lady fell out of the balcony to get a glimpse of "The American Dream," and he danced like a son of a bitch, so I went down to this African-American club, and I walked in, and there he was. He looked like a big, black, Sidney Greenstreet, the guy you see in those old movies. Abdullah had on a white suit and a big, white Panama hat and everybody around him was black and he was out on the dance floor dancing his ass off. And that's what I think about now when I think of Abdullah. Dressing nice and classy, but everyone was scared of him and they still are. Larry was a bad ass and still is.

A couple of years ago, the most fun I had in a long, long time was when Terry Funk, Kevin Sullivan, Abdullah and I did this four-way brawl in Davie, Florida, for a local promoter down there. About 4,500 people showed up at the Davie Rodeo Arena for this independent show, which was really unheard of, just to see the four of us kick the shit out of each other, and we did not disappoint the fans. I love those type of things because it was just so simple. There was no rocket science there that night, just four old fuckers beating the piss out of each other and loving every minute of it.

Wahoo McDaniel was like the first guy I really marked out for. He was an Indian from Oklahoma like my dad, and he had more fire in him than anybody else I had seen. His fire on his comebacks was just phenomenal and you believed in him. I was at this gas station in Canyon, Texas, at West Texas State University once and he stopped in on his way from Amarillo going to the next town for a match. He had a new Mustang at the time—a '66 or '67—and he got out and he was wearing this orange alpaca sweater, a really nice sweater with a turtleneck. Man, he looked immaculate, and I thought to myself he must have $20 million in the bank—that's the way my mind worked back then. He took me in, he grabbed me, he brought me into that realm and made it real. This guy lived his gimmick and what I've been talking about all throughout the book. He got out of the car as Wahoo McDaniel, he didn't get out of the car as Ed McDaniel, the former New York Jets football player. He was Wahoo McDaniel, the pro wrestler and he was at the gas station. To me it was like the fucking Beatles were here. He just drove up in a fucking Mustang instead of a yellow submarine, and that's important because it was about believability. He was a good-hearted guy and a tough guy, too. He did some unbelievable stuff athletics-wise, that people still talk about him doing, like running from Norman, Oklahoma, to Oklahoma City, 18 miles or whatever it is on a bet with Bill Watts and taking on all comers. I had a lot of respect for him. I loved the guy and enjoyed being with him as he was kind of a father figure to me because he reminded me of my dad a little bit the way he looked, dark, and he had that face kind of like my dad. He wasn't that much older than me, but he was kind of like a father figure.

Wahoo bought me a real nice shotgun one time, and I went dove hunting with him. He was one of those pre-Yellow Finger guys, and to watch his early matches would be a study in how to get "over." In the end fans remembered the old, worn-out Wahoo, but that's not him. It's just like when Sitting Bull kicked the shit out of Custer at Little Big Horn, massacred him by the overwhelming numbers. Well, I imagine a few years later, Sitting Bull was a little heavier and wasn't really the same Sitting Bull. So you can't really look at Wahoo at the end of his career, you have to look at it as a whole. As a matter of fact, he did a lot of "Dusty Finishes" during his career. I was sad when he died because I not only respected him, but he was one of my idols.

Dallas Page is a real friend. He works harder than anyone I know to be the very best he can be. He has a very impressive attitude. I think Dallas in a way is an example of doing anything you put your mind to, because he proved everybody wrong who said he couldn't work. In the beginning, he really couldn't. Dallas couldn't do anything. He had no coordination whatsoever. But he worked hard to obtain it and he made history in winning the WCW title for a guy who became an overachiever. He really overachieved and he tried so hard to be in that little clique of guys.

I enjoyed watching him just as he was breaking out, battling Arn Anderson, Ric Flair, and company, who would try to keep him down. We had a real close relationship then as we still do today. We talk about our business of course, but we also talk about our personal lives. He has a real ability to stay focused and positive. In Fort Myers, Florida, one time, I invited him to a Willie Nelson concert. Chelle and I met him there and he was pumped as he took pictures of Willie and me on stage together; he was like a celebrity mark! Little did I know that he took the pictures to put in his resume for later use. He reminded me of "Rambling" Dallas Rhodes. Well, he proved himself, and we are very close. I still was really pissed off when he had Hogan write the foreword for his book—big mistake! Anyway, I got fucking over it! Dallas became a megastar in pro wrestling. Hard work and trusting his instincts paid off.

My favorite story about Dallas was at a pay-per-view when Jim Heard, the blooming idiot of corporate America, was running WCW. Dallas was being pushed big time by me, when in his "Diamond Mine" episode with Vinnie Vegas, aka Kevin Nash, he wanted to use what he called a "Garth Brooks headset" instead of a stick mic. Well, he said the word "fuck" on the broadcast. I remember Jim Ross and his personal bitch, Jim Herd, were in shock; they went off. I was able to get it shut down, but that was the "Diamond Mine," and it was okay as he made it anyway. Dallas is my lifelong friend. Good work, DDP!

> *"If not for Dusty there is no DDP. I went up to Dusty to ask him if I should start wrestling and he said, 'You'll be a fire-breathing dragon … the greatest manager of all time!' There were times I would go to him and he, like Jake Roberts, would smarten me up about how some guys were gonna*

fuck me even though they were making it look like they were gonna help me. I remember asking him how do I get to the next level and he said, 'I don't know how you got here?' There was a defining moment, saying to him that I'm never gonna be you, or Hogan or Flair, and Dusty asked me, 'If you don't want to be world champion, then what are you doing this for?' When I won the WCW title, I was driving through the mountains and Dusty called me on the cell phone and asked, 'How does it feel? Even though it's a work, it's something else, isn't it?' Like I said, if not for Dusty, there is no Diamond Dallas Page."

—Diamond Dallas Page

One guy who I've had a lot of history with, but haven't spoken much about was also one of my favorite guys as tag-team partner—Bugsy McGraw. I first met Mike Davis working for the Sheik in the Detroit territory. We wrestled each other 35 years ago at The Armory in Akron, Ohio. The Main Event was Johnny Powers versus the Sheik. Bugsy and I wrestled to a 20-minute draw. He was known then as "The Big O." He went on to become one of the most charismatic and entertaining men to step into the squared circle. I loved when he put on those flight goggles and spun around, and when he and "Boogie Woogie" Jimmy Valiant tag-teamed back in the '80s ... pure magic. We have been friends a long time. He always seemed to be watching over me, like an angel praying for me! I think we had a lot in common, like our speech impediments, which we both used to our advantage. If you really know him, you are better off than most. My friend Michael will always be in my heart.

Nikita Koloff and Magnum T.A., Terry Allen. To me, when you say one, you have to say the other. I would always try to pick the heir to the throne with me being the guy on the throne. Who is the heir to the throne? Who's the next Babe Ruth? Who's the next guy on the babyface side, and it was Magnum. Jimmy Crocket and I foresaw movies for him, we saw television for him, we saw all kinds of things happening for him, and he deserved it. His heart was as big as gold. He worked his ass off. He never complained. He was tremendous, and he was a close friend and a loyal friend. As I mentioned before, he went to Oklahoma to become a star, and it was my job to make him a bigger star. He drew some money for Bill and then when we began to make a move on the national scene with Jim Crockett Promotions and Mid-Atlantic Wrestling, we bought the UWF and we brought Magnum to Mid-Atlantic. I remember him coming in with his first of two or three wives, and the way he looked when he walked in was one of those things I talked about a lot. He demanded that respect. There was something about him that said this guy is going to be special. When he had the accident, he was in the middle of the hottest angle in the history of Mid-Atlantic. You see, Flair and Tully and Arn and old J.J. believed that I had built everything around them. I had built a lot around them as Flair was the champion of the world and Tully was always tight with me as far as drawing money. But the angle that was the big deal, the one that there was none hotter than, was the Nikita and Magnum TA feud. None. Zero. Period. Nothing ever before that or since then in Mid-Atlantic. When he went down the blow was unbelievable, not only because he was a friend, but because once you got your composure, you had to think about what you're going to do for business. Of course, everybody knows I brought the biggest bad guy, the baddest asshole in the world as far as the public knew "The Russian Nightmare," Nikita Koloff, to be my tag team partner. The rest is history. The roar is still rumbling from the shouting in the coliseum when Nikita walked out as my tag-team partner to create the "Super Powers."

"I don't think I understood the impact it had on the wrestling world. Nobody knew who the mystery partner against the Horsemen was until I walked into the babyface dressing room. I got there one hour earlier. With no internet back then, it was easier to do. I had just gotten back from Japan, and being a wrestler, I thought it was a work. I had only been in the business for two years at that point and even though I stepped in right away, I didn't fully understand what was happening. In that first nanosecond I walked out, you could have heard a pin drop. As we made our way down the aisle it starting getting louder ... the second I jumped on the Horsemen and it sunk in that I was really Dusty's partner and it wasn't some double cross, the place erupted. The next 15 minutes were absolutely mind-boggling. With the fans chanting the name Ni-ki-ta, Ni-ki-ta ... it does something for your ego and overwhelms you. Last week these same people were cursing you, spitting on you, throwing things at you, and now guys had their shirts off doing the Nikita muscle pose."

—NIKITA KOLOFF

CHAPTER ELEVEN

I remember a little while after we did that, Vince had Hogan and Macho up in the WWF do the "Mega Powers." Someone asked me if I was pissed at that, and no I wasn't, not at the time, because I was taking home some big checks. One week I made $80,000 with Crockett and that's pretty good fucking money. I was doing a lot of shit though, so they didn't really piss me off that much. Magnum going down and being told he was going to be paralyzed for life and all that—the real-life angle, the shoot angle, the fans knew it was real and that's why it drew so much money.

Which brings me to "The Dusty Finish." Holy dippity dogshit, did that phrase really come out of my mouth? "The Dusty Finish" is without a doubt the biggest scam in our industry, because it doesn't exist. Just exactly what is the "Dusty Finish?" The phrase was created by sheet writers and picked up by the guys in the business who read them. They say it's where the referee is knocked out, the babyface gets the pin on the heel but it doesn't count, because there's nobody there to count one, two, three, so the babyface helps the ref and in the aftermath somehow gets fucked by the heel with a swerve of some sort. And this is *my* finish?

Sure, I may have brought it to prominence by showing it on TV back in the '80s, but *my* finish? That fucking finish was around a hell of a lot longer than before I was booking. I actually remember seeing a finish like that when I was a kid. And if the swerve is what makes it the "Dusty Finish," well then I guess the Japanese attack on Pearl Harbor was a "Dusty Finish." George Washington crossing the Delaware to surprise the Hessians, that was a "Dusty Finish." The army hiding inside the wooden horse at Troy, that was a "Dusty Finish." Hell, even the snake convincing Eve to bite the apple in the Garden of Eden, that was a "Dusty Finish," Give me a fucking break … there's only one and original "Dusty Finish" and you're just going to have to read the whole book to find out exactly what that is.

The "Dusty Finish?" … *Puhleeease!*

CHAPTER 12

"Dusty is a man that's more than his profession. He's a very creative person who has lived an unconventional life. He's a lot more than a wrestler."

—MICHELLE RUNNELS, WIFE

Pro wrestling is a funny business in the sense that anybody who is involved in it and has any kind of success has two families—their wrestling family and their flesh and blood family. While some in our business will argue that our wrestling families are more business acquaintances than anything else, anyone who has felt the wrath of one knows that the most important thing in our lives is the other.

There have been far too many of us in this unique industry who have allowed the business to fuck up a good thing, and I'm no exception. But I've learned from my mistakes and I know that before anything else in the world, it's my family first. I will never let the business come between me and my family again.

So with that, let's talk about my wife, Michelle, first. Chelle is the love of my life. I know I don't say that often enough, but when we had this party where Henry Gonzalez, my attorney, and Monsignor Laurence Higgins of Tampa and all of our friends were there and in the toast I gave, it was to the woman who I said I love more than my life, everybody cried because it was not only so cool I said it, but that I meant it, and I still do.

I met Chelle in Tampa during my first big run, and there was something about her that was not like anybody else I had ever met. She just had a way about her. I loved Latin women and she not only had Latin blood in her, but there was cracker blood in her as well; her mom was from Alabama and her dad was from Cuba. I can't explain it, but in a strange way, she seemed like she was a lot like me inside. She was much younger than me—she was 19 and I was 30—but she had something about her that just made me feel good inside; just being around her.

We started dating, or actually I should say that I started coming by where she lived, because I was in that egotistical, big-Lincoln-driving stage, and I looked as if I were part of the Mafia or something. I would drive by to pick her up and she had a boyfriend at that time and they were learning how to scuba dive or some shit like that and she always had like this dark brown tan because she loved the sun, and she was just unbelievable to look at. She still is. Her grandmother, who could not speak English, Grandma Rubio, would call me *Virjilio* instead of Virgil, and she would say in Spanish, "*Virjilio* is coming to pick you up."

> *"He was a lot of fun. He was interesting and he was the first person I dated who listened to country music. He was exotic. He was the also the first Texan I had dated and the people from Texas are ... different. The wrestling thing was weird, but I liked it when I was a kid. Dusty was young and good looking."*
>
> —MICHELLE RUNNELS, WIFE

While we had a rocky start, luckily it smoothed out and I eventually asked her to marry me on the banks of Lake Austin, not over the telephone like the legend goes. We had gone to Texas to visit Dustin and Kristin, my two oldest children from my previous marriage. When she said, "Yes," man, I was on cloud nine.

Well, we had planned this wedding and Eddie Graham was out of town, so he had to fly back to Tampa for it. We actually had the wedding party the day before at the Columbia, a nightclub down in Ybor City, Tampa's National Historic Landmark District; thrown for us by Henry Gonzalez. The wedding itself was small with just a few of our friends, Monsignor Higgins, who was Father Higgins at the time, presiding—and nobody else could have married us, not even the Pope, that's how far up the pecking order Monsignor Higgins is with me. He overshadows the Pope because those guys come and go, but the Monsignor doesn't. He doesn't really know how special he is to me.

CHAPTER TWELVE

"Dusty is one of the nicest men I've ever known. He's a man that's very bright, smart, well informed, who has good values. He's a good family man. He's a fine gentleman and top of the line as a person."

—MONSIGNOR LAURENCE HIGGINS

Anyway, we had the wedding and when we moved in to the little horse ranch I had in Lutz, a little community on the north side of Tampa. Chelle didn't like it, I don't think, because it wasn't her house. I had an old girlfriend when I had bought the house, so Chelle picked out a new house off of Dale Mabry Highway in Tampa, and that was kind of our first home together and that was really cool.

But the two of us were really wild back then. We had this tremendous ability for drinking until we couldn't walk anymore. And of course when you drink, you can get loud and you disagree, you can't keep a hard on ... a lot of things happen. So we had a pretty loud, ruckus time, and I used to become somewhat angry and violent at times, and she had that Latino temper that was unbelievable, man. It wasn't like Ricky Ricardo and Lucy, believe me. We had some knockout, drag outs. But everything I had ever said bad to her or whatever, I regretted within hours, and really felt remorseful through the years, because to me she truly is an angel who was sent down to look over me.

She has said to me on numerous occasions, "It's not my job to feed you or take care of you," and that's what she's always said to me. It's not her job. It's not her job to be in the kitchen. But she's unbelievable at helping other people. I truly believe she would pick up every stray dog and homeless person if she won the lottery and she would put them in a home or something; taking care of them. She's got the biggest and kindest heart of anybody I've ever been around.

Chelle always liked to work. She loves that independence. She'll gripe about it as the day is long like anybody would, but she would miss it if she didn't work. I think she really loves being Dusty Rhodes's wife, but not as much as she loves being Michelle. I think that's the important thing.

"I get tired of having a lot of crises in our life and the constant moving around. By the time we moved here (Marietta, Georgia), the kids had been in different places every year. Either business or financially, there's

always a crisis in Dusty's life. It's 'Crisis Central' around here sometimes. But it's his personality. The business and his personality go hand in hand."

—MICHELLE RUNNELS

I can write for pages and pages about her. One day, it was the day after the Super Bowl 15 years ago I believe, she said, "That's it! I'm not drinking anymore!" and we went from being total drunks to just the opposite. Well, she did, anyway. And it was hard for her, but she fought through it and it was amazing to see her overcome that and she never drank again. Cold turkey, buddy, she's amazing.

"The Studio 54 crowd loved Dusty. We had met an old schoolmate of mine, Tommy Sullivan, who looked like Black Bart. His arm was badly burned from a plane crash where he was the pilot. He invited us to Studio 54 for the first time and we met Halston, Bianca Jagger and others. Dusty loved that celebrity shit, but they were the most self-absorbed, boring people you could be around. We later found out Tommy was a drug smuggler, one of the 'Cocaine Cowboys.'"

—MICHELLE RUNNELS

She liked to go around with me when I traveled. She went everywhere with me until she got tired of it. She even went to Japan with me. The guys nowadays would say, "I wouldn't take my wife. I can't take my wife on the road, I'm trying to get some pussy," or something. Back then, I wouldn't go anywhere without her. I did not want to be anywhere without her. I wanted her to be seen with me on the trip to Japan. I remember when she came to the Kyo Plaza in Tokyo for the first time, New Japan Pro Wrestling Chairman Antonio Inoki sent his limousine for her, not a bus or nothing, to pick her up at Narita Airport. I had just dropped the World Heavyweight title and it was very important for me to go over and wrestle for his company, because the NWA would never give him the time of day as they were wrapped up more with Giant Baba's group, even though both were members of the organization. So he sent his limo to pick her up and they brought her into the lobby of the Kyo Plaza Hotel, and even with the time-change difference with it being at night, there were probably between 200 and 500 kids roped off, waiting to see her or just to get a picture of her. She just stayed a week as she had come at the end of a tour, but Chelle went everywhere with me, including to the matches.

"We had no children for the first five years we were married, so we lived on the road. It was a lot of fun, but it's not glamorous like a lot of people think it is. It's pretty much the airport, the hotel, the arena, and a restaurant or a bar. There's not a lot of time for sightseeing."
—MICHELLE RUNNELS

Materialistically, we had every kind of car you can imagine. From Rolls to Bentleys to Fiats to different trucks—any kind of car you can imagine someone would want. Now of course the minute we drove them off the lot, we owed more than we had because we were always backlogged. But man, we had a great time. The same money I made to piss Miami away, she made with me to piss it away.

"I've often felt we were an oddity. My life was very separate from the business. I was a traditional homemaker. We had a very traditional family with him not being in a traditional business. Sometimes it would get on my nerves when others in the business would ask me about personal issues. I didn't have a lot in common with the other wives. I didn't feel I had anything in common with these people. I tried as much as possible to keep myself isolated away from the business. I hate it."
—MICHELLE RUNNELS

When the kids came we moved from that home in Tampa and we went to Charlotte. Chelle always had everything packed up and ready to go, whether she wants to admit it or not. She was like that song, "Stand By Your Man." She was always there. I could always depend on her. Even today, as mad as she gets at me ... she starts ordering food for me nowadays like I'm an old man.

She had an uncle or a cousin or a grandfather or something named Cuspert, and Cuspert right away tells you this is a cracker redneck motherfucker, and Cuspert I guess was so old and ornery he would say shit like, "Hey, God damn it ..." He was always screaming at the kids and everything. So, she treats me like Cuspert now. A perfect example is we were standing to get food the other day and before I could open my mouth to order, she said, "He wants a hotdog and he can't have any mustard and he wants a Diet Coke, and he only wants a medium." And she looked at me like, "What do you want?"

I was getting ready to say, "Now you're fucking Cusperting me, like the old man Cuspert." She's ordering for me now like I'm an old man. I can't imagine four or five years from now. Is she going to go deer hunting with me and open my case and get my gun out and load it for me? So she treats me like I'm an old man already.

But that's just shit married couples do.

"Dusty has got a lot of good points. He's a good father and a good provider. But the thing that gets on my nerves is he can't conform. He can't conform and he lives by his rules. His way is always the right way."

—MICHELLE RUNNELS

Two years ago we went to Mexico and to me she's amazing to look at. And I know she doesn't know that, but she's finding out now because I probably don't say it enough to her … but just to watch her is still amazing to me after all these years.

Mexico

She laughed out loud
She smiled so easily
She had warmth
She has had for 25 years

As of late my dealings
And things I do have kept
That smile, that laughter from us

Mexico reminded me
Which I did not need reminding
That my best friend was with me
Maybe my only friend
My lover and my partner for life

Mexico was good fun for us
It gave us a look at why 25 years ago
We got married
Mexico made the picture clear for me
Mexico met Michelle

Thanks, Mexico!
                                    —DUSTY RHODES, AUGUST 23, 2003

The main thing about Chelle is, unlike me, if she found out that somebody who hated her or did something wrong to her, was on the street starving or really needed help or something, she would pick them up, take them home and help them. Like I said, she's amazing that way. Mother Theresa, maybe not, but she's a hellcat, man. She's done just about everything that could be done.

She's given us some great kids in Teil and Cody and she couldn't have raised the two kids any better, as they are tremendous, and she loves Dustin and Kristin—who were already two loves of my life—like they were and are her own and they love her too. It's hard to say anything else except how amazing we feel and how 29 years together—28 married—it's a phenomenal feat for two people who were as high strung and as crazy as we were when we were younger. We were nuts. But she was the only one who could keep up with me and sometimes I had to keep up with her.

"When we were on the road, we traveled with the Giant a lot. We had a rental car, and it seemed like we were always together. He was a lot of fun, but he was rude as shit. He had a sticker on his suitcase that read, 'If you get any closer, I'll fart.' Well this one time we were in New Orleans and they had a show at the Superdome, and Dusty's mom had joined us for the trip. Well at 3 a.m. Andre called our room and told Dusty that Lee Majors and Farrah Fawcett were down at the bar and wanted to meet him. So Dusty not only gets up and gets dressed, but he wakes me up and then calls his mom's room to wake her up so all of us could go down there and meet them. When we went down to the bar it was deserted except for a cleaning woman who was vacuuming. Andre loved to rib Dusty."
                                                —MICHELLE RUNNELS

Chelle's family is something else, too. Her dad, Ralph Rubio, is a great, cool guy, who is very close to his daughter. She also has two stepdads, Bobby Rodriguez and Tony Gonzales, since her mom remarried twice, and they're all good people. While these names sound like they could come right out of the crime books in New York, when you start saying them like that, they're actually not. Like I said, they're all good people. But when I married her, just seeing the name Henry Gonzalez and Rubio and all at the Columbia, the wedding was like the white champion of the world marrying into this "family." To an outsider, God knows what they must have thought, but who cared? From that point forward, her family and I would always be very close. It was a great time, and she was the one.

As you know, I was married previously, and my ex-wife who still lives in Austin raised tremendous children in Dustin and Kristin. I'd be remiss if I did not mention Sandy. I know she loves our children and watches out for them and takes care of them, and she did a great job bringing them up. We had very little time that we ever actually spent together, with me being on the road, to the point that we hardly knew each other.

But Michelle was without a doubt my best friend before anything else happened, then we fell in love. She's the best friend I have. I have no other confidante than her. She's got her own posse and it's just her. I'm in her posse, buddy.

"[Laughing] He's a real pain in the ass."

—MICHELLE RUNNELS

Dustin is my oldest child and like all my children, I love him with all my heart. But because my situation with him is such a volatile topic and an emotional thing, I'm going to discuss my relationship with him last.

Like Dustin, my daughter Kristin is from my first marriage. And like my other kids, she's a hell of a talent. She was a Dallas Cowboys cheerleader. She had tried out for the squad for four years in a row on different occasions, competing with something like 800 girls. But that is something that she wanted. Kristin is one of those people who says if I want to do something, if I have a dream, nothing can keep me from doing it. She is very strong-willed like that. She wanted to be a Dallas Cowboys cheerleader and she kept trying and trying and trying until she finally made it. Then after doing it for two or three years she retired because she had accomplished what she wanted to.

Kristin and her husband, Don Ditto, took a company from nowhere and made it into one of the top technology companies in the country. About four or five years ago, Dittcomm Technologies was featured in *Fortune* or *Forbes* or one of those magazines, as one of the top 300 independently owned companies in the United States. They're based out of Austin with offices in Dallas-Fort Worth, San Antonio, and Houston. They were very successful and they were young.

The best way to describe Kristin is she is kind of like Maui if you go to Hawaii, because it's so beautiful there. Well, all my kids are gorgeous, but she is drop-dead gorgeous, and Don is a good-looking young guy from Texas and they were kind of like the Barbie doll couple, Ken and Barbie. They were perfect. But Kristin is really high strung as far as having her opinions, and buddy, you don't ever want to get into it with her. She knows exactly what she wants to do and she has her opinions and she's very strong about them. She's the strong one of that family, believe me. They live in a beautiful home out in the country in the hills of Texas, and she just gave us our second grandbaby, Dalton Wayne. Dakota, of course, Dustin's daughter, was our first. Dalton is two years old now. That's some cool thing, to have grandbabies like that.

"My dad is a show stopper. He is the best at what he does. He started so young. He has a passion for the wrestling business and everyone knows about 'The American Dream.' He can go anywhere and they know who he is."

—KRISTIN DITTO, DAUGHTER

I think deep down Kristin missed out on going to Los Angeles, out to Hollywood and being a movie star because she wanted that too, like Teil and Cody, my two youngest ones who I will get to in a bit. She had other priorities though; otherwise she would have done it. But I think she missed out on it and that's why she backed Teil and Cody so much on going out there and chasing that dream. I think not a day goes by that she doesn't wish she was in Hollywood somehow, because all four of them are the most talented kids you can be around, and they all have different ways of expressing their talent. Kristin is very strong and is going to be a great mom.

"My parents got divorced when I was young and so I saw dad only a couple of times a year; a week or so during the holidays. He was gone all the time. He was always traveling. When we got together, it was nice, though. My relationship with my father really developed during my last few years of high school, as I was getting older and maturing more. I also have a wonderful relationship with my stepmom, Michelle."

—Kristin Ditto

I think between the two of them, Kristin was better adjusted when they went through that period of time of being raised and I wasn't there. I tried to make it up to them in a short, two-year period of time, and you cannot do that. Over time, however, we've become very close, Kristin and I. I think she had a half-ass understanding of it, and I would hope as we went along, that the hurt would heal. It's hard to understand why your father is not around when he's alive. You just can't show up once or twice a year with Christmas presents and provide all the money that they need and expect everything to be made right. It doesn't make sense to a child why you weren't there for them and missed that time with them; everything from Little League to school work, all of that. Luckily God gave me the chance to come back and do it right with Teil and Cody, and that I was actually there for them all the way through school. I saw how strong the bond was with my younger two, and I know I should have been there for Dustin and Kristin, too.

"He regrets leaving us behind, but that's him. My dad is very emotional. It's not like he was a deadbeat dad. I don't look for faults in the past. Dustin spent a lot of his younger years crying because his dad wasn't around. But they are different relationships—a father and a daughter, and a father and a son."

—Kristin Ditto

But I was out being "The American Dream," learning my trade and selfishly just not taking care of what really meant something to me. I love them all four the same, and more than anything else going.

CHAPTER TWELVE

"My father has a huge heart. He's always give, give, give to his children and grandchildren. He can come across kind of harsh though, and he used to be rude to people in order to protect his family. Growing up, Dad was popular, so he would be swamped everywhere we went. But when he was home, he did not want anyone to interfere with his time with the family. To me, he's still my dad. I did understand where he was coming from and what he did—it wasn't that he didn't love me and my brother, he was following his dream. When the show was over, he always came home and afterward, always put his family first."

—Kristin Ditto

They'll either say, "I understand" and be okay sooner or later, or they'll really be bitter about it the rest of their lives. I'm sure Kristin thinks about it a lot but, she's not bitter about it. She understands. So I love her for that and I thank her for that. I thank them both, Dustin and Kristin for forgiving me for not being there when they were younger.

"I never resented him not being there. It was different for Dustin, but the best way I can describe it is like you're in the same car wreck, but you come out of it with different injuries."

—Kristin Ditto

Teil, on the other hand, is a movie waiting to happen. She walks around being a movie. She looks a lot like a young Dyan Cannon with her hair the way it is. I was in Los Angeles with Teil and Cody recently since they are enrolled at the Howard Fine Acting Studio there, which is one of the bigger acting schools as they're trying to make their dreams come true.

But she is so naturally talented. Like Dustin was naturally talented for wrestling, she's naturally talented just walking around. And she can't understand why they haven't already made her life story, why she's not in another *Gone With the Wind* with her in the leading role because she doesn't need to practice. "I don't need to practice because I am that good." Where Cody and Dustin work hard on their trade, and are very good at what they do, Teil knows the answers before they ask the questions. Now I know I'm being a bit facetious, as she needs to pay her dues, but I think she's going to be a huge star out there … I really do.

"When we were little he was gone a lot, not as much as when Dustin and Kristin were young, but he was always hands on when he was home. He was always supportive of all our aspirations no matter how outlandish they might have been. He never missed one of my plays or any of Cody's wrestling matches. I think there's a great strength knowing you're loved so much. There was an effort to be a family. Christmases were always my favorite memory. Christmas and special days like birthdays, which were always fun."

—TEIL RUNNELS

I know one thing, if she ever gets married, the guy who marries her or even dates her, better have a lot of money, buddy, because she's high maintenance. She was carrying Louis Vuitton purses when she was six years old, before it was fashionable, when other kids didn't even know what the hell they were. Kristin and Teil both have these bags and they will steal them from each other. If I give one a Louis Vuitton bag, the other will want one. Then they'll find it at each other's house and take them back and they'll go back and forth like that. Jesus! Now I'm talking about all that in a funny way … it's not like that's what they live for.

"It's their fault because they raised me that way, especially him. Dad spoiled me. I could have asked for a pet monkey and could have worked on it with my dad. I remember going on the road with them and I'd have my little red suitcase. I had a little Louis Vuitton like my mom. I think the term 'Princess' is a fair assessment."

—TEIL RUNNELS

Teil didn't like school. Two of the funniest stories about Teil readers will find hard to believe. I wonder who she gets it from?

She went for PE class one day, and it was very hot out. They were running the girls around the track, and Coach Day, Cody's wrestling coach at Lassiter High School and a very close friend of the family, was teaching this class. Teil came out of the locker room carrying a parasol—like an umbrella—to trot around the track with; holding it so she didn't get the sun on her. Well, Coach Day called us and said, "This girl … this isn't going to work."

Another time she was playing softball. In slow pitch she didn't get a hit but she walked a lot, though, and she was always messing with her hair. Well, one of my closest friends and members of the posse, J.D. Douthit, was coaching her, and he would try to get her to slide into bases and she said, "I am not sliding on these legs here. These legs are going to Hollywood." This was back when she was like 14 or 15 years old. So she wouldn't slide into the base because of that. Later she was a little older and playing fast pitch, and the girls she was playing against looked like they weighed about 225 pounds and are on steroids or something, and they're throwing the ball like 100 mph. Well Teil came up to hit and she took the bat and rested it between her knees like she was going to hold it there just for a second while she adjusted her pants or something, but instead she took a brush out of her uniform, and while she was standing in the batter's box, she started brushing her hair to put it up in a ponytail, and the pitcher threw the ball for a strike. The coaches and everybody were hollering at her and I was looking at this scene, shaking my head and saying to myself, "She is not going to be on the U.S. Olympic softball team."

I'm telling you, she's a movie waiting to happen. She just has this knack. They would just walk her and she would trot down to first base. Now she did make a couple of big plays, and I remember that because I went crazy, but she'd always play the game. She sat on the bench most of the time, but they had to play them so many times over the course of the season, and she'd always do her thing. There was also always a big standing ovation for her because every boy in Marietta, in East Cobb County Georgia, who went to Lassiter High School, thought she was it; she was the one.

> *"The [wrestling] business was part of our life. We always compare it to growing up in the circus. There are all these larger-than-life people around you, but it's normal. It wasn't until high school or college that I realized how different our unconventional growing up was. What a crazy environment to grow up in. But there was always so much love in our house. I think that's why Cody and I are so grounded."*
>
> —TEIL RUNNELS

This one time she lost the Miss Odyssey Contest. Now the Miss Odyssey Contest—to a parent—is like who do you know to have your ugly child win this Miss Odyssey Contest? It's a bigger "work" than they say our business is. It's unbelievable. Teil was so beautiful and both of my girls could have won that thing if they would have went out there with no makeup on. Teil went out there—and it was always some big dress she had to have for whatever the occasion that would be a financial setback—and we were watching her and there was not even anyone close. Not because she's my daughter, but because she really was beautiful. This girl who won it … and as a parent you want to stand up like a parent at the Little League game who just saw a bogus call and say, "Oh, this is bullshit! This is fucking bullshit!" You're not knocking the other little girl, but you're just saying, "Somebody's got to know someone." And then she was going to try to be a cheerleader. She really didn't want to be a cheerleader, but she thought she did. Teil couldn't do the jumping that she wanted to do, as she didn't want to put that much effort into doing the jumping, so she lost that. Well, she thought that was the end of the world; her heart was broken.

The thing about Teil is, in a way she's like me deep down because she has no prejudice whatsoever. She has a tremendous amount of African-American friends, both girls and guys, and there's never been a line drawn with her and she can't understand anybody who doesn't understand that. For example, George W. Bush. She knows I voted for "W" and it eats her alive. She cannot stand him. But the biggest thing she has in common with me is she's a huge Yankee fan! She loves Derek Jeter, and we never miss a Yankee game together when we have the opportunity.

"Sometimes dad gets a raw deal. For all the success he's had, he worked very hard. Nothing was handed to him. His work ethic was so strong. There's a misconception of him by total strangers. He really is kind and has a big heart. In his business I think it's rare to find such a standup, loyal person. His character is exemplary. He has pride and dignity. What a dedicated, family person."

—TEIL RUNNELS

So both of those girls are just the most talented, special people any father could have. They're tremendous.

"I think all of us are performers. We are performers. No matter how that manifests itself, it's influenced by him."

—TEIL RUNNELS

CHAPTER TWELVE

Which brings me to my youngest son, Cody.

Cody was a two-time State of Georgia high school wrestling champion who now has his sights set on acting. I call him the hardest working man in show business, because once he puts his mind to doing something, there's not anything at all that will stop him. I remember reading in a book this guy wrote about the last season that he wrestled—he said that when he walked into a gymnasium, it was like he had walked into an alley that was dark and you were scared when you walked in there because you had seen him step out of the shadows and you pissed your pants. Well, Cody had that ability to instill fear into his opponent that he learned; he had an intimidation on the mat and in the gyms.

> *"When I was wrestling, my opponent's parents wanted their kids to beat Dusty Rhodes, not Cody Runnels, so the pressure was on them. When you're born into that type of situation, you're almost given a choice to step out of that shadow. There's nothing selfish about matching or being better than your famous father. That would motivate me ... get my ire up. I'm my father's son. I never complained about it, because it made me stronger."*
>
> —CODY RUNNELS, SON

When he walked into a high school gym, in his junior and senior years, you knew who he was. He was like a rock star and he owned it, he owned that place. He would walk around for two to three hours before his match, with headsets on, just walking around the gym, while everybody else was laughing and joking and training, and of course the guy he was going to wrestle never took his eyes off of Cody, and so he was already beat. The guy was so intimidated because Cody was the most menacing wrestler I think I've seen on an amateur scale, ever, and I think a lot of local reporters have written that about him. So to beat him, you had to beat him. He wasn't going to beat himself. He was amazing in that aspect, but he loved drama too, and watching his plays with his school as well as watching him wrestle was equally exciting. When it came down to having to make a choice, he chose drama, also at the Howard Fine Acting Studio in Los Angeles.

Cody and Teil shared an apartment in L.A. as they went there together to chase that dream. Since she had already completed college while he was finishing up high school, she waited on him. He's 20 years old and she's 24.

I think he's the next big thing out there. A lot of people say that, but I think he is because of his work ethic—it's so amazing ... unbelievable ... I can't imagine that.

> *"When I discontinued playing football and said I just wanted to wrestle, my dad supported my decision with reluctance, because he was unsure if I was going down the right path. He wanted to see the work and not the talk. He wanted to see the actions. Now when I made my choice for acting, he was less reluctant about me going to Hollywood because he saw my earlier decision flower into the right decision."*
>
> —CODY RUNNELS

The funny thing is that both of them weren't worth a shit in school. They got through school to get through school. I remember the Penn State coach wanted to know what Cody's grade point average was for wrestling, but Cody knew he was going to go to California; he was headed there. He doesn't like California that much, but he knows he's got a job to do, and he's going to get it done. He's going to do his thing and make it happen.

Like Dustin, he was just a little pretty baby when he was born. He loves wrestling. He saved all the dolls. He watched all the matches. He went through that whole phase. I could always tell through him if wrestling was hot or not, because he'd be watching both shows: *Nitro* and *Raw*, with a clicker, and pretty soon you didn't hear the clicker. When that happened, you could tell one of those shows were not as hot. Then when he stopped talking about wrestling with his friends, you knew it was bad.

> *"You don't know my dad's a celebrity unless you ask someone else. He's actually a very humble person. My dad's fame has this mystique ... it's like a Cuban cigar, so you know it's the best. In* The Odyssey *Homer describes certain gods as 'Earth Shakers' and my dad was like that in the wrestling biz. He was an 'Earth Shaker.'"*
>
> —CODY RUNNELS

Cody and Dustin both taped all of their early matches that they put together in the backyard. They did the same things in our backyard that I did in my parents' backyard, except we didn't have any videos back in the '50s. But they did the identical thing I did. They promoted matches, both of them. It was amazing to see how they kind of did the same thing that I did when I was a kid about the business. And then Cody of course, in his junior year in high school, refereed his first Turnbuckle Championship Wrestling match, like Dustin did when he was younger. But Cody wanted to be in a different industry, and I think that's good.

> *"Wrestling is all I wanted to do and the only thing I thought I was going to do. Watching WrestleMania and the Academy Awards were the two things that gave me chills. In my own personal time, I think I could—as dad calls it—tell a better story wrestling, but at this time I want to concentrate on acting and eventually win an Oscar."*
> —CODY RUNNELS

When Cody got his first truck, we bought him this $9,000 old Chevy. It had all the lifts and everything, so then it cost $22,000. The motor blew up, so I'd say it eventually cost $25,000. Like I said, we paid $9,000 for it and sold it for $7,000, so I really lost my ass on that truck. But you knew it when you saw him coming.

And he's like Dustin in that they're drop-dead handsome guys. He's got the cold blue eyes and a look that's amazing. But I think one of his best attributes is that he's a great writer and has published a couple of poems, even as a young high school student in the big artsy books that are published in Atlanta, and he's very deep in what he says and what he believes.

Remember

Remember the sound of bacon crackling, me rushing to make morning tasty for you...

Remember the tears that come from my solid, broken only by you...

Remember my trembling lips, as you teased me with a first kiss you have forgotten...

Remember the clock hands that danced in circles, the time I handed to you...

Remember the flash bulbs, my hands raised high, I had conquered, without you...

Remember the soft drops that fell from your eyes, in fear you might lose me...

Remember the love that drove that fear, the love that encompassed me and you...

—CODY RUNNELS, ARETE,
LASSITER HIGH SCHOOL LITERARY MAGAZINE, FALL 2003

He's always on me and Teil about stuff, like the Yankees. Whether he likes the other team or not, he'd call Roger Clemens a fat ass during the World Series when they played the Marlins. He'd do it just to make me mad. He'd say shit like in 2004 Roger Clemens went over to Randy Johnson's house to have dinner and not only stole his dinner, but his Cy Young award off his table and took it back to Texas. He'd just say stuff like that.

I remember Cody breaking his leg, it was after Little League and he was 12 years old. He broke it riding a four-wheeler out behind our house on a hill. I heard it running and then I heard it stop, and then I didn't hear anything. He got up and tried to walk. He had broken his leg, and Dustin had broken his leg on a four-wheeler too, when he was younger. Those things are pretty dangerous.

Anyway, he's close to his brother and sisters. He takes great pride in taking care of Teil out in California, or should I say he thinks he is, and Paul Jones, my very close friend with Limited Brands helped get them jobs in loss prevention out there, and he takes them out to eat, watches over them for me and Chelle. Even Dallas Page, who I was kind of a mentor to, is kind of Cody's mentor. Cody understands him, but knows where to draw the line with Dallas, and they are very close.

"Dad always says and puts family first. It's not just rhetoric. He still has his family to take care of. I've had the best two parents possible. Dad is the ultimate family man in an unconventional manner. ... I can't think of him as anything but a family man."

—CODY RUNNELS

So Cody's a kid who almost tried too hard to achieve that goal instead of just letting it fall into place. So, it's cool.

Okay, now with all that said, it's time to talk about my eldest son, Dustin, and you better pay close attention, because this is only going to be said and written about once.

CHAPTER TWELVE

There are a lot of stories about Dustin and me, whom I love and am so very, very proud of. But of all those stories, there's only one that the fans of wrestling really want to know about, and so I am going to bare my soul and tell it like it is.

For five years, a piece of my heart was missing. It was the hardest thing in the world for me to go through, because I knew I fucked up. But I also knew deep down, that with time, patience, understanding, and the grace of God, that deep, deep wound would eventually heal, and Dustin and I would be closer than ever.

For years I did not want to talk about this, and I couldn't because the hurt was that deep. When we were in that place, emotionally, I had refused interview after interview with wrestling magazines, with *The New York Times*, with everybody, not only because it was so upsetting for me to discuss, but for fear that if I talked about it openly while it was still going on, I could somehow damage the chances for future reconciliation. I was not willing to risk losing my son and granddaughter forever.

Many people who really didn't understand the relationship between Dustin and me, thought the feud between us became public when he went on his own and became "Goldust," a character that seemingly mocked me and my old "Stardust" persona. But in reality, the Goldust creation that he and Vince put together was creative genius, because it allowed Dustin to feed off of an emotion and step out of my shadow and be his own person … and that made me proud. When anybody would ask me how could I be so proud of him for doing that, I'd say because I understand the wrestling business.

While it's true that Vince tried to play our emotions at one point and attempted to get me to do an angle with Dustin—and it would have been very easy to go there and make a million dollars because I was in need of money at the time—neither one of us would shoot that angle for Vince or anybody else to draw money on this real-life family battle that was going on. Even today, as close as we are, we wouldn't do it because it would hurt everything that Dustin worked so hard for to establish his own name. But that battle was festering for a long time, and it actually came to a head when I was in full control at WCW.

Terri Boatright was a makeup artist there. I knew she had talent when I first got there, as she was a manager for Terry Taylor doing the Alexandra York character. She had a great knack for wanting to move up. She didn't want to be mediocre, she wanted to be on top, but I paid little attention to her.

Well, one night I was in a hotel room, and Dustin showed up and said that they were going to get married. I was drunk and just went off on him, because in my opinion they were not right for each other and that's all that needs to be said. But Dustin loved her to death, and the more I said, the worse it probably would have gotten. So I kept my mouth shut and I accepted Terri as my daughter-in-law. All I cared about was that she was going to be a good wife to Dustin and a good mother when they had kids. Whatever happened between them is their business, because in my opinion the best thing that came out of that marriage was that it gave Chelle and me a beautiful granddaughter; my first grandbaby, Dakota.

Anyway, Dustin had all this resentment building in him from when he was younger, and the whole thing came to a head over a golf game or something when he said Terri had a headache and he couldn't go with me. Well, things were said that shouldn't have been said on my part, and all the resentment on his part came pouring out like an open water hose.

They were powerful times, they were powerful moments, and powerful things were said, and as that went down, Terri would write me these letters saying what an unbelievably bad father I had been to Dustin and that he would never speak to me again. It ate my fucking heart out. I felt she was pushing him away from me, but Dustin was in on it at the time, so they were hard times for us, rocky times that we eventually worked through.

As time passed, Teil and Cody were getting older and I was also closer to Kristin now. Dakota was growing up, and Chelle and I wanted to see our grandbaby. But not seeing Dustin, I got really depressed not having him around; really discouraged, especially since I could see him on TV.

Dustin was the most gifted, the most natural worker there was, probably one of the top five wrestlers in our business today, and without a doubt, the smoothest. He and Barry Windham are two of the most natural athletes to come into our industry systematically. Anyway, with that said, I was going to fly to a town and I always had a fear or big knot in my stomach that I would see Dustin at the airport or something, and sure enough it came to pass. About four years after the big blow up, he was standing in line at Delta Airlines in Atlanta and I walked up, and he turned around, and we spoke for the first time in a very long time. That didn't mean jack shit to anybody, except to family, and we started talking about what had happened between us and it was just an amazing, surreal moment, and when we were done, we went our separate ways.

Shortly after that I gave him a call and for all those years of me being this dominating figure, this controlling guy that I am perceived to be by many, who usually dominates our conversations by never letting him talk, never letting him say what he needed to say, it finally came to a head on the telephone.

He said things to me that I can tell myself, but I couldn't even say to his face. I couldn't even repeat some of the things that were said to me about what he wanted to do with me. It was amazing, shocking, but he had to get it off his chest to heal. Not one word. But once he got it all out, once he finally got all that out of his system, I knew for the first time we legitimately might have a chance to patch the thing up, because for the first time I listened to him ... and I agreed with him.

"I'm not one of those people who can come off the cuff with words with your father. I was very intimidated by my father. He was very intimidating ... and he still is and I love him to death ... and I would never cross that path again, ever ... so I started writing stuff down like a script to tell him over the phone. When the call finally happened, for the start of that five-year stint, I read everything off the piece of paper ... I was scared to death and so fucking nervous my heart was beating, butterflies were racing, but I told him this and that and that was it. Boom! That was it! I didn't talk to him for five years. That was a tough five years. I regret the decision that I made, but I made it. I'm the one who did it. I can't put the blame on anyone else. I blame myself for that. But I regret it and it was tough."

—DUSTIN RUNNELS, SON

"You're right. ..." What could I say about a guy who takes off for 14 fucking years except for a visit here and there, while his son's whole life he's felt that way? I can say a lot about guys in the wrestling business, but I wasn't any better than they were in that respect.

Now that I was older, I wanted my children to be close to me. I wanted them to be a part of my life, and I wanted to be a part of theirs, and that comes to pass with just about everybody who has been in that position as they get older. And like a wish on a shooting star that came true, it finally was made possible, and Barry Windham was involved in helping me make it happen.

I was still with WCW and we were at the Jacksonville Coliseum. We were doing this angle with the late Bobby Duncum, Jr. who was doing the good old boys thing with Curt Hennig, Barry and Kendall Windham, and that's what was going down on this particular day. They were going to shoot this video of them riding bikes on Barry's property, which was real close by. Well, Dustin had just bought a new truck and Barry talked him into coming over. I didn't know this and I didn't even know where Dustin lived at that point. Well, Barry came in and walked over to me and said, "Dustin is in the parking lot. He wants to see you."

> *"I was on Barry's property when they were shooting this video, just hanging out with him and having fun and he said, come on to Jacksonville. Dad was there, though. I thought about it for a little bit and at this point it was like, what the hell. I'm making good money, who gives a shit? So I pulled into the back of the Jacksonville Coliseum, Barry and Curt are standing out back and Barry went inside and told dad that I was there and I was like, oh shit ... first time I've seen him, talked to him in five years ... about 15 minutes went by or so and here he comes walking outside. It was one of those moments that you can't explain to anybody ... it's so electrified and so scary too, at the same time. He started walking from the back door of the Coliseum and I was back up there kind of by the gate sitting in my truck ... and he was walking toward me with his head down and walking toward me with his hat on and he didn't stop, and I was looking at him and I was like, God, oh God ... what the hell ... scared to death and wanting so much and my dad ... my dad walked up and he grabbed me, and ... Barry and Curt, they walked off ."*
>
> —DUSTIN RUNNELS

I don't know why, but I knew, I just knew he was coming because this meeting had to happen. I had those same knots in my stomach that I'd get when I traveled, thinking I would bump into him. Anticipation, trepidation, whatever you want to call it, and I walked outside and I saw my son. It was a very cool moment with a lot of love there and just like loads of love on my shoulder. The emotion was unbelievable. The guilt was always there and will always be there, it will be my guilt forever. But that was the real moment I waited for and there was nothing better at that particular moment in time; just him and me locked in that love hug.

"... and he grabbed me and put his arms around me, I put my arms around him and ... whew ... it was fucking intense ... an intense moment, man. It was so intense ... I just can't explain it. It was coming out of my eyes and I was just shaking. It was one of those moments. I'm holding him and he's holding me and I don't even remember the conversation. It was so good to be in his arms, and for me to be putting my arms around him. Standing up three, four inches taller than him, I had gone and stepped off and did Goldust and done this and that and stepped out of his shadow a little bit. But right then and there, that's one of those moments that I will never, ever, ever forget."

—DUSTIN RUNNELS

Not long after that magical moment, I was driving back home and Chelle was in the house and there was Dustin's truck in the driveway. Right out of the blue he came to visit and stay the night and we talked over things, so I barely slept and that was okay, because we had a lot of catching up to do. And so it would go on like that every time we'd get together.

"I don't think my dad understood at the time what Dustin was going through. He understands today, but he had to listen to Dustin. He had to make up for a lot of lost time."

—KRISTIN RUNNELS

And so Chelle and Dakota got to be pretty close, and all my kids are closer now because everybody's talking and they're getting closer each time they see each other, which does my heart good. So I'm a very lucky guy that I've been given another chance to try to understand what was going on in their life while I wasn't there.

And now I think I understand just how hard Dustin had it, because no matter what I think, being my son in the same profession comes with a price, because he is the son of a very famous father. I think when you meet a lot of folks who talk about their fathers being great athletes or famous people, they have the same hurdles and obstacles to overcome when they are in the same profession. I can't go back and erase that, I can only support him in whatever he wants to do. I can't go back and change that he's my son and wants to be whatever he wanted back then. But like I said, I never felt he did not love me. I felt that I did not understand him and he wanted me to know what he went through, and my God, he showed me what he went through and he put me through some shit to get me to that point. There were times he was defiant and he'd call me a motherfucker and said I deserved it, and I'd say, "You're right, I do deserve it."

Right after that period of time Dustin and Terri got a divorce and then later on she was let go by WWE, so they had something else in common aside from Dakota; they both knew what it was like to be fired by the WWE.

"When we touched, it was big ... big, big ... because people knew. They knew we had our falling out. I made it apparent during that five-year stint that I hated him for what he had done to me, which I regret ... and Pops, I'm so sorry ... and I know he's forgiven me and we've tied our ties and stuff, but I was wrong and I regret it, and if you got your dad, you hold on to him tight man, for the rest of your life, no matter how bad or good he is. Your dad's your dad and you have to take care of him and he has to take care of you. You have your differences, you set them aside, you talk tomorrow. I don't look to the past now, I don't look to the future, I look to right now, today, and what's going on in my life today."

—DUSTIN RUNNELS

In looking back on all that, it seems like it happened in another time. Dustin is still a young man and I think he's going to make great strides in the wrestling industry and do a lot of other great things. So that's the story there. There's nothing else in between and nothing else pulled over it.

"Dusty is a loyal person. He is very devoted to his family—to the kids and me. Even as mad as he gets sometimes, he never admits we have any faults."

—MICHELLE RUNNELS

I thank God that Chelle has been by my side for all these years and I want my four children to know that whatever they're doing, I want to be part of that ride they take, because I took them on a ride at times that wasn't worth a shit except financially. It's a really great place to be right now mentally and emotionally with being able to worry about them all as parents.

"I'd like to see my father do more movies, move away from Marietta and go to Texas or Florida and coach high school football. I've had trouble watching him get in the ring without breaking down. It's time for us kids to start paying him back."

—CODY RUNNELS

It makes me proud to say, "Man, I got the greatest gift of all and the greatest children of all."

CHAPTER 13

Man, that last chapter was an emotional one for me, talking about my family and all that. So I think it'd be a good idea to shift gears here and just have a little fun, because I know this is the area that all you readers really want to know about and hopefully I won't disappoint you.

Every wrestler who has ever laced up a pair of boots for more than a few months has them. From the main-event guy you see at WrestleMania to the opening-match guy you watch at the high school show near your house. For some, they are simple. For others, they are more elaborate. And if you haven't figured it out by now, I'm not talking about boots or trunks or arena rats (groupies) or injuries. I'm talking about those little glimpses of our life, those quick snapshots, those Polaroid minutes if you will, that make us who we are when we sit in dressing rooms and tell our war stories, our conquests, our stories from the road to our fellow workers.

Willie Nelson probably says it best and even though he's talking about music, it really relates to our business too. So come on, and sing this little part along with me, because I know you know it!

> *"On the road again,*
> *Just can't wait to get on the road again.*
> *The life I love is makin' music with my friends,*
> *And I can't wait to get on the road again."*
>
> —WILLIE NELSON, "ON THE ROAD AGAIN"

Up and down the highways, town to town, rain, heat, snow, sleet … for us guys in the business, sometimes I think we're the only people who've done more miles behind the wheel than truck drivers or been to more zip codes than postmen.

175

But even with all the traveling, all the hotels, all the fast food or greasy spoon restaurants, there's nothing quite like being on the road with the boys. The camaraderie is unbelievable. But the experiences we have are sometimes even more unbelievable. I'm sure some of the stories I've already told here will be met with their fair share of "He's full of shit," but if I didn't live these things myself, even I would question some of them.

Like the time Terry Funk and I were driving in the Southwest with two midgets in the back seat. The two of us were dog tired and we had to get from Albuquerque, New Mexico to Amarillo, Texas, but we had already done a little recreational drinking and were in no condition to drive. So we asked Little Crusher—I think that's who it was—if he could drive. He said, "Sure," but his feet couldn't reach the pedals. So Terry took one of my boots and he taped it to the midget's foot, wrapped it right around his fucking foot, so he could reach the gas pedal. Well, we get into the back to sleep it off and the midget was driving down the highway, looking like a little kid behind the wheel. The next thing that happened is we were in Truth or Consequences and we heard police sirens, which woke us up. The cops pulled the midget over, and now we were laughing our asses off in the back seat. The sheriff looked in the car, saw the midget with his foot taped to the boot and couldn't believe his eyes. He said something like, "I have never seen anything like this in my life. One of you get up here and don't ever let me see you in my county like this again!" He wouldn't even write us up because it was so crazy. He just wanted us to get the fuck out of his county! You can't make up shit like that, buddy!

Being on the road with Terry was always a trip, but sometimes just going to his house was an adventure, even if he wasn't with you.

This one particular time Nick Bockwinkle was with me. Nick reminds me of when you go to the dentist and you sit there getting ready to have your teeth drilled or your mouth wired up and they are playing this music—Muzak—that you can't stand, the kind they wouldn't even play in an elevator to get you in the mood. To me Nick was always like elevator music. He would just kind of move on through, never getting excited, never getting pissed off. I've seen him have some great matches. He was the complete opposite of Ray Stevens, when they were partners, my God, they were like the odd couple.

But I would say Bockwinkle was one of the classiest guys besides Thesz. When I'd seen him, he was the second or third classiest guy in our business for the way he dressed, the way he carried himself; demanding that respect, and that's what it's all about! Nick was just a mediocre hand, but he never got out of character from being Nick Bockwinkle, the elevator music or the dentist's office. It's just like you bought a new Cadillac and after you got in, there is this tape from the manufacturer. Well, just like in the fucking dentist's office, you wanted to scream … and they would listen to this tape going down the road. He would have a new Cadillac, but not buy any new tapes or anything. He would still have the tape that Cadillac would give him and it would be like … *ugh!*

You'd be drinking beer and going along and he would try to be like an outlaw or something when he was with me. Anyway, we came from Amarillo and it was about 3:30 in the morning and he said, "Let's go by Terry's house down in the canyon."

Terry Funk literally lived in the canyon outside of Canyon, Texas. This is a motherfucker of a ride, so Nick was driving the whole way and it was 195 degrees outside. I was sweating to death and he still had that fucking shooter sport coat on that all the old guys wore, that had the shoulder pads in them that made them stick out a lot more, and they all wore them. Every time you would see a picture of those guys, they had the shooter shoulder pads. He had this coat on and we drank about 20 beers, and I like Nick! He's right there with me drinking beers, but he's immaculate. He didn't spill any on his shirt, unlike me. I was shooting guns off and shit in the night, being loud and obnoxious as we were driving down the road, and he's calm and cool. We drove and we got down there and he said, "What are you going to do?"

My plan was to sneak around to the back because at the ranch house Terry had a screened-in deal, and knowing he probably had the windows up because it was so hot, I was going to take the water hose, stick it through the window into the bedroom where he and Vicky were, and turn the son of a bitch on full blast at 3:30 in the morning!

Nick says, "My boy…" talking like Jim Barnett, "that sounds like fun."

I said, "All right, motherfucker. …"

We got there. Stopped the car. Turned the lights off … just like a jewel heist or something. We walked down into the canyon, Nick still immaculate; he didn't even break a sweat. He was down there and he said, "Dusto," he always called me Dusto—he said, "Dusto, what you want me to do?"

"When I give you the signal, you turn that water hose on full blast."

I crawled around to the back and I ran the water hose through the window. Nick was standing by the faucet, shoulder pads sticking out in the moonlight. You could see this motherfucker—I turned around and standing right behind Nick was Terry holding a double-barreled shotgun.

Nick was looking at me waiting for the signal, and I was just staring at him.

Terry put the double-barreled shotgun behind Nick's head, sticking straight up in the air of course, and he pulled both barrels!

Brother, I've never seen a white man turn whiter than this motherfucker, and the sound that thing made in the still of the night was like a cannon went off right in my eardrum.

Terry ran back around to the front of the house and locked himself in, while Nick was running around in a circle like a chicken that just had its head cut off and didn't know which way to go or what the fuck happened. He was running around with his mouth open but nothing was coming out. It was like *mwah... mwah...*

Nick turned out to be cool about everything, but those were the types of things we experienced on the road. Sometimes, some of the best stories didn't happen in or around a car at all. Sometimes it was on a boat, or in an airplane, or at an airport.

Like this one time we were coming back from the Bahamas. The Florida office would frequently run Nassau or Freeport, and on a dare from one of the guys, I walked with a few others from Eddie's plane on the tarmac at Miami's Opa-Locka Airport to the hangar, completely naked! Except for my cowboy hat and boots, I was naked as a jaybird.

But that's how we were back then. Crazy. Funny. Just out there, buddy, experiencing life and living this unbelievable dream.

For those of you who may doubt me, even for just one minute ... no matter what I say you're going to think what you will, but before passing judgment, I suggest you ask some of the people who I traveled the roads with or who hung out with me and they'll probably tell you their own favorite road story about us.

CHAPTER THIRTEEN

Janie Engle, former assistant

"This is so gross, but Dusty picks his nose and wipes the boogers under the car seat! So don't ever stick your hand under the passenger seat of a rental car. You never know what you will find there!

Anyway, we traveled together for many miles during the WCW years. He would sing silly songs that would crack me up, or we would both be singing to Willie and Waylon songs and drinking a beer. I loved to hear all of the stories about him and Dick Murdoch and Black Jack Mulligan. One time I was traveling with Dusty, Dustin and [former WCW security chief] Doug Dellinger to a TV taping, PPV or something ... I think we were headed to Augusta, Georgia. At the time Doug was a heavy chain smoker and would choke the rest of us in the car to death with all of the secondhand smoke. I had bought some cigarette loads to set Doug up on this trip. A cigarette load will blow up when it is lit. Dusty and Dustin were in on the joke with me. Doug was driving the car, so this was really a stupid prank to pull on him, but we did it, anyway. We tried over and over to get Doug to stop and get out of the car so we could get his cigarettes from over the visor where he kept them. Well, he would stop each time we wanted to, but he wouldn't get out of the car! I bet we stopped about five times before Dustin finally got him to go into the store with him. So, Dusty and I loaded two of his cigarettes, but I put two loads instead of one in each, just to make sure there was a nice impact! When he got back in the car, Dusty, Dustin and I kept giggling, waiting for him to light the darn thing ... and of course it seemed like it took forever. He kept asking us what was so funny, but we wouldn't tell him. Finally, he got his cigarettes down and Dusty, who was riding in the front with him, started to lean away from him. When Doug lit that cigarette, it blew completely up all the way back to the filter! He just sat there with the filter still in his mouth and tobacco all over him. He looked at us and said, 'Fuck every one of ya'll!' We were cracking up! I'm sure he paid us back somehow ... and I'm sure this was Dusty's idea and not mine!"

"Superstar" Billy Graham

"Dusty was a free spirit. One time, while working the Minneapolis territory, we were at O'Hare Airport in Chicago and he took my bag with my wrestling gear and threw it out in front of a Greyhound Bus. Everything was crushed. It was a spur-of-the-moment rib."

Mike Graham

"I have a few favorite Dusty stories. When he first came to Florida, being from Texas, he was not a big boating guy. I'd say, 'Hey Dream, come out on the boat,' he'd say no, and finally I got him to go out on the boat with us. He'd never been out in the water or anything, he'd been out on a mud bank in Texas, so he was used to seeing the bottom, so he didn't know how deep the water was or anything. Anyway, I noticed the boat up on the beach, and when I noticed it, I told him earlier, 'I'll pull the boat right up on the beach, just hop off the side and walk the anchor up on the beach and set it down.' That's all, in case the waves come or whatever, it'll keep the boat from going back out into the water. Well, where the water came off the beach, it came out about two feet and then it dropped to about ten feet. When I pulled the boat up on the beach, I knew he was smart enough to back off the bow of the boat, that when he hopped off the boat, he was just going to go straight down. He had his ball cap on, a cigar in his mouth, and he was playing big shooter out for riding the boat. He had the anchor in his arms and when he hopped off the boat, he just disappeared. He went right off, completely underwater! I started laughing real hard and as I was getting myself back up, I looked ... and when he hit the bottom, he hit the bottom standing up. I guess he realized which was the way out. He walked, with the anchor in his arms, up the bank, coming up to the beach. As he was walking, his head came out of the water, cigar came out of the water, he slowly walked right up out of the water, walked up on the beach, put the anchor down in the sand and he said, 'Goddamn it! Is this what you wanted me to do?' His cigar's hanging out of his mouth, and his hat rim is all hanging down. We were laughing hysterically.

One of my other favorite Dusty stories is when we were coming back from Jacksonville. Steve Keirn, Dusty and I were in my dad's airplane. We used to always stop at an ABC liquor store to get beer, wine; whatever we're gonna drink coming home. Dusty bought a bottle of Penn-Rose sausages, like the little Vienna sausages, but they got hot peppers in them. So we got in the airplane and took off and cracked a beer ... for some reason Dusty was always trying to be Mr. 'The American Dream' better than everybody. So Keirn took a sausage, I took a sausage and Dusty reached in and pulled out one of these little jalapenos or whatever kind of peppers they used to season these sausages ... he took one out and just—'These ain't from Texas, I'm tough. We boys from Texas eat this hot stuff'—and he threw the pepper in his mouth. Keirn and I didn't think anything about it because we guessed that was what he did. Well, I was sitting right in front of him and Keirn was sitting next to him and the cooler was on the floor between all three of us. I looked at Dusty and his face went pale, starting at his chin ... and as the color went out of his face, over his lips, up his cheeks, and when it got to his nose ... literally his cheeks and nose turned white. Fluid started running from his nose, his mouth ... he started coughing and hacking and just making all kinds of noises and crying and snifflin' ... and Steve and I were laughing—he grabbed the cooler and blew all the stuff into the cooler. It took him about ten minutes to get his shit together; he couldn't even talk! Finally, when he could talk, he looked at Keirn and I and said, 'Well boys, I guess the American Dream ain't as tough as he says he is.'

Georgia Senator Richard Green

"When you travel on the road with Dusty, he's the type of guy who has to have breakfast at the Waffle House. Well, one day we were in Conyers, Georgia, and we were sitting at the counter. This real skinny cook came over ... tall, about six-one, six-two, maybe 175 pounds, tattoos, sleeveless T-shirt ... he came over and asked, 'You Dusty Rhodes? Is that true?' Dusty had just signed an autograph. Then he asked, 'Is this wrestling really true?' Well, Dusty looked at the guy and flexed his arm and clinched his fists together in front of his chest and replied, 'If you don't think so,

why don't you come get some of this!' The guy's expression was priceless. He sauntered away, never saying a word."

"Playboy" Gary Hart

"Dusty had this long, white Cadillac with stars on the side of it. Dusty, Haystacks Calhoun, and Danny Hodge were riding in it, while Humpy [Sir Oliver Humperdink], Pak Song, the Hollywood Blonds, and I were riding in a van behind them. As we pulled up alongside them at a roadside rest area, Dusty and Danny were outside the car doing the stroll, dancing, and singing along with the song 'Working at the Car Wash Blues' by Jim Croce, which was playing on the radio. Dusty kept trying to get Haystacks out of the car, and Danny finally got so mad, saying to Dusty, 'Leave the fat man alone!' Dusty turned to Danny and smacked him in the face … in a long way. They stopped, looked at each other and started to laugh, then started dancing again. It just went too far."

Monsignor Laurence Higgins

"One of my fondest memories was when Dusty couldn't come to my 25th anniversary to the priesthood, so he did a video wishing me all the best. In it, he did a skit making up stories about me … some were true.

I also remember doing a radio interview together, and I brought back an Irish flag from Ireland and gave it to him because he had won the world title. He showed me the tag on the flag … 'Made in China.'"

Nikita Koloff

"We were in Hamilton, Ontario, and we jumped on the private plane to go see the Big Apple. I'm not a big partier, but I hadn't been there before, so I was game. It was Dusty, Jim Crockett, Barry Windham, the Horsemen, and me. When we landed in the Apple, there were two limos waiting for us. The Horsemen went in one limo and went one way, and we got in the other limo and did our thing. Windham had contacts in the

city from when he worked for the WWF, so he came up with the idea to go to a gay club, the Palladium, as a rib. We pulled up to this joint, we went inside, and sure enough, it was a bunch of gays in there. I didn't even want to touch anything. ... It must have been a staggering thing to witness, as I'm sure we were sticking out like sore thumbs. I was getting looks and stares that I wasn't real receptive to. One of the high spots, however, was that I was up on the second level, looking down, and I saw Dusty and it looked like he was up to something. The next thing I saw is he was at the edge of this jammed dance floor. Then out of nowhere he did the John Wayne swagger across the dance floor. It was hilarious to watch. It was like Moses parting the Red Sea ... as he walked, people parted in front of him, and as he passed them, the crowd closed in behind him. He was just Dusty being Dusty. We ended up at this little café. ... 'You've got to try this pate,' he said. It was steak tartare! I about wanted to gag! I ordered normal food and passed the steak tartare along to him."

Black Jack Mulligan

"Dusty liked to rib me. He ribbed me the first time I had a payoff. He had a stack of ones, but I didn't know they were ones and he said, 'How would you like one of these?'

Well, that was nothing compared to what Dusty and Dickie did to me one time. In Texas they have these big, six-foot rattlesnakes. We were going from Austin to Corpus Christi and they put a dead rattlesnake on my car. It scared the shit out of me and I never forgot that. Years later, Dusty and I stopped in Ocala [Florida] for some chili dogs. He had this brand-new Dodge that was kept immaculately clean. We start driving again and I started talking about how I think there are bigger rattlesnakes in Florida than in Texas. Well, he started lisping and as soon as he does, you know he's bullshitting. Anyway, I had bought this plastic snake and I popped it out while he's driving and ... he starts screaming like a woman ... chili all over the place. There were tears in his eyes from laughing so hard. He said, 'Bobby, sometimes you go way down too far with shit.' What fun it was ... I enjoyed it all the way."

Harley Race

"Dusty won the NWA World Heavyweight title in Tampa, and the following night we were in Key West for Fantasyfest. I booked a charter flight ... Dusty rented a Lear Jet. I got there just in time to see the big parade, and Dusty was in it. Three beautiful women jumped on the float with him, and Dusty grabbed one and kissed her and then the second one kissed him. At this point he realized he had just swapped spit with two guys who were dressed in drag. The third looked at him and said, 'Aren't you going to kiss me, too?'"

Jim Ross

"The Dream used to like to get ready, well, almost ready, for his matches early in the evening in the locker room. By that I mean he would get undressed, put on his Austin Hall cowboy-styled wrestling boots and, well, that's it. So here you have a 300-pound man standing around a locker room full of male wrestlers wearing absolutely nothing but a pair of boots. I remember one time in Raleigh, North Carolina, at the old Dorton Arena on a hot summer's night that the Dream's pre-match locker room attire sent the late Jim Barnett running for the hills when James E. saw The Dream in all his glory."

So that's a little bit of what it was like on the road or interacting with some of the boys and all the crazy shit that went on; stuff that always puts a smile on my face when I think back because we had so much fun. Sometimes we were like little kids in this crazy business we call pro wrestling.

As we get a little closer to the end of the book, I remind myself that our business is not all fun and games, but it sure is easy to remember the good times, like the time Eddie took me fishing for the first time.

We were on his boat right near the Howard Frankland Bridge and when I cast my reel I accidentally cast it up on the highway, snagging a passing truck. Well, there went my rod and reel ... flying out of my hands. Eddie looked at me and just shook his head.

Funny shit. As unbelievable as they sound, these things really did happen ... and I wouldn't give up any of them for any price!

CHAPTER 14

I was driving back home from an independent show in Lenoir, North Carolina, where it was another sellout for "The American Dream" Dusty Rhodes—1,500 fans—as I teamed with the Rock-n-Roll Express, Ricky Morton and Robert Gibson, to defeat the Midnight Express, Dennis Condrey, Bobby Eaton, and Stan Lane, and it just struck me how quickly 20 years had passed ... just like that—*snap!*—In the blink of an eye.

On the card this particular December night were not only the guys I just mentioned, but Nikita Koloff was there as the special guest referee. "Sensational" Sherri Martel, Gary Royal, David Isley, and George South were also on the card, as was "The Ugandan Giant" Kamala. Wonderful Willie himself, Bill Apter, was there, too. And to top it all off, to culminate the night of *déjà vu* for me, up on the wall doing a promo to challenge me for a card the next month was a video projection of Tully Blanchard.

As I gave my rebuttal to the video, I not only realized I was talking to a wall, but I remembered that nearly every one of those guys on that card had worked for me at some point in their careers. It's was like a one point twenty-one gigawatt lighting ride to 1985, but when the night was over and I was looking at the long road home in front of me, it was I who was back to the future of 2004 ... 2005 ... and it got me thinking of just how I got here ... in this new and often treacherous world of independent wrestling.

After the fall of the small Roman Empire known as World Championship Wrestling in the late '90s, I found myself fucked over— first by my assistant for many years, James J. Dillon, and then by a real half-witted accountant who Turner properties put in charge of WCW, Bill Bush. Man, the business was shot to hell in a handbag. Anyway, out of work for about 20 minutes, I formed my own companies, Turnbuckle Entertainment and Turnbuckle Championship Wrestling, TCW.

Little did I know, however, that the independent wrestling business was more fucked up than WCW. What I mostly found, aside from the handful of legit guys out there who were really trying, was that the business was now made up of kids promoting shows, because they went on the internet and bought a promotion book or something, or they read the sheets from the guys who never promoted a show in their life and ran those shows off of what these guys thought was good ... and then they made or bought a belt— champion of the world, of course—and made themselves champion. It was no longer a blueprint of the Mafia with regional Godfathers, but rather a blueprint of "Our Gang Comedy" and the local wrestlers were Alfalfa and Butch ... with Spanky and Darla as the promoters.

And if all that wasn't bad enough, some of these guys who never drew a dime's worth of business with anybody and couldn't draw flies if they were covered with shit, were opening wrestling schools teaching other guys who knew even less than they did, all the stuff they knew ... which could fit on the head of a pin and still have room left over for some of the other promoters who were doing the same thing. That's why I said earlier Murdoch would fart on them.

I think you get the picture, and it ain't really a pretty one.

So, when I got let go by General Bush, the IRS agent, accountant, or whatever he was there, I started TCW and went into that, but I also started working independents. I never really worked independents before, and Terry Funk warned me it's really rough out there but I didn't believe it, because he'd been doing it for so long, making a living. He said, "It's a constant hustle ... it's just really a hustle to do it." So I kind of started out on my own, making myself available for independents, and in the process, one day out of the blue, I got a call from Paul E. Dangerously.

Extreme Championship Wrestling at that time already had that cult niche going on around the country ... around the world ... and Paul E., Paul Heyman, called me to say they were going to be at the Tabernacle in Atlanta, Georgia, a building that used to be the "House of Blues." He and his partner at the time asked me, "Would you like to come to ECW?"

With ECW I knew that their unique fans were a group of loyal followers, kind of like the "Insane Clown Posse" followers, who were dedicated to the wrestling papers, the sheets, and the home of ECW of course, was in

Philadelphia at Viking Hall, a bingo parlor that the fans renamed the ECW Arena. I met with Paul at a time when I was really down business-wise, because the independents were not paying what I wanted. I figured my price was a certain amount, and I wasn't going to come off of it.

Turnbuckle Entertainment did well the first year, but then it went on a downward spiral because we just didn't do things right. While the people I had surrounding it and actually working for me, worked very hard, we just all didn't do anything right. If I had to do it over again, I would, but you can't go back. At that point I said to myself, "I'm going to have to go out and hustle some like Terry told me."

As a result I went down there and made a deal with them, a very lucrative deal at the time, and I really thought it was payback from Paul E. from when I hired him at WCW to do the original Midnight Express angle with the new Midnight Express and Jim Cornette. Anyway, he picked me up and it was like he said, "Come on, I'm gonna give you this amount of money, no matter what you do." At that point in time it was kind of a Godsend, because it was really rough. Because of that, I was always very appreciative, and I honestly didn't know at the time what was going on with their innerworkings or anything like that. So I went to the Tabernacle in Atlanta and I did the spot with me hitting the ring on Steve Corino; the first time I'd ever seen him.

The guys I had been around on the independent circuit have all been so respectful, but never was there a group of guys, the ones Paul E. had, who were as respectful as these guys were to the old school and what I brought to the dance. They made me feel really at home, and it was really cool.

> *"I remember the day I met him like it was yesterday. It was December 2, 1999, in Atlanta, and I thought that 'The Dream,' who had just left WCW, was there to say hi to some people he knew who were working for ECW at the time. Never in my wildest dreams had I thought I would be eye to eye with him in the ring less than three hours later!"*
>
> —"KING OF OLD SCHOOL" STEVE CORINO

There was a TV taping there and when I hit the ring, it was a phenomenal response. My debut was a surprise, but Corino and I went on to have a feud and I helped further his career when he beat me in a bull rope match at the ECW Arena. So we went on and made TV and I was still working, trying to make independents at the time on my own.

Paul E. brought me up to the ECW Arena for the first time. It was about 20 degrees outside, ice on the street, cold as shit. I had read different articles on the internet about how the fans in this place received certain wrestlers, and I wondered how they were going to receive me if I didn't go there. Well, of course, the fans knew I was in Philly, but they didn't know how I was going to have it, how I was going to make my entrance there. Paul E. had me go outside and wait for the right time to run in from the side door. Like I said, it was about 20 degrees outside and I stood there about 20 minutes, just about freezing my balls off, and then the time came, and I hadn't received a reception like I did from those fans in quite a long time. Anyhow, I think it was more out of the respect for me in coming down to their building, because it really was the fans' building, coming into their home, coming into that organization, and they really respected me for it. That spot really gave me a shot in the arm at that point in time. So we went on and just kept on with ECW and I wasn't doing a lot, just showing up, but I was getting paid and doing a lot of things.

"I am sure most people would say that they admire Dream's charisma or the way he sold for the heels or even his booking style. The thing I admire most about Dusty Rhodes is his heart. This is a guy who didn't have to do what he did for a 27-year-old kid. Dusty was already a legend, he didn't need to do a program with an unknown Steve Corino, but he did. Not only did he do it, but he made me look like a superstar and I became an instant success [with the ECW fans]. I was already claiming to be the 'King of Old School,' but Dusty made the nickname a reality, all for the purpose of 'making' someone. ECW didn't have the money to pay Dusty what he deserved, he did it because that is the type of guy he is. In a few words, Dusty Rhodes made Steve Corino! There is no doubt about it. Before Dream came to ECW, I was a mid-level heel that had just prematurely finished a program with Taz and Tommy Dreamer. I had heat, but to the ECW fans Taz and Dreamer were not 'Old School,' they were ECW born. But when Dusty came to ECW, he legitimized my beliefs in old-school wrestling and put me at the top of the card almost right away. Steve Corino would never have been either the ECW World or NWA World champion without Dusty Rhodes."

—"KING OF OLD SCHOOL" STEVE CORINO

CHAPTER FOURTEEN

Tommy Dreamer was a cool guy. Not only did he show me a lot of respect when I was there, but I have a lot of respect for him as he really took his time to hone his craft. A lot of people don't realize just how much of ECW was Tommy's. He had his heart and soul in that thing, which is why I booked him a few times with TCW.

So anyway, I was still running Turnbuckle at the time, still trying to take independent bookings, and then shortly after ECW, Jerry Lawler's booking agent, and that's what he is—people say, "Aw, he's just a guy you have," and that shit—but booking agent Mike O'Brien came to me in Nashville when Lawler and I did an independent date for the first time where we had actually wrestled each other. "The King" introduced me to Mike and right away he said, "Let me handle this."

Since that time, Mike's been my agent and we've made a lot of money together. He's a hardcore guy in that he knows how to negotiate, and because of that, everybody who does business with him doesn't like him on most occasions. But the bottom line is he gets the job done. They don't like it because they think it's just the old school and they should be dealing directly with me, but I'll deal with my heart instead of my wallet; Michael deals with the wallet. He's been a great asset, and we've come to be good friends.

> *"Part of the problem some of these promoters have with me is they don't understand that the fee can change depending on where the show is, what type of match it is and who Dusty's wrestling. For example, a promoter in the Carolinas or Florida is going to pay more if he is working with Terry Funk or Tully Blanchard than let's say a promoter in Wisconsin where Dusty would be working a local guy. Sometimes it depends on the economic situation of the area too, as typically they can pay a little more if their ticket prices are higher because they can afford to."*
>
> —MICHAEL O'BRIEN

Meanwhile, time marched on for ECW, and they were getting ready to fold their camp. There were a lot of guys not getting paid, not getting checks, bitching and complaining, but Paul E. had that old-school promoter's way of talking to his guys when they said, "I'm going to go in there tonight, I'm going to get my money, I'm going to tell that son of a bitch that I'm through and it's all over. ..." and they'd go in and have a meeting, and by the time they finished talking with Paul E. they were ready to knock down a wall—

and that's the way the old promoters were. You'd get ready to quit: "I'm leaving ... I hate this territory ... the money ain't right here..." they would be leaving, one foot out the door, but that old fucking mentality talks them into staying.

I have a lot of respect for Paul E. He was a guy who when I was in charge of Jim Crockett Promotions and TBS, he always came to the production meetings. I never ran him off because he was always there, involved, but he took mental notes. It was kind of like he went to school and got paid to go by WCW. And as we know, back then they threw money around like it was fucking chocolate bars at a Hershey convention in Hershey, Pennsylvania. ECW was a good time, and it was a time that helped me out a lot and made me appreciate how people really respected the industry. Of course the matches with Corino and me, and the matches with Funk and me—that's just legendary shit that went down during that period of time.

The independents were a little bit different. We had some huge houses. The biggest one, besides Lawler and me in Butler, Pennsylvania, outside of Pittsburgh, where we did 6,800 people, was in Davie, Florida, at the Rodeo Arena when they had Abdullah and Kevin Sullivan and Terry Funk and me. I talked about this briefly earlier, but it was a tremendous night because it was the old Miami, the old Fort Lauderdale crowd. I believe it was like 4,000 paid and it was great.

So the independents were off and on. I never went to a place that Mike got a booking for me where I didn't get my money. It was usually waiting for me when I get there. The only time was for this guy Norm Connors in Pittsburgh, where we did the 6,800 house just before that—the bastard still owes me $750. But I don't want to come across like it's all about money, because it ain't. It's not the money, because $750 is beer money. It's the point of what was going on, and I took him at his word. As I write this, it's been almost two years now.

"I get a lot of requests literally from all over the world to book Dusty, and the most difficult thing I have to deal with, especially if I never heard of the group making the request, is researching who the person is and what wrestling organization it's for; it's important that the person and group are reputable. There are a lot of good promoters out there like William Moody and Marvin Ward in Virginia, Tony Hunter in North Carolina, and Jonathan Gold among others. These are the type of

promoters who are businessmen and try to make their promotions successful through hard work. Unfortunately, there are also promoters out there who are really just fans who've found money somewhere and want to wrestle, making themselves the star."

—MIKE O'BRIEN

Independents are tough, and Terry warned me, "There have been many nights I've seen guys go and not get their money; the houses being the shits." I've often thought, "Here I am, 'The American Dream.' I've wrestled in front of 35,000 people or more, and now here I am in front of 35 people because this promoter doesn't have a fucking clue."

But I was just out doing what I knew how to do best. That was my job and vocation, to be in this industry. It was rough at the beginning, and even though I work for WWE, independents are still a big part of my life. I'm determined to always do my best when I go to work for somebody and they pay me big bucks.

"Well, having Dusty in my NWA Arena for Hardcore Hell 2004 was literally a 'dream' come true. And it wasn't just the genuine thrill all of us felt when he was introduced, when he hit the 'flip, flop and fly' at the end of his match, or when he pointed at the Wildside sign. What was amazing was that Dusty sat in the go area nearly the whole night, watched every match, and talked with all the wrestlers. Here was one of the biggest stars ever in professional wrestling making everyone feel special. So, having Dusty at NWA Wildside was 'special' because he is."

—BILL BEHRENS

But, getting back to ECW, they let me into their inner circle, and I made some really great friends while I was over there like Sandman and my brother New Jack, and those guys were really great to me, and I will never forget it, because Paul E. took me in and picked me up when I was really down.

Jim Ross talks on occasion about those of us who've fallen from grace. I think we all fell from grace at one time, even the biggest stars do. I remember when Ross had gotten fired by Eric Bischoff—that's falling from grace because Ross had so much power at the time. But he worked his way back, reinvented himself, and now is in a good position with Vince. And that's what I've done too, but instead of with Vince, I did it with TNA. I enjoy being around the young kids like A.J. Styles, Monty Brown, and Abyss, and seeing some of the old stars too, like Jeff Jarrett, Scott Hall, and Kevin Nash.

ECW was a good thing. I made a lot of money on the Acclaim ECW game. There were some good times there. I enjoyed working with those guys at ECW. Every single one of them put his heart and soul and life on the line, really, literally, every night. Sabu and Terry Funk had one of the most brutal, unbelievable matches I've ever seen in the history of wrestling to this day, and they had a great heel in Shane Douglas. Shane to me is a throwback to Rick Rude, who I thought was the greatest heel of the '90s. I think Shane was that type of heel, just a tremendous talker and savvy about what's going on in the ring. I got to see a lot of guys, a lot of young guys while I was there, seeing them performing as best they could, and they took it serious! They were all pissed at Paul E. at the start of the night and they rallied around him at the end of the night. ECW was a great experience for me at a time when I really needed to get back up from that fall from grace or whatever you call it, but I never stopped being "The American Dream," and that was really cool.

In a way ECW was like Japan, as respect was so important there; well, respect was important in Japan until recently, anyhow.

My first trip to the land of the Rising Sun was when I with the AWA working for Verne Gagne. In Japan I went to work for Hisashi Shinma as that's who Verne used to deal with. In the late '70s Shinma would actually be a figurehead president of the WWWF for Vince Sr. Anyway, Murdoch went with me there and he had been with Baba all of those years, but I talked him into going with me. He remained with Baba most of his career there as that was where his loyalties were. I loved Baba and I worked for him a little bit, but when I became a star, my loyalties were with Inoki for a couple of reasons. Not only because he treated me right—the respect was unbelievable toward me—but because Eddie Graham, Duke Keomuka, and Hiro Matsuda, pretty much the whole Florida office was affiliated with Inoki, and I had respect for them.

And respect in Japan was so much different than in the U.S. even to this day up until just recently. There was real respect for the guys who went over and the ones who brought them there, and I remember Inoki would bring some of the older guys there all the time like Lord Blears. They would even bring Barnett over there one time with me. Inoki had a tremendous respect for the past—and so did Baba for that matter—it was unbelievable the way they treated the American wrestlers.

The way they treated the business, up until just recently, was with a handshake, and that was all you needed. But my entire perspective was changed about that with the new breed of promoters there. I was scheduled to work a Hustle show for Dream Stage Entertainment (DSE)—a PRIDE/Zero-One co-promotion—for a certain amount of money, and those guys, Yoshi Nakamura and company, took years of honor and respect and threw it to the wind. The new regimes over there, the people who are running the companies, have no respect for the business whatsoever. What they did to me, as far as waiting until the last week and actually canceling me out of the tour, would have never been done before. It was all over something like $3,000 more than what they were going to give, which they promised on a handshake and came on top of what I was making; just to ensure I would make the same amount as before. And they also canceled Dustin with no explanation, just cutting us off at that point with no respect letter to come later or any offer of "Here's half of it up front," or whatever. So, as far as I'm concerned, it's changed from that time—from when my mentor in Japan was Matsuda, and like I said, I respected him unbelievably. Massa Saito, better known to fans in the U.S. as Mr. Saito, was my closest friend from Japan as he also worked for the Inoki office, and I made a lot of great friends over there. Inoki I respect to this day.

Being able to get in there was whatever it was, but to be told a week before you're getting your bags packed and ready to go, at a time in my life and my age where you count on certain contracts to be fulfilled, it just looks and smells like a bad independent deal, man. "No, we can't run. ... We're not running this weekend. ... We can't pay you this amount of money, we can only pay you this amount. If you want to take a pay cut, you can come. ..." Take a cut? Come to what? Shit, it was very disheartening to know that all the ones who had come before them, the Japanese guys, the amount of respect they had for the industry and for me ... and what had been done, that this group, Zero-One, and Hashimoto was a big fan of mine, and I'm sure he wasn't involved in the decision making on this thing, I'm sure it was people higher up, or with this new regime that wanted wrestling and shoot-fighting to be all in one, when we know it's not. So, it was just amazing and has left a sour taste in my mouth.

Back in the early days, Japan was some fun times. We'd stay six to seven or eight weeks, like the Australian tours; 13 weeks with Murdoch. They were fun, but man, you wanted to go home. You weren't making a lot of money, but it was a great experience for a young guy in the business. Even when the business started to get tarnished and exposed in the States, Japan was still sacred ground. Everyone from the top promoter to the bottom fan held you in high esteem and treated you with a level of respect that rivaled the great sumo wrestlers. And it grew from the time Michelle went over there with me to when Inoki and I were working. I would go over for one week or whatever. It was phenomenal. I love Japan, second only to Mexico, as far as my favorite countries to go visit. I have a lot of respect for those who brought us to the dance. There's not much more I can say about that except when they disrespected me at the end, Zero-One, PRIDE and DSE will always remain in the back of my head ... phenomenal ... not even a letter.

It's kind of like when I first started with TNA. There were times I thought the TNA office ran their place like a leper colony. A lot of guys were kept in the dark unnecessarily, as they never knew if they were going to be on TV or not. I guess the office just really appeared disorganized and unfocused, and to me there was no mystery how they got 10 or 15 million dollars in the hole in two and a half years. Their focus was in the wrong place, and a lot of the young guys felt they weren't being respected. Jerry Jarrett had me in there, and I have a tremendous amount of respect and admiration for Jerry, as he's one of the leftover Godfathers from the old days—I often said to him up in the office that he and I were playing poker while everybody else was playing Go Fish—but to have a 50-something-year-old as your biggest babyface, well right there it tells you there is something wrong with that whole picture.

The money was great and I enjoyed doing what I did, and the office respected me tremendously. But me being the top draw was like the Grammy Awards a few years ago when Tony Bennett walked out and won a Grammy away from those younger guys—he took away the spotlight from the kids who really needed it, just like I was taking away the focus from the young lions at TNA. "Who the fuck is this guy and why is he singing? Why is he wrestling? Why is he still here?" Well, I felt like Tony Bennett. So when I became executive producer of TNA, I still kept my on-air personality, but I de-emphasized the focus on me and put it back on the guys it should be on, like A.J. Styles, Monty Brown, and even Dustin. It's all about respect. If you want to be respected by others, you have to start by respecting others. It's like Bob and Dixie Carter, the majority owners of TNA. They had a tremendous amount of respect for me, and I in turn had an enormous amount of respect for and gratitude for them.

In a way it's like this new thing I'm doing, motivational speaking, even though I suppose you can say I've always been a motivational speaker through my interviews and promos. After all, isn't that what we're supposed to do in pro wrestling—motivate people to buy an arena ticket or to buy our pay-per-view?

But in a way, it's a lot deeper than that, and I guess I always knew that. I guess I always understood that my story was the story of the people and that's really what people respected about me, and because it was their story, that's what I really, deep down respected about them.

> *"I have been a longtime fan of Dusty. I was a young boy who was captivated with professional wrestling. I watched Dusty Rhodes come into the Boston area of the WWWF where I lived and stand up to the bully of the day, 'Superstar' Billy Graham. He electrified the city of Boston and the WWWF fans ... I was raised in humble settings and was a professional wrestling fan and played the sport of judo. Dusty became my motivation in judo. The story of 'The American Dream,' the son of a plumber who went on to sell out Madison Square Garden and win the world title is one I latched onto and believed in. I was the son of an electrician and was inspired by Dusty to never give up, stand up against the odds and be what you want to be ... live 'The American Dream.' I went on to win the state championships and was the National Judo Champion for several years and went on to be the captain of the U.S. Judo team that toured South Africa. I kept the vision of 'The American Dream' with me as I competed for years. So besides entertaining me for years, Dusty inspired me to reach for my goal, be persistent, and make it happen."*
>
> —PAUL JONES, SVP, LIMITED BRANDS

How can I get in front of more than a hundred corporate executives from a company like Limited Brands and talk about wrestling? I can't, because it's not about wrestling and never has been. If you read this book and walk away from it without understanding that these words are really about family and friends and sacrifice and overcoming obstacles and being everything you push yourself to be ... and you respect yourself for who you are, what you do and how you do it ... well, then read the book again.

"I asked Dusty to speak with a group of 110-plus Loss Prevention executives who are on the top of their game. My goal was to have Dusty articulate his journey of 'The American Dream.' Most of the people were not wrestling fans, but all of the people got fired up, reenergized, and were ready to live their 'American Dream' after hearing Dusty speak. He speaks from his heart, is a straight shooter and captivated the audience. Dusty's story is so much more than wrestling. It's a story of passion, guts and achievement. He has a career as a motivational speaker, for sure."

—PAUL JONES, SVP, LIMITED BRANDS

So, getting back to Japan, that disrespect ate at me. They had Steve Corino email me and put him in the middle of the thing and caused heat between him and me, which there shouldn't have been, because even a letter of apology from Nakamura would have been acceptable. You see, this is Dusty Rhodes, Hulk Hogan, Ric Flair, and an email that says, "Oh yeah, they want you to take that cut in pay if you want to come." What's not to want to go? The first time I was there with Zero-One, we did 14,000 people with me against Mil Mascaras in a six-man that drew as much as anything they had over there at that point in time. So, as far as I was concerned, I earned my way back over even at my age now, to go over there and have the right to be respected.

When I called Nakamura in Japan, he acted so surprised, but I felt he was full of shit. I told him in all my years of being in this business I had seen it all, but this was very embarrassing. He said he would call Corino, who handled the bookings for the American guys, or as the Japanese refer to the foreigners, gaijins. Quite frankly, at that stage in my life, I was too old for that shit! But if Matsuda were alive, it wouldn't have happened, because that's how much respect he had in Japan, whether it was with New Japan or All Japan. If he'd even been with a different company, it wouldn't have happened. He probably would have had somebody's legs broken. But that's the way it was, and that's the way it is, because "business is business," and mutual respect is such an important and integral part of our business.

How important and integral is it?

As I look back at things that happened in my career, there are people that are so outstanding, you forget about what you love or respect about them times and situations.

CHAPTER FOURTEEN

In January 2005, I had an opportunity over an unbelievable two week period to see so many of the guys I've talked so much about all in one place, nearly 90 of them that were a part of my life, and it really humbled me to be in the presence of guys that have helped mold my career and I've helped in some way mold their careers.

At this one thing called Wrestle Reunion in Tampa, Florida, of the 80 guys booked, 79 actually showed up. Guys who I hadn't seen in years were there. Everybody from Ron Bass to Dewey Robertson, the Missing Link, to "Beezer" Brian Blair, who's now a politician down in Tampa ... all those guys ... Mike Graham, Jake "the Snake" Roberts, Dallas Page ...

During this three day deal, one of the things that stand out is when Mick Foley, Bill Apter, Terry Funk, Kevin von Erich and I were doing this question and answer session. It was so amazing for the fans that were there. And it was so amazing for all of us to be together. I was really overwhelmed. I was in awe of some of these guys. And yet when I walked in, the egotistical bastard that I am, in my opinion, and reflecting back for a moment, we were the selected Godfathers from that era. And I feel like I'm in charge or responsible for them guys. I want them all to prevail. I don't want them to be sick ... they're like my babies. It was just tremendous seeing them all.

One of the guys I got a real chance to observe was "Big Sexy" Kevin Nash. I'm associated with him a lot these days as he's been working with TNA. I was sitting there at the autograph session and I looked over at him when he was signing autographs and talking to people and I thought to myself, of this new era, he is the most charismatic fucking guy that we have on our roster. He just exuberates charisma in the way he talks, the way he walks, the way he moves ... he actually reminds me of my own chubby self back the way of how sure I was about things. But knowing too that money has been what drove him, and for a lot of baseball players, and a lot of football players, and a lot of basketball players, and a lot of hockey players, it's the money. But it's also about the athlete. And I thought to myself as I'm looking at him, something that had stood out lately at TNA, now that I'm writing and executive producing the show, is being around him, he has really taught me a lot because I always thought he was really creative. But I wish I really could have produced him back—which I did a little bit with the Oz character— but not to the point that I wish I had the full Kevin Nash like I have right now because he has that intangible ability to make you think it's all about the money, man. But in reality he's a throw back to that era where some guys would come in and say, "You don't have to pay me tonight, just give me a belt. I want to be champion." And when I watched him, I saw in his eyes that he may be kidding somebody, but he ain't kidding me; it's not all just about the money. It's about the performance and the athletic ability ... it's about his respect for himself and for our business. So I took that away from there and I thought that was really cool as it made me look at him a little differently.

And then I looked at Ron Bass, and I thought about when he was in Florida, he was as hot as can be and we drew a lot of money together. Jake Roberts, who, at this point in time, just came off another conviction or something. But there he was and he looked the same. Ronnie Garvin, Jimmy Garvin, Bobby "the Brain" Heenan, Cowboy Bill Watts ... like I said, there were just so many guys from my past running around there.

It was a great time to reflect and see all of these great stars in one place at one time and actually talking about the past. It was a beautiful, beautiful time.

I just remember sitting there with Humperdink and Harley Race, and as I looked around the room, there were different people that would go up to a guy and a picture would snap, or someone would move to me and a different picture would snap.

Just in the past few months, in finishing this book and writing about the things in my life and this business, I've really grown to understand how important an industry we have and how important it is to the fans and how important it is for the people to actually be able to touch us. And what a great justice we do for mankind in telling some unbelievable stories and doing some unbelievable things.

It's just like looking at A.J. Styles now and Jeff Jarrett with the NWA title, and Chris Daniels and America's Most Wanted, and all these guys that are good ... looking at these guys and seeing them do this unbelievable stuff, and seeing Dustin in there ... it just makes me proud that I'm doing what I'm doing ... and this reunion brought all that back to me.

It actually took this egotistical son-of-a-bitch Dusty Rhodes out of character and made me the most humble man I could possibly be, being around this group of guys.

But the one guy that really stood out, who I had an opportunity to see and talk to after 20 years, but not until the following week in Tucson, Arizona, was "Superstar" Billy Graham. Although we've talked on the phone on numerous occasions, to see him in person was something else. And he looked fabulous. He looked great. This was a guy who was supposed to be dead ... liver transplant ... and it was a 20 year reunion of us actually being face-to-face; he remembered to the day.

My good friend Dallas Page was there and it was supposed to be kind of a surprise for me. The thing about Dallas is he understands the industry and what it means to me and what different guys meant to me and he was like in awe ... it was like John Lennon was still alive and Paul McCartney walked in ... and then to actually witness the meeting.

As I walked in and looked at him, he stood up and we hugged for a long time. I had tears in my eyes ... and my first instinct was to start to tell my stories. We talked about the industry and what happened, how many towns we'd sold out and we were just talking, man, recollecting ... and "Superstar" and me have lived our lives together as this band of brothers on the Bob Dylan road.

Bobby Dylan—Bobby D—was somebody that we would play every album, we would take every bit of what he said, and in my interviews, I would turn them into what the interviews were talking about. When a guy would turn on me, a bad guy, someone would do something to me, in Orlando I'd say, "I offered up my innocence and he paid me back in scorn, Orlando said come in I'll give you shelter from the storm."

We said these things and interjected them at a time when it was unheard of in our business. We were the poet laureates from '74 on up in our industry and an opportunity to face off on that mega stage in New York City, Madison Square Garden, when Vince, Sr. was still alive. Or the next unforgettable moment was still to this day where people still call it the Garden, said they never heard a roar like that ... there was no music, there was nothing that was played like a video or anything before you came out ... instead the people stood to get a glimpse of these two guys, "Superstar" Billy Graham against "the American Dream" Dusty Rhodes.

So we're sitting there and having this conversation, and Dallas was sitting there too, listening, as he's always at my side, and this Indian kid walks up who was in the opening match at the show—AWA show in Tucson, Arizona at the Casino Del Sol—he said, "Mr. Rhodes, excuse me ..." not even thinking of what a moment he just walked in on. Not even thinking for a second how the Earth was moving right there as he walked in with these two guys sitting there.

Jesse Ventura and Hulk Hogan admit to this day that we were the two guys that took their careers and where they wanted to be and took it to that different level.

So the Indian kid looks at us and he said, "Excuse me, sir ... Mr. Rhodes ... I'm in the opening match. Would you please come out and watch my match and tell me how I did? It would be a great honor."

I said, "Sure, kid, I'll do it." Then he walked away.

"Superstar" Billy Graham looked at me and said, "Brother ... we're on an Indian reservation ... in Tucson, Arizona ...two guys that filled up back to back to back Madison Square Garden ... and this young kid wants you to go out and watch the opener?" And he laughed so hard, and we laughed at the moment ... the kid didn't even know what the moment was all about.

And I did watch him, and he wasn't bad and it was cool, but it was just something that took the edge off and it was something the two of us could relate to together.

Then "Superstar" Billy presented me with a tape he had recorded of an interview that recently had showed Bob Dylan on 20/20 or some show like that. He was our way of thinking and how we interjected it in our talk and how we felt about him and we talked about that and as it went down to the old wrestling genre, Dallas would ask questions about this and that, people would come in and they'd trade off pictures and take pictures with us, of us ... I was just sitting there looking at him and he said he was just amazed.

"You look a little older in the face." Obviously my body hadn't changed, but he said, "You look the same."

His face looked the same too.

I told him I could remember him posing and just walking around and interviewing and the interviews were unscripted. They were a battle back and forth between us as we talked about the match, whether it'd be in the Boston Gardens or Madison Square Garden or whether it'd be in Tampa, Florida.

The only guy that really didn't understand our gimmick, our stuff, our shtick, was Verne Gage and the AWA. He didn't understand how charismatic and how unbelievable this thing could be between me and "Superstar." He was heavy into the arm wrestling thing and that was working for him ... Wahoo and the strap matches, that was working ... and me and "Superstar" talked about that.

So he left it with me and it was pretty chilly in Tucson, a beautiful day, but chilly for there and he'd come outside, watch a little bit of the match, watch Dallas and Erik Watts, and he had to go in as he couldn't stay out because of the liver ... he couldn't stay out in the air a long time, but he looked great. We went inside ... back and forth ... he was getting tired toward the end of the show and finally it was just me and him left in the dressing room.

Everybody was gone and I was taking the wraps off my leg and he would sit there in amazement. Then he said something that was so cool. He said, "You know, all of the people in our industry from our era, all of them, owe you and me a tremendous amount of gratitude because we proved that two polar opposites, two guys that don't even look like each other, bodies that are not even close ... that there's a common bond of human nature in imagination that could talk 21,000 people, 20,000 people, whatever it was, into a building and have them in a fever pitch with a shake of the ass, a pose from the arm ... in a fever pitch for them thirty seconds, and not do anything but tell a soft, easy to read story. It was that simple."

I said, "Man, it was so unbelievable what you just said. Dallas told me this one time when I was really down. He said to me, 'You're gonna get up and go over to the mirror and tell me what you see.' He said, 'I'll tell you what you see. You see Dusty Rhodes, the American Dream. And no industry on this Earth, nowhere, no place, is there a bigger star.'"

And then I told him. I said, "'Superstar,' you look in the mirror and you tell me what you see. Because the guy that revolutionized and changed the way we do our business is looking back at you."

And we hugged a long hug, said our goodbyes, and went out to the car ... you know, life is so short sometimes, and we turned to each other and Bobby Dylan on an album that he came out a while back says, "It's getting dark, I can barely see the light." And he looked at me and he said, "You know, the darker it gets, the only light you'll see next, is that light that takes you home."

What a great moment in the life of two guys that relived what they meant to the industry, but what they really meant to each other. All of that built on mutual respect.

Now you know what the industry really means and how it's come full circle.

NOTE: *According to the May-June 2004 edition of Loss Prevention magazine, Paul Jones is senior vice president of loss prevention for Limited*

Brands. He is responsible for overseeing the loss prevention, shortage control, and safety functions for more than 4,000 specialty retail stores, the supply-chain function, call centers, headquarters, and sixteen worldwide offices. Limited Brands includes Express, The Limited, Victoria's Secret, Victoria's secret direct and catalogue, Bath & Body Works, Henri Bendel, and the White Barn Candle Company.

CHAPTER 15

W hen you've been in the wrestling business for as long as I have, been at the creative forefront like I have, and seen or worked with the caliber of performers that I have over the years, you sometimes find yourself thinking, "Wow, I wonder what it would be like to work with this guy?"

In that same instance, that question goes one step further from working a match to working a whole program. Then, sometimes strictly from a creative aspect, whether you were the "booker" in the old days or the executive producer today, you might start to wonder how this guy would work with this other guy? And then going one step further from there, taking the business aspect into account, you ask yourself the ultimate question, which is at the root of the wrestling business, "Would they draw a house?"

You can have the greatest match in the history of the business, but if it's between two guys who couldn't draw flies if they were covered with shit, it means absolutely nothing. The bottom line is while this fancy stunt wrestling shit today is well and good, the business is not based on how many hurricaranas you can do, but whether or not you can draw money. If you don't have the ability to talk and if you don't have that natural charisma, it doesn't matter how good you are in the ring; you won't draw money. I'd rather have a guy who is a mediocre wrestler, but who can give a great interview and has great charisma, because of the two, the mediocre wrestler will draw more money than the guy who can do a quadruple somersault. In the old days it was drawing money at the arena. Today it's drawing money through pay-per-view buys.

One of the things people both in and out of the business often ask me is how do I do what I do? In other words, how do I come up with a particular idea about a specific match? What is my thought process about creating a new tag team? How do I determine which wrestlers will face each other and for what titles?

While I've given you just a little bit of an idea above of what goes through the mind of an executive producer like myself, I thought it would be both fun and educational to really show you what crosses the mind of a matchmaker by actually booking a fictional card that I'd like to call "Starrcade Prime."

I'm calling it "Starrcade Prime" for two reasons. First, because "Starrcade" was the biggest show there ever was before the advent of pay-per-view; and second, because every performer who I've chosen to be on this super card was considered as if he were in the "prime" of his career.

Now, there's a lot that goes into a selection process, so let's consider the following: "Starrcade Prime" will be a televised event, but not a pay-per-view. Because of the caliber of matches, there'll be two announcing teams that will switch off during the show. The first team will be the legendary Gordon Solie and Jim Ross, while the second team will be Gorilla Monsoon, Jesse "The Body" Ventura, and Bobby "The Brain" Heenan.

I chose Gordon because he's the guy who will be able to "tell the story" to the viewers of what is unfolding in the ring, while keeping it "real," especially with the types of wrestlers I've chosen, because he had the big call. I teamed him up with J.R. because in many ways they are similar. J.R. would be able to add to the realism as he too has the knack for the big call, reinforcing what Gordon would be saying. Plus J.R. is the guy who I said earlier I would have when going to war. When he's on his game, there's no better. None. Because these guys are the best solo announcers there ever were in my opinion, and because they loved the business like no other two announcers I ever saw or heard, I think they would complement each other perfectly.

Now, like a great tag team, the second team was chosen because of their chemistry. In my opinion, when it came to announcing teams, there was none better than when Gorilla teamed with either Jesse or Bobby. As a team, they had style, charisma, and were just plain entertaining. Gorilla was a great straight man to his more flamboyant partners. So, in order to keep the chemistry intact, I've decided to make this announcing team a three-man squad with Gorilla being the play-by-play pivot man between two really great color analysts.

While no fan ever bought a ticket to come to an arena to see a television announcer, they certainly didn't buy a ticket to see the referee. However, the great referees knew not only when to be seen and heard, but more importantly when to be the most important invisible person in the ring. The two guys in my opinion who had this quality the best, and therefore are my referees for this card, are Tommy Young and Earl Hebner.

Just as important as the matches themselves, sometimes you've got to have the right building to create something special and the right person to promote that building. There are a lot of great buildings that come to mind. Some of my favorites include the old Sportatorium in Dallas, the Cow Palace in San Francisco, the Omni in Atlanta, the Kiel Auditorium in St. Louis, Cobo Hall in Detroit, the Olympic Auditorium in Los Angeles, and the Miami Beach Convention Center.

Now, if "Starrcade Prime" were to be a pay-per-view, then hands down Madison Square Garden, the Mecca of wrestling if you will, would be the location and Vince McMahon Jr. would be the promoter, because he would know how to hype this thing like no one else. But since it's not a pay-per-view, then the building of choice would be what I always considered the Madison Square Garden of the south—the Fort Homer W. Hesterly Armory in Tampa—and the local promoter would be Sam Mushnick, the legendary president of the NWA and promoter from St. Louis. In its heyday the Armory could hold about 5,800 people, 6,000 with standing room only. The ambiance of that building with that single spotlight over the ring in the darkened, smoke-filled building … well, that's what wrestling was all about; every eye on that ring with no distractions. Man, I get goosebumps just thinking about that. While Sam never promoted Tampa, nobody knew how to promote a local event like him, not even the great Paul Boesch who became a multimillionaire by running just one city, Houston. Sam was one of the first promoters who utilized every medium there was to draw a house, and so he gets the nod for "Starrcade Prime."

There's no doubt that there will be many raised eyebrows, both for my selection of matches and for the apparent absence of some people on the card, many of who I've discussed previously in the book. Plus, I've decided that it's not up to me to decide who would win or lose these fantasy matches, because if a card is booked the right way, it really doesn't matter who wins or loses, only that it draws a profitable house and keeps everyone on it strong to ensure they will be able to continue drawing strong houses going forward.

With that in mind, I've also chosen who would be the booker and assistant bookers for this historic card. These would be the guys who would make sure there would be a good rhythm to the show, that all the finishes would be executed correctly and that the goals of keeping everyone on the card strong and ensuring they will be able to continue drawing strong houses after this card would be met.

The booker would be Eddie Graham. His assistants would be Jim Barnett and Jerry Jarrett. These three guys would probably come up with more creative stuff than you could imagine, while keeping everything very simple. Over the years I enjoyed listening to their bullshit, because they were even better at bullshitting than me. What's great from my perspective is these three guys together wouldn't try to reinvent the wheel. They'd use their knowledge of the business, current events and knack of reading the fans to book the greatest card in the history of the business.

While there would be many other factors to consider in putting a card of this magnitude together, it would probably take a whole book itself to explain the angles and buildups to get to this point, but we don't have the luxury of time here.

So, with all that said, and without further delay, here now is "Starrcade Prime," 10 main-event matches courtesy of that little ol' matchmaker, me!

"The American Dream"
Dusty Rhodes vs. Harley Race

This would be for the NWA World Heavyweight Championship. I could have chosen a number of opponents to face on this card who would guarantee a sellout, such as Ric Flair, Tully Blanchard, Terry Funk, Abdullah the Butcher, or Kevin Sullivan. I drew great money with all these guys, but I never drew the type of money with them like I did with Harley. This is the match that drew the most arena money during our prime than anything else. The match itself would be a classic, and because we've worked so many times against each other, it would be spot on. The bottom line is this match is a proven commodity, so this is the match that gets my nod to close out "Starrcade Prime."

Hulk Hogan vs. Bruno Sammartino

This one would be for the WWWF title. If the card would be at Madison Square Garden instead of the Armory, this would be the one that everyone would line up to see. It's the one match everyone wanted to see take place, but it never happened. I believe Bruno had more sellouts at the Garden than any wrestler in history, while Hogan was the king of the PPVs. While both were enormously popular in their prime, Bruno never played the bad guy to my knowledge, so you'd have to figure that the Hulkster would take that role here. "Well, you know something brother," while Bruno saw very little action in Florida, Tampa is Hogan's hometown, so it would be interesting to see who would come out on top, "Doggone it!"

The Sheik vs. Mark Lewin

This match would be for the United States title. I personally witnessed this match as a young lad first hand in the Detroit territory and of all the matches I've ever seen, this is the one I "mark" for as they say. As I mentioned earlier, The Sheik and Mark Lewin were the greatest heel and babyface I'd ever seen, which is saying a lot. I probably learned more from watching these two work each other than any other match in my career. I don't know what more I can say about these two that I haven't already said earlier, except don't confuse the Sheik with the guy who was the Iron Sheik, because the original Sheik is the measuring stick for which all other heels are judged.

Jose Lothario vs. Ric Flair

With the exception of one other match, this is the one that I think could be the potential "show stealer," as these two would battle for the Texas Heavyweight Championship. Lothario was one of the greatest natural workers I've both seen and worked against, and when you talk about owning a town, he was the guy. There were some cities that you couldn't even imagine beating Lothario for fear of a riot breaking out. So I think with the strong Hispanic population in Tampa and Flair's ability to be a natural heel, the heat here would potentially be nothing short of tremendous. While I've said a lot about Ric's style and ability, he has always risen to the occasion when the money is on the line, and so I think his approach going into this match would fit perfectly with Jose's.

PROFESSIONAL WRESTLING

FORT HOMER W. HESTERLY ARMORY ✳ TAMPA

STARRCADE PRIME

TUESDAY NIGHT 7:30 P.M.

Dusty Rhodes vs. Harley Race

Hulk Hogan vs. Bruno Sammartino

The Sheik vs. Mark Lewin

Jose Lothario vs. Ric Flair

Terry & Dory Funk Jr. vs. "Cowboy" Bill Watts & Black Jack Mulligan

Jack Brisco vs. Dick Murdoch

Fritz von Erich vs. Gene Kiniski

Wahoo McDaniel vs. Johnny Valentine

Goldust vs. Freddie Blassie

The Fabulous Moolah vs. Kay Noble

Terry and Dory Funk Jr. vs. "Cowboy" Bill Watts and Black Jack Mulligan

Being the only tag-team match on the card, there are a lot of tag teams I could have chosen, but in a match for the World Tag-Team titles, there's no other team that would belong there except the Funks. The Rock-n-Roll Express, the Midnight Express, the Fabulous Freebirds, the Wild Samoans, the Brisco Brothers, and Arn Anderson and Tully Blanchard, are among countless others as some of the great tag teams that drew money over the years. But in my opinion, Terry and Dory were the greatest tag team ever, period. I know a lot of people say the "Minnesota Wrecking Crew" of Gene and Ole Anderson were the very best, but I personally think they were overrated. The Funks had a chemistry that was unmatched in any team I had seen before or since. As for their opponents, I chose Watts and Mulligan for the sheer brutality of them being a babyface tandem in this match up. To my knowledge Bill and Bobby Jack never teamed up before and I think it would be a good fit to work the Funks. I've already said plenty about Dory and Terry, but Bill and Black Jack were two guys who could do some legitimate ass whooping. When Bobby Jack made up his mind to kick your ass, you knew you were going to get your ass handed to you. Bill was also a tough S.O.B. If you've ever heard the word "stiff" used in the business before as a description of how guys work in the ring for their believability factor, this would be the match that would illustrate that style.

Jack Brisco vs. Dick Murdoch

In this contest for the Florida Heavyweight Championship, you have the guy who was a hero to me in Jack facing the guy who was my soul mate in this business and the person who should have been the NWA World Heavyweight Champion. This is another match that is a proven product as I witnessed this match up many times and it was really a cool program. Like I said, when Hoyt was on, there was none better, and Jack was so smooth in the ring, he had that special instinct on knowing how to read a crowd by listening to its reaction. From a pure wrestling perspective, this could potentially be the best match on the card.

Fritz von Erich vs. "Big Thunder" Gene Kiniski

With America's Title on the line, this is another proven match for drawing money by standing on its own. If the match were held in Texas, it could probably be the only match on the card and still draw a huge house. This was the match that was the headliner for the first big outdoor show I remember in Arlington. While many will remember Fritz as a fan favorite in his later years, in his early days he was one of the most hated heels ever, portraying a goose-stepping, iron cross-wearing Nazi. Kiniski, on the other hand, was a former Canadian Football League player with the Edmonton Eskimos, who won the NWA World Heavyweight Championship by defeating my first hero, Lou Thesz, in 1966, only to lose it in this very building to Dory Funk, Jr. three years later. It would be interesting to see if Fritz's claw could make "Big Thunder" submit in the same building he submitted to Funk in when the Spinning Toe Hold was applied.

"Chief" Wahoo McDaniel vs. Johnny Valentine

This match would be for the North America Title and recreates one of the greatest feuds of all time. While both men had successful stints in Florida during their respective careers, both received their legendary status for taking two very different paths. Wahoo was very aware of being a role model for Native Americans and therefore was the perfect babyface at times, while Valentine personified the heel role with his cocky mannerisms and arrogance. While Wahoo was one of the most intense and violent performers in the ring, often opening up cuts on his opponent's chest with his tomahawk chops, Valentine is considered by many to be the best ever in getting his story across to the fans, something I personally witnessed and learned from. In 1970 Wahoo defeated Valentine in a vicious match for the Texas Heavyweight title, therefore making this "Starrcade Prime" match up the other bout that could potentially be the "show stealer."

Goldust vs. Freddie Blassie

In a match that would probably be more suited for the Olympic Auditorium in Los Angeles than the Tampa Armory because of it being a Hollywood type of match, there would be no title on the line necessary for this one. In what I believe to be the best gimmick to hit wrestling since

"Gorgeous" George Wagner in the 1950s, Goldust, to have him against the "Hollywood Fashion Plate" Freddie Blassie, just fits. I have always thought of Dustin as being one of the greatest athletes in the business, not because he is my son, but because of his ability. He makes what he does in the ring look so easy, almost effortless. Take those qualities and put it with the guy who was one of the first people in our business who understood the power of exposure beyond wrestling in Blassie, who guest starred on different TV shows like The Dick van Dyke Show and such, and you have a match that's a perfect ten on the entertainment scale.

The Fabulous Moolah vs. Kay Noble

As the only females on the card, this one would be for the Women's World title and features Lillian Ellison, who dominated the women's division of pro wrestling as The Fabulous Moolah for some 30 years in a match against the toughest woman who I've ever seen around a wrestling ring, Kay Noble. While Moolah was salty in her prime, personally I would pay to see this match because Kay was one of those rare women who could put an ass whooping on a guy if she were so inclined to. I'd expect this match to be nothing short of stiff, tight and something that is a bit more meaningful than the tits and ass shows we see today with women's wrestling.

So there you have it. That's my All-Star line up for "Starrcade Prime." I'm sure it included a few surprises and even a couple of disappointments, but that's the way the wrestling business is. It can't be perfect all the time.

It's pretty common that after I put together a creation, I often think that what I've done is both good and bad. I think it's important for you to know that in order to be successful in the wrestling business as a booker or executive producer, the person who has creative control, you have to be critical of yourself in order to push yourself to the next level and in order to stay on top of your game. If you don't, you're not only letting your fans down, but yourself as well.

While I would have loved to work some other top people onto the card like Andre the Giant, "Superstar" Billy Graham, and Magnum T.A. to name just a few, sometimes you have to know when not to book people for fear of overkill, because as we've been saying all along here, "business is business."

It was also hard not to include the two best managers in the history of wrestling in my opinion, "Playboy" Gary Hart and Sir Oliver Humperdink. Like the great referees who knew when to be seen and heard and when to be invisible, these two guys were the best at knowing when to keep their hands off and when to be involved. Their timing was impeccable. While having two very distinct styles, they knew how important it was to keep the focus on the wrestlers and not on themselves. They knew how far they could go without going over the top and they knew when to actually go over that line in order to make a statement for the good of the business. Plus, by being around the business from an early age, they each had that very important sixth sense of knowing what was the right thing to do in order to protect their talent.

While there were very good managers throughout the years, and I'm sure some of you will argue with me saying that Lou Albano or Jimmy Hart or The Grand Wizard or Jim Cornette or Paul E or even J.J. Dillon was the best, and they were all great in their own regards, but to me Gary and Hump were simply a cut above the rest and just the best of the best.

I was glad, however, that I was able to find spots for four of my top five performers of all-time onto the card: Jose Lothario, Dick Murdoch, Fritz von Erich, and Wahoo McDaniel. The only one who didn't find his way on the card actually wrestling was Eddie Graham, but because he would have been the head booker, well, hell, I guess that makes up for it.

So there you go. Now you've had the chance to get inside my head for just a little bit and understand more of what it takes to play matchmaker in the greatest business on Earth, professional wrestling.

So, who do you think would win these matches? Go to
http://www.dustyrhodeswrestling.com/starrcadeprime.htm
to cast your vote and to see how other fans voted.

CHAPTER 16

In late 2004 we ran a contest on my new web site, dustyrhodeswrestling.com, to search for the top ten fans of "The American Dream," Dusty Rhodes. While I've always said that if not for you, my fans, there would be no "Dream," we were overwhelmed by the thousands of responses and heartfelt sentiments that were sent in through the web site or by email.

To say that it was hard to pick the top ten from all of those submissions would be an understatement. That is why in addition to the top ten, I've also chosen 15 fans to receive Honorable Mention here.

They are in alphabetical order: Robbie Boyette (Greer, South Carolina); Frank Cabanski (Houston, Texas); Dominick Giorgianni (Gresham, Oregon); Rick Ingram (Longmont, Colorado); Dan Keefe (Falconer, New York); Malcolm A. Madison (Hilton Head Island, South Carolina); Reginald Moody (Cincinnati, Ohio); Dale L. Murphy (Lakeside, Arizona); Mark Roth (Hartford, Connecticut); Zach Thompson (Topeka, Kansas); Robert D. VanKavelaar (Williston, Florida); Andrew B. Weiner (Atlanta, Georgia); Brian Westcott (Meridian, Idaho); Ben Williams (Lusby, Maryland); and Dan Wojcik (Davenport, Iowa).

Like those who were chosen for the top ten, each of these fans captured a unique memory of me, and I thank them as I do you for letting me be a part of their life and yours, even if it has only been for a short period of time in the grand scheme of things.

So without any further delay, here now are my personal top ten selections and the winners of the "Why I am Dusty Rhodes's Biggest Fan Contest," each of who has received an autographed copy of this book from me.

10. Marc Wiggins. Sacramento, California

As a youngster growing up in Oakland, California during the '70s, I was right in the middle of the Big Time Wrestling territory, so I was introduced to the sport by guys like Rocky Johnson, Pat Patterson and Ray Stevens. As I got older, during junior high school, I began reading wrestling magazines like The Wrestler, Inside Wrestling *and later,* Pro Wrestling Illustrated.

It was in early 1976 when I read how Dusty Rhodes was on the trail of the current NWA World Champion, Terry Funk. I was riveted. Everything about him, his appearance, his relentless pursuit of the title and the way he talked, it was as if he was talking to me personally because he didn't try to portray himself as noble or heroic or above the fans. He was one of the guys, who at that point I still hadn't seen wrestle yet; I had just seen the pictures in the magazines.

In seventh grade I began to wear a gold elbow pad. My own "Bionic Elbow," if you will. I started my own wrestling organization, featuring myself and several other eighth graders, but I was the champ [it was my idea] and had a new name ... "Dusty" Wiggins. I used the "Bionic Elbow" to ward off the bullies, it only took one taste and they left me alone—and that is a direct result of "The American Dream's" influence on me.

The first time I saw Dusty wrestle was on TV during the summer of 1977. My cable company had an all-sports channel; this was in the days before ESPN or Fox Sports Net. This particular all-sports channel would show the WWWF shows from Madison Square Garden, and at the time that was a huge deal since there was no way to see those wrestlers who were on the east coast.

One day the champ, "Superstar" Billy Graham was going to defend against Dusty Rhodes. I was on the ceiling for the entire match! I had never seen anyone light up an arena like that before. It was electric.

The match ended in a count out loss by Graham. After the match, Rhodes took the house mic from Howard Finkel, the ring announcer, and said, "I came a long way to whoop your ass Graham, and this ain't over, baby!"

Now that I had actually seen him wrestle, that was it. I was hooked. I remember seeing a picture of him in a satin jacket, so of course I had to have one. He wore a ZZ Top T-shirt in another photo; I had to have one, even though at the time I had no idea who ZZ Top was.

The next time that I saw Rhodes was again on TV. But this time it was from the Central States area. Big Time Wrestling had gone out of business and the Central States promotion had begun to show their TV show out here and Rhodes was having a match with Tank Patton. After the match he was in the ring doing a live interview and during the interview there was a black woman in the crowd who was completely beside herself at the sight of Rhodes. She was jumping around and running in the aisles. Rhodes saw this and stopped the interview, saying, and I remember this like it was yesterday, "Come here, baby. Come here and gimme some of that brown sugar!" With that she jumped into the ring and he kissed her, which sent her into orbit. I thought that was the coolest thing that I ever saw.

The critics said that he couldn't win the NWA title, that if he didn't win it in 1976, then he would never win it. He refused to listen and while he didn't get it from Terry Funk, he did take it from Harley Race and he went on to win it on two other occasions. He never stopped competing.

It wasn't until 1980 or so that I actually got a chance to see "The American Dream" live. He was working with the Florida promotion and they had decided to run a few shows in San Francisco. Rhodes had a U.S. title shot against Dick Slater. I was there and he won the U.S. title that night! Watching the "Bionic Elbow" live was like nothing I had ever seen. I had been to the Cow Palace many times to see Pat Patterson and Ray Stevens, but this was like a rock concert … it was an event … this was Dusty Rhodes in my city! It didn't get any better than that!

In 1984 Oakland cable systems finally got TBS and World Championship Wrestling, this was right around the time before Starrcade '84, which unfortunately was before pay-per-view so I didn't get to see it. But I was riveted at 3:05 every Saturday afternoon until January 1986 when I left for college. But all those Saturdays had so many memories: Rhodes unveiling his "Gorilla," "The Midnight Rider," battles with Ric Flair and the Four Horsemen, teaming with Magnum T.A. and in later years forming the "Superpowers" with Nikita Koloff and being in six-man tag-team matches with the Road Warriors.

In 1989 or so I was at a friend's house who had a big satellite dish and he wanted to show me the WWF show from Boston on NESN (New England Sports Network), and there he was in the WWF! I knew that he hadn't been on TBS in a while and now he was there. That was during the time that WWF was in their "marketing to nine-year-olds" phase, so as a rule I would never watch, but that all changed with the arrival of Dusty.

I got such a kick out the vignettes of Rhodes as "the Common Man," especially the one where he played a gas station attendant and asked the timeless question, "Ever seen a dipstick before, baby?"

I have followed Rhodes's career back to WCW, ECW, and now NWA-TNA. There are so many more memories of watching and reading about him that I could probably fill a book myself, but to the man known as "The American Dream," I just want to say thanks for helping me become the man that I am today.

9. Ron Heim. Honolulu, Hawaii

I consider myself to be Dusty Rhodes's biggest fan because we go way back. From those humble days in Hollywood, Florida, to the present day in Honolulu, Hawaii, Dusty has been a hero, an entertainer and as I have come to look back, a teacher. This essay has allowed me to reflect on over 30 years of "The American Dream."

CHAPTER SIXTEEN

I am looking at these words on a color monitor but I think about the black and white television set on Saturday mornings in Hollywood, Florida. We were too young to learn much from Dusty Rhodes back then except how to deliver the "Bionic Elbow" on our couches [and each other] and to talk with that southern drawl. We all tried to be like Dusty using his words and mannerisms, but as I got older, those words began to have meaning, and "The American Dream" became more than entertainment, it became lessons of life.

The entertainment turned into teaching when I entered high school. I first learned that I was different and not accepted by other people because of my social background. My father worked two jobs to support us, but I was on a subsidized lunch program. When I pulled out that card to pay, people would make fun of me. I resented my parents for the shame it caused me. Now it was one of the best motivators of my life. Another lesson I learned was when I joined the wrestling team. I was still watching Dusty each weekend and I thought that with my confidence and charisma, I would become a champion. I was wrong, and learned about it quick. It took talent, which took dedication, discipline and focus. I learned the hard way, but I learned.

One of the biggest lessons Dusty taught me came later in my life as I live so far from my parents and have become someone they are proud of. Like I said, my dad worked two jobs to support us and he gave his all for his family. As I sat down to write this, I began to think of the times my dad took us all to see Dusty wrestling at the Hollywood Sportatorium or the Miami Beach Convention Center. I remember my mom crying when Dusty got hit from behind and knocked out and I remember how our energy was drained and we all lost our voices after the matches. We always went to see Dusty. It was exciting, fun and pure energy. Today though, I see a lesson of how my father must have been so tired from working and still managed to take us to the matches. I don't think he loved wrestling as much as we did. He loved to see us love something like wrestling and "The American Dream."

In the '80s we got a color television with cable! Dusty was still in Florida, but he was on the move too, in Georgia. It was also time for me to move on if I was going to be "The American Dream." The U.S. Army was my ticket to "The American Dream." It became the "ring" in which I would win many championships. It no longer mattered who you were, or how much money you came from. Everything started out equal and you moved up only with talent, drive and focus. Combined with the charisma I learned from those Saturday mornings in Hollywood, Florida, it was easy and fun. I went from buck private to a commissioned officer in three years and along the way picked up medals with the words "the best" on them. Those were my championship belts.

I took on all challenges, was never afraid of losing and always gaining more confidence. While in the Army, I was stationed in Hawaii and I didn't get to watch wrestling. One time though, in the mid-eighties, Dusty came to visit and I saw him at Aloha Stadium. Just like the old days, I was seated far from the ring, but I could tell that when Dusty was going to drop the elbow, he would pause, look straight at me for just a brief second until I yelled, "Go get him, Dust" and then lay it on. I bet lots of people felt Dusty was looking right at them as well, but I knew it was me.

Here I am today, retired from the Army, but still in Hawaii. After getting out, I had to start from the bottom again, but I had good practice by that point. Right now I think of what's valuable to me. Maybe it's this $750,000 house, or the membership in the private club I belong to, or the private school my son goes to. Nope. I still love my truck, I still rock to the Allman Brothers and I still pour Sonny's Barbecue Sauce on my ribs. I am who I was and always will be. I'm proud of that fact, that's my tradition, and I learned that from Dusty Rhodes and that black and white television.

My son is three and his environment in Hawaii is much different than mine was in Hollywood. I try to give him the best and things I never had. I already see from his school there are the same kinds of people who didn't accept me because of how I paid for my lunch. He'll be okay because he has my spirit and pride. He will know where he came from and to value his tradition. He may not be the "Son of a Plumber," but he is the "Grandson of a Corrections Officer." My son and I still watch Dusty's matches on DVD, just him and me. He is too young to understand any lessons, so it is just pure entertainment. He takes off his shirt, yells "My Bidness" and jumps on the couch with his "Ebb-low."

Over 30 years and 6,000 miles later, Dusty is still entertaining me and I hope helping me teach my son a lesson about "The American Dream."

Thanks and Aloha Big Dust!

8. Tyre Davis. Phoenix, Arizona

If you polled wrestling fans with the question, "Who is the greatest of all time?" it would be interesting to see that those who "looked the part" would usually be the first names mentioned. Those raised in the era of ruggedness would point out Harley Race, while those in the era of style, it was Ric Flair. For unabridged charisma you loved Hulk Hogan and when it came to attitude, the name "Stone Cold" Steve Austin would easily top the list.

However, there is one man who transcended it all. One man exhibited ruggedness, style, charisma and attitude in its purest form. That man was Virgil Runnels. That man was Dusty Rhodes!

For today's generation Dusty wouldn't be what one visualizes as an athlete, but the greatness of Big Dust was that he turned something so vague and so intangible as "The American Dream" into something you could easily latch onto. In a sport and art form where authenticity is always questioned, Dusty Rhodes was the one guy you ALWAYS believed in. With that unforgettable drawl and cadence of a Baptist preacher, "The American Dream" took his opponents not only to school, but to church as well. Dusty was the "feel good" wrestler of his and future eras to come.

Dusty could not only talk the talk, but in the ring he consistently walked the walk. When the term great worker is thrown around, for me, two things come to mind: a performer who has the ability to tell an awesome story with ANYONE in the ring; and someone who could draw the big crowds and the big money. While he may never be given credit, based on that criteria, Dusty is one of the greatest workers of all time. As much as their own abilities made the Horsemen legends, it was Dusty Rhodes who made them deities. Dusty could tell a story with Flair, Arn, Tully, Windham, Luger and if given the chance would have made a monster out of Sid. Dusty told great stories with each of them and consequently sold out, sold out and sold out.

Why am I a Dusty Rhodes fan? It's simple. Out of all the wrestlers I've seen in 20 years, Dusty is the one I could most relate to. It wasn't because he was big and bad or the "Bull of the Woods." It wasn't because of his genius or his talent or his magnetism. It's not for being a successful businessman or a three-time NWA World Champion. It's because Dusty taught us all, taught me how make reality out of a dream!

7. Craig Whyel. Belle Vernon, Pennsylvania

When the renowned Studio Wrestling out of Pittsburgh bit the dust in the early seventies after several incarnations, we wrestling fans in Southwestern Pennsylvania were bummed. No Internet. No cable TV. The five VHF stations we received contained no wrestling whatsoever.

When my brother and I got our first twelve-inch black and white TV for Christmas, we found a new wonder to television: UHF stations. After nearly electrocuting myself trying to attach a World War II era set of rabbit ears atop the set, we found that we could pick up other stations. At one point, we were up to a whopping eleven stations. One night, while maneuvering the rabbit ears about with an effort equal to a Tae Bo workout, my brother stopped me in my tracks with a magic word: Wrestling.

I had stumbled onto a station, I think out of Parma or somewhere in Ohio that was carrying some sort of promotion. It seemed that there was a great amount of guys coming out of Pittsburgh, Buffalo, Cleveland, Detroit, and beyond [before the great monopoly, there seemed to be a great amount of talent exchanged between the territories that brought in fresh faces].

The show would fade in and out with the persistent UHF snow being a constant nuisance.

I had a brainstorm. If I opened up the front window and sat the TV into the window sill and reached those damned rabbit ears out of the window, I could keep the show on fairly intact, and I'm glad I did, because one night I got to see a young stud from Texas [through what I believe was the Detroit promotion] wrestle. I remember hearing the name "Dusty" and I didn't catch the last name but that certainly would come in time. Regardless, he was an instant favorite in my book.

I don't remember who he wrestled, because the bitter Pittsburgh evening was kicking up a nasty wind through the window so much so that I had to wrap myself in a blanket. Anyhow, this guy from Texas, a big dude with a thick build entered the ring wearing a tie die shirt, a cap we called a "pimp hat" that covered an Afro hairdo, and carried a cowbell. When he got down to business between the ropes, I saw that he was without the great muscle-head physiques that we were used to seeing out of Pittsburgh. It didn't matter. He was as slick as a puma, he hit with power and when he dropped the "Bionic Elbow" on his opponent, the studio audience went nuts. I did too, but I kept it quiet because my parents were downstairs bellowing about someone letting in the cold air. [I lied, of course].

Eventually the TV died and I once again was without wrestling until the late 1970s when Dusty was making his way through the WWWF and a monster riff with "Superstar" Billy Graham. I got to see him in glorious color and was never disappointed. Always fun. Always entertaining.

I wish I had a better tale about getting out of my sick bed and riding hundreds of miles in a blinding storm just to shake hands with him as he made his way to the ring, but I don't. There's no tear-jerking inspirational homily about meeting him in person and tell what a great guy he was. [Maybe someday I'll get a chance].

There's just me, with a blanket wrapped around skinny shoulders, sticking my little black and white TV out of the upstairs bedroom window of our family house, freezing my ass off just to get a chance to see Big Dusty.

It was worth every shivering second of it.

I lied to my folks, raised the heating bill and nearly fell out of the window a few times trying to get it right. Now, almost thirty years later, I can tell you without hesitation that I would do it all again in a heartbeat just for the chance to see Dusty Rhodes wrestle.

I love you, Dusty. Thanks for the great memories.

6. Randy Bodell. Pittsburgh, Pennsylvania

Dusty Rhodes's larger than life yet "common man" persona had a direct impact on the culturing and development of my own personal growth as a human being.

As a child from an average middle class family, my parents always somehow managed to squeak out a week's summer vacation. In the mid- to late '70s one of our weeks was in Miami, Florida. Already a wrestling fan and avid reader of wrestling magazines, the legend that was evolving—Dusty Rhodes—was of great anticipation to possibly witnessing him in action on this particular vacation.

While staying at the Dunes Hotel on Miami Beach and reading the Miami Herald, *the ad was there in black and white. Luck had it. We were in town the perfect time when Dusty was wrestling. I was so excited, my father took me and I was a hooked Dusty fanatic.*

The Dusty charisma and persona was such a strong influence on me that after that vacation, I urged my parents to vacation every summer in Miami so I could at least catch Dusty once a year in person! My family may have liked Florida for other reasons as well, but I like to think that the return trips—ten years in a row —were in part due to my urgings to go back to see Dusty wrestle and perform.

At the same time I was in my adolescence, growing up in the inner city of Pittsburgh, Pennsylvania, with the diverseness of ethnicity, races, religions, etc. I found communicating, connecting, and cultivating relationships with other kids was very important to getting along in life. Through Dusty's mannerisms, witticisms, and general communication, I found myself emulating and embodying many of those same characteristics. I was able to get along with the black kid, the Puerto Rican kid, the German kid, the super-smart kid, the not-so-smart kid— as a Jewish kid. Dusty gave me that.

My father is most definitely the strongest figure in my life for several reasons; far too deep to explore here. But Dusty Rhodes was a figure to relate to on several levels. My personality has roots of Rhodes. The clothing, the gift of gab, the "presence" of being somebody, all of which Dusty embodied took form in myself. Respect for others and treating everyone, as I wanted to be treated—with that sincere knowledge of good and bad, right and wrong, just and unjust—all have a base Dusty getting those attributes across from the TV and the arena to my life. For that I am forever grateful to Dusty Rhodes.

Besides starting to collect wrestling magazines that began in the '70s, so I could read and see more of Dusty while living in the northeast, I also purchased by mail from photographers who would shoot in Florida, as I would buy photos of Dusty as well. I loved the sport as a whole, but Dusty was definitely my favorite wrestler through the years.

To fast forward, I was fortunate enough to meet Dusty in 2003 on an independent show in the Pittsburgh area. Doing backstage work for a local show, I got to spend some time around Dusty. Although I didn't show it in my outside demeanor, on the inside I was "marking out" big time. The man I literally grew with from my youth to being a 40-year-old was right there in living color, IF YOU WILL!

I didn't have a long conversation with him, but I got a few items autographed, listened to a few stories, and came away with a genuine feeling that after all those years, Dusty truly was and is "The American Dream."

Thank you, Dusty!

5. David Cottom Jr. Ambler, Pennsylvania

I first saw Dusty Rhodes on TV about 1975 or 1976. Since I lived in the Northeast [WWWF Philadelphia area], I had only seen Dusty Rhodes a couple of times before in the wrestling magazines of the time and briefly on Florida and Georgia wrestling shows of the '70s and '80s that I would see infrequently on Philly UHF channels or when I would visit my cousins down in Atlanta during the summer.

However, to a kid growing up during that time, Dusty looked and acted cool. No wrestler was even close to Dusty's big-time Texas style; big stars on the wrestling boots, red, white and blue jacket and tights, bushy blonde hair, an Apple Jack hat and preaching about "the American Dream." I loved hearing his "jive" talk and telling fans WHAT he was going to do an opponent, BEFORE a match, and then actually DOING IT during the match.

For those of us that were childhood wrestling fans back in the '70s and early '80s, Dusty Rhodes was Muhammad Ali, Evil Knievel and Bruce Lee all wrapped up into one. Dusty's matches were classic "old school" and what pro wrestling should always be —two guys either settling a score or the stories of competition, the eternal quest for the championship. No matter what it was, Dusty Rhodes was the guy you needed to see get the best of Ric Flair or any of the major heels of the time. No one, as I remember, rooted for the "bad guy" when Dusty was in the ring.

I have been a wrestling fan since 1967. There aren't many times that I can remember crying during a wrestling show, but two events quickly come to mind:

CHAPTER SIXTEEN

Whenever Dusty talked about "the best day of his life being also the worst day of his life," referring to his father dying on the same day that his son, Dustin was born. You could always hear the hurt AND the pride every time he referred to this. I've always thought about how hard that must be to live with and how there must not be a day that goes by where he doesn't think about it. It is one of those things that you just have to hear.

When Dusty gave an emotional speech to his son Dustin about "being your own man" and "being the best" and if you end up always being a "follower," how "the view never changes." Anytime I might be feeling low, I pull out the tape and watch this interview. I know that was real because my own father has given me the same speech many, many times. It is one of those rare moments where you could see the true passion and the feeling between father and son.

Dusty Rhodes always made me feel good about being a pro wrestling fan. This was at a time when you couldn't talk about being a fan Professional Wrestling even in CASUAL situations. These were the days when most people weren't sure whether wrestling was real or fake. Because of Dusty, I didn't care what people thought of professional wrestling, I remain a fan even to this day.

Go back and look at some of the old NWA tapes and look at the crowd response during a Dusty match. No matter who the opponent was, whether it was when the Andersons turned on him during the match with the Assassins, Dusty winning his NWA titles or the Barry Windham heel turn, Dusty made it real for everyone watching. He made you believe.

"The American Dream" was a concept that I had heard many times during my life, and damn it, America is STILL the greatest country on Earth. Going to work, making a living for your family and having time to enjoy yourself IS "the American Dream." During his career, Dusty Rhodes has embodied that spirit and all that it entails.

Dusty Rhodes is truly the most charismatic wrestler that has ever lived. No one has combined telling a story during a match in the ring in combination with real life personal events like Dusty has. For me, it has been 30 years of seeing Dusty during his many, many high points and his times of "pain, blues and agony."

I wouldn't trade that for anything in the world. Thanks, Big Dust.

4. Allen L. Kelso. Amarillo, Texas

I started watching wrestling at a very early age. My parents hated it and always said it was not real, but Dusty Rhodes was MORE REAL to me than anyone in any type of sports. He would fight anyone at anytime in any place. I was always the little skinny kid, but when I turned on the TV and saw Dusty kicking ass and taking names, I knew you didn't have to be a huge, muscle-bound giant to be the very best at whatever you wanted to do in life.

As I grew older I lost track of wrestling for a few years because of fast cars and running around after the ladies. But in 1985 I joined the U.S. Army as a military policeman and I once again started watching wrestling. Once again it was Dusty and he was one hundred percent "The American Dream" fighting for everything he was worth against the evil force of the Four Horsemen.

When I was not deployed to different places around the world, I was stuck to the NWA watching Rhodes fight off Ric Flair and the other Horsemen. In 1989 I got to go to Starrcade with my wife who was seven months pregnant with my daughter. I would be leaving for Europe in a few months and my wife got me the tickets for Christmas. I got to shake Dusty's hand as he was leaving the ring covered in his own blood and I have the tape of us sitting three rows back and loving every minute of the action.

Now I am out of the Army living back in Amarillo, Texas, and I have achieved a "Dream" of my own. Still not the biggest guy in the area, but I have a great job and an even better family. I have only been back home for 11 months now, but I have been lucky enough to be part of a local wrestling promotion as a manager and I only hope to be able to put on a show here and one day have one of the kids at ringside see us and say, "Even though I am not the biggest one around, if they can do what they do every week, then I also have a very good shot in life." One day I hope to work a show where Dusty is booked on the very same card.

Thank you, Dusty, for all the great memories!

3. Jeff Lumpkin. Huntsville, Texas

Why I'm Dream's biggest fan? Um, how to even start? I was a chunky kid, kind of athletic, but so shy. ... I had come to believe that you had to have a great body to be popular or be an athlete.

That all changed for me in the early '70s. I had started watching Houston Wrestling with Paul Boesch every Saturday night. One night Bad Leroy Brown was fighting Killer Karl Krupp and was in the midst of the claw hold, when down the aisle came a man with blonde curly hair and a stove top hat with a chicken foot on it ... not an Adonis by any means, but even at that early age I knew he was electric

He got on the house mic and said, "Mr. Promoter play it one more time," and they started playing Brown's music and he came alive ... someone else came down to help Krupp and soon the man I later learned was Dusty Rhodes, came in and helped clean house with the "Bionic Elbow" and a charisma I'd never before or since. The next thing I saw was an interview with the "man of the hour, too sweet to be sour, the tower of power" ... and by God, the "Son of a Plumber" from Austin Texas ... and who could ever forget the million-dollar smile?

I was hooked from then on and developed a new self-image that propelled me to be very popular in high school ... watching every week on Houston Wrestling, Mid-south, Atlanta and WCW ... through his feuds with the Sheik, Abdullah the Butcher, the Four Horsemen, and a hundred others. To pick one favorite moment would be tough, but if put to the task I believe it would be back in Mid-South after Dusty lost a loser leaves town match and then came the first promo for the Midnight Rider. I marked out, as they say, so bad that I could hardly breathe.

But in truth "The American Dream" has given me so many moments in the last 30-plus years that I can't pick one, but can only hope that I can relay in my own little way how grateful I am that Virgil Runnels became my hero, Dusty Rhodes "The American Dream" and helped me see how much more I could be.

Thanks Dusty, and God bless you.

2. Greg Fiske. Homestead, Florida

For a wrestling fan growing up in New York in 1980, there was one hour of WWWF wrestling a week at midnight. At that point, the only exposure to the wrestling world outside of New York came from the wrestling magazines.

The wrestling magazines loved Dusty and painted a picture of him being a gritty, gutsy competitor who seemed to win against all odds. Dusty was a New York favorite, primarily for his run at "Superstar" Billy Graham's title reign in 1977. After his WWWF stint, Dusty would appear at Madison Square Garden once a year or on special occasions.

Unfortunately, I became a fan of wrestling at a time in between one of his Madison Square Garden appearances. So, all I really knew of Dusty was from the bloody pictures and romantic articles in Pro Wrestling Illustrated.

I was a regular at the monthly Monday night Garden cards and at some point in 1981 it was announced that Dusty was going to make a guest appearance against King Kong Angelo Mosca. I was pretty psyched because this was my first chance to see "The American Dream" live.

When I got to the Garden on the night of the event, I noticed from the program that Dusty's match was last. Back in those days, they would put the World Title match in the middle of the card and not at the end. On this night I am fairly sure that there were two big main event matches with Bob Backlund and Pedro Morales that would go on before Dusty's match, so it was almost guaranteed that the crowd would be burned out and ready to go home by the time Dusty faced Mosca.

I have to laugh, because this is the funniest part of the story. Halfway through the show, I got really sick. I started to run a fever and have really bad stomach cramps. By the main event I had gone to the bathroom seven times with diarrhea. I was feeling really bad. I had some sort of stomach virus or flu; however, I waited and waited because I wanted to see Dusty.

Finally, at 10:40 p.m., King Kong Mosca entered the ring and grabbed the microphone and yelled, "Dusty Rhodes get your big fat ass out here." Dusty came prancing out and jumped in the ring and the crowd went nuts. It was amazing because the crowd had already seen a few other big matches, but they gladly stayed until the end and were going nuts for Dusty. This formula would never work today, because everyone is patterned on going home after the so-called main event.

I momentarily forgot about my situation and jumped up and down for Dusty. Unfortunately I forgot about everything and had an accident in my pants. It was horrible. You can imagine the subway ride home.

Soon after this incident, cable television brought WTBS to where I lived and I saw Dusty every week. Years later, I moved to Florida and actually became a professional wrestler for a short period of time.

Dusty, thanks again for the memories!

1. Frank Ginocchio. Wilmington, Delaware

When people meet one of their heroes, they're always concerned about either the person or the experience living up to their expectations. I can wholeheartedly say that whatever expectations or hopes of meeting Dusty

Rhodes I may have ever had were definitely exceeded! The magical part of it all is that I never thought it would happen.

I have been a fan of Dusty Rhodes for 29 years. I was eight years old when I first saw Dusty wrestle. It was 1976 on TV and I have been a fan of his from then to this very day. I saw Dusty wrestle "Superstar" Billy Graham in a bull rope match at the Philadelphia Spectrum from the second row. It was one of the most memorable matches I've ever seen. Every time Dusty would get the upper hand on Graham, there was a thunderous roar and when Dusty was down, the crowd stomped so loudly I thought the roof was caving in.

Then around 1979, we started to get the Superstation TBS and I saw Dusty on Georgia Championship Wrestling. I was glued to the TV every Saturday night from 6:05 to 8:05.

I grew up in a lower middle-class neighborhood. I was 11 years old and pretty insecure and the more I saw Dusty on TV and how he carried himself, he made me feel better about myself and I started to gain more confidence. Dusty was the good guy, the hero that thwarted evil. When he got knocked down, he got right back up and eventually prevailed, and oh boy, could he talk. He was the common man, the plumber's son, and the simple unassuming man that just wanted what was rightfully his and fought long and hard to get it and keep it. I totally related to this on a personal level. Whatever Dusty was selling, I was buying every bit of it. He made me truly believe that I could be somebody if I kept trying. He was my role model growing up. If he did something, like winning the NWA belt, I believed I could achieve my goals. Now that's much more powerful than being told to say my prayers and take my vitamins.

In 1996, I finally realized my childhood dream of meeting Dusty at a WCW promotional event at Tower Records near Philly. I brought my camera and some pictures in the hopes that he would sign them and take a picture with me. As I was waiting in line I kept thinking about what I would say to him when I got there. I swore I wouldn't do the cliché "Hey, I'm a longtime fan!" I got up there, showed him the pictures and he signed them and stood for a picture with me but I was so nervous, the first thing that came out of my mouth was "Hey Dusty, I've been fan of yours for over 20 years!"

In 2000, I came across Dusty's then-brand new web site and noticed that the webmaster, Clyde Sherman, was looking for anyone that had pictures of Dusty that he could use for the web site. I contacted Clyde and told him what a huge fan I was of Dusty and that I had some pictures for him to use and offered to help any way I could. During the course of our conversations, Clyde mentioned a wrestling show coming up in Rome, Georgia, and that I should come and check it out. He said I could show up early and meet Dusty! Without any consideration, I immediately decided that I was going to drive over 1,400 miles to Rome, Georgia, and meet Dusty Rhodes! I grabbed everything I had for Dusty to sign and hit the road. I met Clyde at the venue and he introduced me to Dusty. I went to shake his hand and Dusty pulled me in and gave me a big hug and thanked me for coming down! Here I am meeting my all-time ultimate hero and he's thanking me! He gave me a couple of T-shirts and told me to go get whatever I wanted him to sign. We sat down and talked while he was signing my stuff and he was telling the stories behind some of my memorabilia.

After that, he slapped an all-access pass on my shirt and put me to work setting up chairs. The whole Turnbuckle crew treated me like family, almost as if they knew how significant this was for me. It was truly one of the greatest highlights of my life.

About a year later, I went back down for another show in Carrollton, Georgia. Since then, I've seen him several times at shows and fan conventions in Philly. It is amazing that he always remembers me when I go up to him.

So were my expectations exceeded? I'll put it this way, if the first time I met Dusty at Tower Records was the only time, it would have been fine with me, but to have lived the experience of actually laughing, talking, and listening to stories from the man who was so influential throughout my life was an incredibly significant moment. That is why I am, and always will be Dusty Rhodes #1 fan, bar none!

Now if that hasn't convinced you, try my Top Ten List:

10. *I have an entire wall dedicated to all the Dusty memorabilia I've collected and had signed by Dusty over the years.*
9. *I submitted photos from my collection for Dusty's first website and had the honor of being asked to give ideas for and to be a part of The Dusty Rhodes Fan Club.*
8. *I'm an official Dustyism translator.*
7. *I actually saw Dusty's Stanback commercials when they first aired.*
6. *I was once restrained by security at an ECW show for climbing over the rail to save Dusty from being jumped. [What can I say? I'm still a mark]*
5. *I drove over 1,400 miles from DE to GA twice to see Dusty.*
4. *Dusty's agent contacted me to work Dusty's merchandise table at a show in Philly.*
3. *The picture of Dusty and me is on my living room   mantle along with our wedding and other family photos. [Married guys or guys who live with a   woman should understand why this is noteworthy].*
2. *I stuck with him through the polka-dot years.*
1. *Two words: "Paradise Park" [Only a real fan knows   what that is].*

Isn't that something else? You have no idea how it makes me feel to know that I affected so many people across such a wide scope in so many different ways.

Like that old television show used to say, there are a million stories in the naked city, and these ten each had their own unique quality to me that set them apart from all the others.

Like I've said before, if not for you, my fans, "The American Dream," Dusty Rhodes would not have come into being.

So, thanks again for letting me live "the American Dream" by being "The American Dream."

CHAPTER 17

Being able to change is not what they call "the flow of the book." But fuck the flow of the book; Johnny Cash is dead. I remember when he died ... man, it's hard to say this, but his impact on me when I was a child was even more than Elvis. When I was older, we traveled many nights on the road together.

It was around 5 a.m. and I was leaving Baton Rouge, Louisiana, for Oklahoma City after one of those all-night wrestling-type parties. With no sleep, still being half-drunk and taking speed to stay awake, I hit the road and was driving somewhere through Mississippi on a backwoods road. It was about 11 a.m. I was on a winding road through cotton-pickin' U.S.A.; fields of white balls on both sides of the road, black men and women bent over with cotton sacks on their back.

On the radio, or maybe the eight-track tape player—if you don't know what an eight-track is, ask someone older than 35, because you won't know what I am talking about—was the Johnny Cash song "Ring of Fire." It was blasting as loud as could be as both my windows were down because my air-conditioner was not working and it was already about a hundred degrees outside.

"Love is a burning thing
And it makes a fiery ring
Bound by wild desire
I fell into a ring of fire..."

Half asleep, I lost control of my car and suddenly found myself speeding wildly through the cotton fields ... men, women and children were running away; shear pandemonium at hand … the look of horror on their faces and the panic on mine … finally coming to a stop as the dust, cotton and heat filled my car. I can close my eyes and I still hear "Ring of Fire" playing so loud; the stillness of the area in the aftermath was almost deafening.

> *"I fell into a burning ring of fire*
> *I went down, down, down*
> *And the flames went higher.*
> *And it burns, burns, burns*
> *The ring of fire*
> *The ring of fire"*
>
> *—Johnny Cash "Ring of Fire*

I made sure everyone was all right; I climbed back up on Johnny's back and headed for Oklahoma City! All I can remember was thinking, "How many of those haul working cotton pickers realized that 'The American Dream,' Dusty Rhodes, just visited their work site?"

I know you've walked through the light, Johnny. So long, my old friend.

When I think back on the business, I always go back to the road because that's where I've spent most of my life. Even now, when driving in my car, sometimes I'll listen to Johnny, but most of the time I'll listen to Willie Nelson or if it's in the morning, I'll listen to one of my favorite radio personalities, Don Imus. I spent a lot of time on the road listening to Don and he's a great thinker, when you get past all the crap and silliness. If they ever asked me who I would want as a manager in the wrestling business, I'd have to say that it would be Imus, but back in the era of Woodstock, when he would be in a stupor, because that was my era too.

But, of all the places I've been, and I've said this a lot to you fans and to the people who covered me through the years, Florida is that place that brought me to the dance. So when I think back on my career, I reflect back on that era in Tampa, because that is where the majority of the people were, who've touched me and touched our industry back then. You have to remember, back then there were no Tampa Bay Buccaneers, or Tampa Bay Devil Rays, wrestling was the only game in town, produced by the Godfather of the region, Eddie Graham and Championship Wrestling from Florida.

Tuesday nights were when I held court and I held it at the Imperial Lounge Room where Yolie and Doc Castellano were the owners. That was the happening place. It was after the matches at the Armory on Tuesday nights and the old country stars would come in there ... the country boys. Captain Lewis, my bro, my posse, led the house band and we would go there and we'd hold court. A lot of really great stories came out of there like the attack by Terry Funk that I talked about earlier, but I remember Doc and his wife so fondly as we would eat Sunday dinner over their house—Cuban beans and rice. As a matter of fact, Michelle's and my first meeting came at the Imperial Lounge after the matches.

It's a lot of great memories, and when I talk about Tampa, I can't help reflecting back about how the legendary newspaperman Tom McEwen of the *Tampa Tribune*, an icon of his own industry, covered the sport of wrestling for Eddie there like it was a real sport; because that's what it was to us! Andy Hardy, another Bay-area icon at Channel 13, covered us on the local news, and then there was "Salty" Saul Fleischmann, the local sportscaster way back then, who'd give the results from the matches at the Armory on TV ... the Armory back then was as I called it, the Madison Square Garden of the south.

Everybody who was anybody in our industry wrestled at the Fort Homer W. Hesterly Armory on Howard Avenue in Tampa except for the ultimate sports entertainer of our era, yellow finger himself, Hulk Hogan. That was one of his dreams, to wrestle there. But he sure as shit saw plenty of matches there involving me, Sullivan, Matsuda, Eddie ... he saw us all ... and he took it all in. The Macho Man, Randy Savage was there too, as a frequent visitor who watched the matches. So those were great times.

I had my posse as we talked about, but my leaders were the old statesmen of the industry who, just like the Mafia consigliore—who you would go to confide with and seek their wisdom and advice—Henry Gonzalez, still my attorney today, was one of the most famous attorneys in the entire world.

Somebody who is really dear to me in some of things he said about me, George Steinbrenner, is a guy who is, to me, the greatest sports figure in the history of sports, even more than the figures of the NFL like Pete Rozelle and those guys. George is also the most powerful owner of the most recognizable property in all of sports, my favorite team, of course as you know, the New York Yankees. He was a guy who came to the Armory, came to the Sun Dome, and despite his larger-than-life persona, would always be inconspicuous. He would sit and watch the matches and he loved it. And I always respected that about him because he could have easily overshadowed us, but he didn't, because he supported me so much, and the times that we'd talk, it was an unbelievable experience for me. I always called him "the Boss" as he was and is just that, "the Boss" ... not a bigger sports figure in our era, and I'm talking about every aspect of sports. The fact that I can call him a friend is really cool.

The fact Steinbrenner was friends with many of my friends was also cool. One of those friends was Father Laurence Higgins, who later received the title of Monsignor. When he became Monsignor Higgins, it was like he had gotten this award, and I didn't know where he got it from. I still don't know what they do to go from being a father to a monsignor, how they go from being at a Willie Nelson concert with me drinking the wine that goes to the church out of the back of a car. I don't know where they get that from, but when he became a monsignor, that was a big deal, because he got pictures of him and the Pope together.

I think about him every day, not a day goes by where he doesn't come into my thoughts. I remember one time asking him for a favor, when he was going to Rome to visit the Pope, and I think he and the Pope were on like an "I'll call you on the cell phone"–type basis. He had the Pope's number on speed dial. I guess he would say, "Hey Pope, it's me, Monsignor Higgins, what's going on?" Well, we had this big picnic called the "Rhodes Picnic," which he was a part of; he came out. I knew he was going to Rome and I wanted him to take the Pope a T-shirt, one of my Dusty Rhodes T-shirts! In my head, I was imagining this scene—as egotistical as I am—where the Pope comes out on the balcony in Vatican City, looking over the vast sea of people ... thousands standing below like they usually do, and he has his white robe on ... and he just rips open the robe and there it is ... he's wearing a black "Rhodes Picnic" T-shirt that Monsignor Higgins gave him from me. So when I knew that wasn't gonna fly, I asked Monsignor Higgins to wear it underneath his deal and then bring it back to me ... this way it'd be close to me and God and all of those things. I don't know who gave him that award, but I know God gave it to him, so it's really cool with me. I don't think anybody is as close to God as Monsignor Higgins, and I think that's why he's continuously on my mind, in my thoughts. Reflecting back on him was so important.

And when I talk about my posse and everybody else who was involved in it, I've got to talk about the guys who were just part of that whole experience. Dick Slater to me was one of the great performers in our industry, and he was a big bud of mine back then and he was part of everything that was going on and that Imperial Lounge. I think about Miami too, not just Tampa, and I think about "Peanut" and Judy; they were two of my biggest fans, still to this day two of my biggest fans ... and they were fans when fans were fans, man! They were just cool about everything.

I reflect back to Bobby Jack—big Black Jack Mulligan—who's one of my closest friends and somebody I love so dearly. Watching that big bastard do things was unbelievable, and I remember back on some of those times and smile.

I remember the times when the Bucs first played in the NFL and won their first game. Chelle and I were sitting in the owners box with Hugh Culverhouse when they won their first game ever! Doug Williams was the fucking quarterback.

All of those things that happened in Yeehaw Junction, like the time I pulled into this gas station and there was Arlo Guthrie's tour bus and I saw two legs sticking out from underneath and I said, "Arlo?" and he said, "Dream?" and I said, "Where the fuck is your bus driver?" and he said, "You're looking at him. I'm the bus driver, the mechanic, and the singer. ..."

It was just a great time.

So really everything kind of came out of Florida, came out of that area, came out of that time. The Willie Nelson and Boxcar Willie concerts, David Allan Coe and Hank Williams Jr., being on the road and crossing paths with these guys, like Dickie Betts. Michelle used to say nobody played a guitar like Dickie and it was the coolest thing to see him play his guitar with the cigarette he was smoking, sucking the top of it while he's playing on stage.

And of course Chelle's family and the party that Henry Gonzalez threw for our wedding at that Columbia restaurant in Ybor City, it was right out of *The Godfather* movie. If you had the same music, it was the same thing, it was phenomenal.

Art Wiggins, who later passed away, was the president of the bank and he took Lee Roy Selmon, who was one of the Tampa Bay Bucs, who became a bank executive, under his wing. Hell, the Lee Roy Selmon Expressway is one of the city's major thoroughfares, and in 2000, he partnered with Outback Steakhouse to open Lee Roy Selman's, a restaurant that claims "Soul Satisfying Southern Cooking." I think about that a lot, what it meant just to drive around Tampa and have everybody be a fan of yours. All of those guys and all of those people I mentioned, that's really what made Dusty Rhodes "The American Dream," and what means the most to me.

I think about Michelle's family and our current family, and Bobbi Ann, Bobby Rodriguez's daughter. I call Bobby "Notorious" and "Black Robert," names that you would only read in magazines that you probably shouldn't be reading. But Bobby is a cool guy. And Michelle's dad, Ralph Rubio, is the greatest Domino player of all time. When I think about it, he was in Cuba when Che Guevara came down the street and they were taking over Havana. He was still the manager of the hotel and the big casino at the time, before Cuba fell to Fidel Castro and communism.

Great stories, great times and an era that can't be matched or duplicated, and so it's our memories that we tend to savor and sometimes you just had to think back and see what you really remember. I always say that you have to give credit to the guys who brought you to where you are, they really brought "The American Dream," Dusty Rhodes, to the dance. They were great times, great posse members and great senior members.

When you think about Tampa Bay, it's always the Armory. It's unbelievable, you just think of all the things that went down in there, angles, feuds, all the emotion that was in that place, the old dressing rooms, history, just great times.

But now, it's an empty house.

The kids—Teil and Cody—have gone to California to be movie stars. Dustin is in Florida and Kristin is in our home of Austin, Texas. Michelle and I and Cody's dog Goober are in what Cody calls our ancestral home in Marietta, Georgia.

I am still on the road with promoters. Bert Prentice and Bob Ryder were with me when my mom died two years ago; they are two of her angels because they watched over me.

My best buddies, Greg Troupe, David Qualls, Captain Lewis, Banny Rooster, Dallas Page, Senator Green and J.D. Douthit stay close too, along with my new posse, Big Tillie, Smoothie Kane, Ray Lloyd (aka Glacier), and Red River Pete (Keith Mitchell). They are good people, as are Peanut, Judy and Janie Engle.

I am working every weekend, writing on *Smackdown*. Mike O'Brien keeps me working; he is a good agent and we are friends.

The business has really changed. I can't complain, because the new boys and girls have only learned one way to go at it in the ring. Every once in a while one of them will surprise me and it gives me hope for our business. They are the future. They need to find a leader out of the pack or they will stay lost. I like them all. They are my kids, just like they are Hogan's, Flair's, and the Funks', all of our kids!

Wrestling in the future will go on as I've said before. I won't retire until Terry Funk hangs them up. He has semi-retired something like ten times. Oh well, the road is still my life and it always has been. Michelle has been with me the whole time. She is my strength, my drive, my best friend, and the thing I love along with my kids and grandbabies, more than life itself.

My dream is to go back in time to the old West, cowboy days, living on the vast land of Texas, riding the wide-open spaces.

God gave me the greatest gift of all, my children, and then let me make a living in the greatest business ever thought up by man. If I truly am a star, it's all because of the people who made me—you, the fans! Without that roar, that sound of walking into the arena, that chant of your name, that knowledge that you did your best to entertain everyone there, it would never be worth it all. So to all of you I say, "Thanks for making *my* dream come true! I love you."

To all wrestlers and wrestling fans reading this, just remember that the future is the past.

And finally to my co-author Howard Brody, thanks for working on this with me.

"L.A. Dream Land"

Morning breaks a new day
Providing us with chance
But only doers and dream makers
Will have the chance to dance

Break away from the smoggy morning
Clear the sky to blue
For in this L.A. dream land
Your dreams they wait for you

DUSTY RHODES: REFLECTIONS OF AN AMERICAN DREAM

Leave nothing here to chance
For your trip down stardust lane
Make sure nothing is overlooked
That could keep you from your fame

Break away from the smoggy morning
Clear the sky to blue
For in this L.A. dream land
Your dreams they wait for you

—*Dusty Rhodes, Los Angeles, 1994*

EPILOGUE

Many of you are probably saying to yourselves, "Okay, Dream, that was great. But, what about tits and ass in this book?"

Well, for those of you who really want tits and ass, I came up with this story. ...

It was a hot Austin, Texas summer. I was 16 years old and me and my boys were sitting around talking on a Wednesday night after running the streets all day. We were in the backyard under the big and bright star filled-night, when one of us, I don't remember which one said, "Let's go to Mexico this weekend."

Well, due to the fact that they were all of Mexican heritage and spoke Spanish, I thought, "What the hell ... why not?"

The plan was to tell our parents that we would be spending the weekend over at Ronnie Angle's house, who was one of our friends. Ronnie, however, was out of town and we would actually leave on Friday after we pooled our money. We'd head to San Antonio, go down through Uvalde—the home of the infamous Uvalde Slim—and on over to the border. We'd cross at a border town and finally go to some bar and bordello. The word for years was that there was a show with a dog or donkey fucking a "lady of the night" on a stage and we were determined to see that. Holy shit! What a vision of grandeur and utter perversion.

The four of us headed out early Friday morning to see the dog and pony show in Mexico. I ended up getting sick after about four hot Pearl beers. To me Pearl beer always tasted like panther piss, whatever panther piss tastes like. The first day was fun, even though the front of my T-shirt, which read "Baseball All-American," was now caked with vomit. The smell would start a riot in Waxahachie, Texas. We took turns driving and by morning we were close to the border.

We stopped to sleep it off at an old Texas off road. At about noon the smell in the car woke us up and all of a sudden it didn't seem to be as much fun anymore. The heat had hit the car like a fucking oven that had been left on for eight hours. You can imagine what it was like. We put some money together and bought something to eat, then washed our faces. I washed my shirt too, because I knew it would dry in about 30 seconds, which it did.

We reached the border around four o'clock Saturday afternoon and the plan was we were going to leave for home Sunday morning. Getting over the border was easy. As we drove through the dirty streets of old Mexico, we thought, "Hell, this ain't much," although our '55 Chevy fit right in with the ambiance.

We stopped and asked about this dog or donkey fucking show and everyone said it would be at the Texania Club that night. I saw federales everywhere. We killed about four hours drinking a beer or two in some real dive bars, but the party was about to pick up. We were feeling good again and ready to see this wild thing.

The time came and we got to the club. When we walked inside, it was like a scene right out of the Robert Rodriguez movie Desperado, it was dark until the neon lights came on. I had butterflies in my stomach as if I was playing in the seventh game of the World Series and batter cleanup for my beloved Yankees.

We took a table and all of the working girls came over and said something about me in Spanish. My boys would point at me and laugh. Shit, I was brutally handsome, white, and they knew I was a virgin.

Then the best-looking whore in the entire place came over and sat on my lap. By now we were roaring like the Wild Bunch. The whore said something in Spanish and one of my boys told me she wanted to take me to a room and do the deed with me. I asked, "Is it free?"

"Fuck no," he said. "It's going to cost about two dollars."

Shit, I had ten dollars, so with wobbly legs and being half drunk, she took my hand and led me to a room.

The room had lit candles all around it, but it was still dark. The only furniture was a bed and a table that had a big washbowl sitting on it. I fell onto the bed.

She undressed.

EPILOGUE

The next thing that happened has to go down in history as the most unbelievable shit a 16-year-old boy could even imagine.

All at once, like an Olympic gymnast, she leapt on the table like a monkey leaping on the cage at the San Antonio Zoo. She straddled the bowl and began to splash water on her private parts.

"Holy shit!" I was so excited by the show that I shot the whole thing without ever taking off my jeans. I guess you could say it was the original "Dusty Finish."

Next, the shit hit the fan.

Seeing what was happening, she began to curse at me in Spanish as she splashed the water faster. All at once she picked up the bowl and threw it on me ... I guess to fucking cool me off. She quickly dressed, helped me up and led me back in the club.

As we walked in, the crowd was going crazy. My boys were standing on the table yelling, "Ole, Ole!" At this point I saw them leading a donkey off the floor. I had missed the donkey show.

"What the fuck. ..."

She began to tell them what happened. I just let it go in one ear and out the other. Holy shit, I was embarrassed in a bad way.

The rest of the night was a blur.

Early in the morning we headed back to Austin. We made it home late Sunday night. Not much was said coming back as we mostly slept. But the trip to Mexico was not talked about again except only between the four of us ... until now.

For those of you wondering, I have purposely kept the names of my amigos out of this story because I think one of them ended up marrying that whore.

So now every time I see someone splashing water in a bowl, the visions of that trip to Mexico vividly come back and I can't help do anything but smile.

How was that for tits and ass?